FELLRUNNER

It takes legs of steel and armoured lungs ...
suicide really, unless you've got the stamina
for it. They're probably the fittest men alive.

By the time he was twenty-four, Lakeland
shepherd Jonas Caudale had clocked up six
fell-running records. When Jonas decided
to run home to Buttermere across Nazi-
occupied Europe, nobody knew he would
become an international *cause-celebre*, but
then no-one knew about the sinister
mystery hidden within the Lakeland Peaks,
or the secret torment eating at Jonas's soul.
Why did the Official Secrets Act suppress
the extraordinary story of Jonas Caudale's
epic run for over fifty years?...

FELLRUNNER

FELLRUNNER

by
Bob Langley

Magna Large Print Books
Long Preston, North Yorkshire,
England.

British Library Cataloguing in Publication Data.

Langley, Bob
  Fellrunner.

  A catalogue record for this book is
  available from the British Library

  ISBN 0-7505-1266-0

First published in Great Britain by Severn House Publishers
Ltd., 1996

Published in Large Print 1998 by arrangement with Severn
House Publishers Ltd.

Magna Large Print is an imprint of
Library Magna Books Ltd.
Printed and bound in Great Britain by
T.J. International Ltd., Cornwall, PL28 8RW.

Chapter One

The sun was behind him as Jonas Caudale breasted the hill. Sweat streamed from his body, drenching the flimsy singlet he wore but he felt better than he had a right to, after six miles across open country. Below, he saw the twin lakes of Crummock and Buttermere, and the steep dirt crack winding over Newlands Pass; a faint mist hung over the water, blending eerily with the fading daylight.

He started down the final stretch, conscious of the other competitors pounding painfully in his wake. Faces drawn, singlets saturated, they moved with the desperation of men who had pushed their bodies to the limit.

He had taken the lead on the very first climb, drawing ahead with that indomitable stubbornness that confounded rivals and spectators alike, and now as the track dipped sharply through Burtness Wood, only Bobby Teasdale, the one-armed runner from Pooley Bridge who had shortened his lead on the gruelling drag over Scarth's Gap, still clung resolutely to his rear. He felt no sense of alarm

9

at the unexpected challenge; with the wind fanning his cheeks and the scent of sun-warmed bracken in his nostrils, he knew intuitively he was going to win.

They charged through Burtness Wood, Teasdale pinned like a limpet to his left shoulder. A ditch loomed up and they sailed over it, neck and neck. He heard Teasdale's breath rasping in his ear, smelled the rank odour of the man's body sweat, yet he felt no strain, that was the curious thing; he had gone beyond strain, and now his primary sensation was the elation which always accompanied the final stages of a major race. There was little subtlety to his movements, only the numbing application of feet on soil as if his body was engaging the earth in some primitive, timeworn ritual.

The trees fell back to reveal the dry-stone wall and the billowing tents where the spectators waited. He quickened his pace, sensing Teasdale's dismay as he drew steadily, inexorably ahead. He took the wall in a flying leap, his limbs clearing the parapet with graceful ease, then he was sprinting like the wind, body and legs moving in perfect unison. He saw the crowds waiting at the finishing line, heard their voices blending into a single obsessive chorus and with a thrill of triumph realized they were calling his name. 'Jonas,' they shouted hysterically, 'Jonas, Jonas, Jonas, Jonas, Jonas, Jonas, Jonas, Jonas, Jonas ...'

'He's sick,' the sentry said. He tapped his forehead meaningfully. 'Up here.'

His companion, a sallow-cheeked young man with a moody expression eased his rifle more comfortably over his shoulder and stared through the barbed wire fence at Jonas Caudale pounding around the compound with his lips drawn back in a painful grimace. The Englishman certainly looked crazy enough, he reflected; his face was like a battering ram and his eyes carried the impassioned fervour of an ageing lion making its last desperate kill. He seemed scarcely conscious of his surroundings, as if by some magical process he had drifted into a different time zone.

'He runs like that every morning,' the first sentry said. 'Round and round the compound, never stopping. He must be covering twenty to thirty miles a day.'

'What's he doing it for?' his companion asked.

'Stir-crazy probably. Been cooped up too long in those Nazi prison camps.'

The second guard was silent for a moment, watching Jonas sprinting toward the main administrative building. He was a curious one and no mistake; lean as a lehmbuck and imbued with a supple, elusive grace, he seemed to have a fire

11

smouldering inside, as if he couldn't stop until it had burned itself out. He had arrived at the internment centre barely two weeks earlier, having crossed the Swiss frontier with a party of SS *Gebirgsjager* hot on his heels. It was a common enough occurrence in war-ravaged Europe; they appeared every day, refugees flooding into the only neutral country within striking distance, escaping Allied POWs, American airmen shot down over enemy territory, Jews fleeing the concentration camps; in fear and hope, they delivered themselves into the hands of the Swiss authorities to be placed in special detention centres and await repatriation through the International Red Cross.

Jonas Caudale had run his pursuers to a standstill across seventy-nine miles of forbidding mountain territory, a feat which had turned him into something of a celebrity among the other internees. Nevertheless, there was one thing the young sentry felt certain of; Caudale was no psycho case. 'I think he's training like this for a reason,' he said. 'I think he has some secret purpose in mind.'

'Purpose? What purpose?'

'I don't know.' The sentry rubbed his rifle strap reflectively as Jonas vanished from sight around the side of the building, his flashing heels leaving a feathery dust haze above the gravel drive. 'But I have the strangest feeling we're about to find out.'

In the early hours of March 2nd 1944, fourteen weeks before the Allied invasion of Normandy, in that area of rural France known as *la petite Bretagne,* Resistance leader Jacqueline Broussard, plump-cheeked, full-bosomed, forty-two years old, sped through the darkened countryside in a charcoal-burning *gazogene.* Huddled uncomfortably in the truck's rear, her little band of followers sat with bodies braced against the chill, their stubbled faces silent and withdrawn.

The slitted headlamps picked up sections of open grassland, lighting them briefly before passing on, creating a curious kaleidoscope effect like a film being played at a very fast speed; rabbits caught in their glare bounded cheekily into the darkness. Jacqueline's breasts bounced up and down as she steered the *gazogene* across the sloping meadowland, straining to see through the dust-grimed windshield.

She was a handsome woman, shrewd, intelligent and—though she distrusted this quality—inherently maternal toward the youthful *résistants* under her command. Before the war she had worked as a

13

milliner in the city of Quimper but when her husband Simon had been conscripted for work in the German labour camps, had devoted her life to the task of driving out the hated invaders.

The reason for her night-time sortie lay sleeping in the vehicle rear, his angular body curled foetus-like against the cold March air. He wore a tattered raincoat with ripped pockets, a cloth cap frayed at the edges and a pair of corduroy farmer's breeches, tied beneath the knees with pieces of knotted string.

He was hardly a *beau monde*, she thought, reflecting idly that the American major whom she had been ordered to smuggle to London was not really human at all in the normal sense. She had met many intelligence agents during the long, interminable years of war—she had even, for strategic purposes, made friends with some of the hated *Boche*—but she had to admit that she had seldom encountered anyone quite so dispiriting as the young American.

She struggled for a word to describe him. He was aloof certainly. Distant, solitary and insular. He was also haughty and impolite. True, he spoke French like a native and had an intimate knowledge of survival in occupied territory, but as a goodwill ambassador he was the last person in the world to win hearts, minds, or anything else.

Trees flanked the river bluffs on Jacqueline's right, their foliage blending into an impenetrable blur; mist gathered among the branches, imbuing the scene with a strangely ethereal air.

'How far's the landing site?' she asked the young man in the passenger seat beside her.

'Just over the next hill,' he said. 'It's a good level spot. Luc and I picked it out yesterday. There's a sixty-yard run-out and we've cleared it of rocks. I spoke to the local farmer and he hasn't seen a German in weeks.'

'Good.' She eased to one side. 'Grab the driving wheel while I wake our sleeping beauty.'

When she touched his shoulder the American opened his eyes with a start, peering up at her with a quizzical, faintly resentful air as if he disliked being disturbed, even in such uncomfortable circumstances. Shadows darted across his cheeks, forming myriad patterns on his craggy chin.

'You were dead to the world,' she said. 'We'll be there in a minute or two.'

He sat up, stretching his legs, massaging warmth into the cramped, stiff muscles. Steam trailed from his nostrils as he expelled the air from his lungs, shaking his head to clear it. 'What's the time?'

'Almost three.'

'Cutting it a bit fine,' he grunted.

'Better than sitting around like whores at a church benefit. Trust us, major. We've been doing this a lot longer than you have and timing's what it's all about.'

Close, he really was quite an attractive man, she thought. His body was lean and athletic and his features were pleasantly-sculpted, but there was something in his eyes she found difficult to accommodate. He looked cold and austere, like a fortress with its drawbridge pulled up.

'I understand you carry France's future in your pocket,' she said conversationally.

He seemed surprised at her directness, and slightly defensive as if he felt she had overstepped the mark. 'Who told you that?' he asked.

'Friends. I hope they're right. We've been waiting a long time for liberation.'

'Well, maybe it's a good deal closer than you think.'

She was about to speak again when the truck skidded suddenly to a halt and her driver leaned forward, rubbing the windshield with his sleeve. He was squinting into the darkness as she wriggled toward him. 'What's wrong?' she whispered.

'Thought I saw movement over by the trees.'

She examined the thicket fearfully. The branches stirred in the wind, making a sibilant rustling sound that came drifting across the meadowland. She picked up her rifle and motioned to a figure in the *gazogene* rear. 'Millar, take a flashlight and scout those woods.'

Millar, a coarse-faced man in a Basque beret, headed toward the pines and for several seconds they saw his flashlight darting among the foliage. Jacqueline's nerves were strained to breaking point and sweat formed tiny globules on her cheeks as she waited in silence, cradling the carbine across her knees.

After a while, Millar returned, moving more casually this time. 'Clean as a whistle,' he declared.

She chuckled with relief, digging her driver with her elbow. 'Getting jumpy in your old age, *chérie?*'

'I could have sworn I heard something,' the young man insisted.

'Probably my heart. It's been going like a steam-hammer ever since we left Quimper.'

They continued on, rumbling over a little knoll, then the land levelled in the pale glow of the headlamps and she realized they had reached the landing site. 'Everybody out,' she snapped. 'Set the flares and check for obstructions. We've got four minutes to zero hour.'

The *résistants* tumbled from the truck and began laying out marker lights, metal drums packed with bundles of oil-soaked rags. She watched the operation in silence, stamping her feet in the pre-dawn chill. The American stood alone at the side of the truck, his raincoat fluttering in the wind. He looked like a scarecrow which was beginning to disintegrate from the inside out. She wondered if he was married. If he was, she felt heartily sorry for his wife.

She heard a droning sound in the distance and held her breath. Clouds floated across the moon and the droning grew louder. 'Here it comes,' she said. 'Light the flares.'

The *résistants* moved among the metal drums, setting fire to the rags inside. Columns of thick black smoke belched into the night. The droning developed into a deafening roar and she watched the shadows taking on shape and substance, forming an elongated hull that emerged out of the darkness like a phantom spectre. The aircraft's undercarriage looked slightly lopsided as it belly-flopped in for the difficult landing, the pilot struggling to gauge the distance between his wheels and the unstable meadowland. He dropped into the ribbon of light and touched down awkwardly, bouncing across the tufted grass clumps, the slipstream from his propellers sending Jacqueline's hair streaming out behind her. She saw the pilot staring down at them from the camouflaged windshield.

'There's your ticket out of here, Major,' she shouted.

The American nodded, his lean face expressionless. The pilot taxied to a halt and turned his plane into the wind. The smell of diesel fumes filled her nostrils mingling with the pungent odour of the blazing oilrags.

When the ambush came it was almost an anticlimax, as if she had been expecting it all along in some curious, intuitive way. She heard a sound in the thicket behind her and turned to examine the trees, a sudden tension gathering in her stomach. There was no sign of any threat. She let herself relax. Then there was a flash of light, blinding in its intensity, and she saw her adjutant, Jean Angelvin, catapult backwards into the grass, his head disintegrating into a million pieces.

A barrage of shots rang out, catching the helpless *résistants* in a blistering crossfire, and she hurled herself behind the truck wheel with the American crouching at her side. The gun blasts blended into a single discordant roll which echoed deafeningly in her eardrums. A sob burst from her lips as she saw André Vegan, the butcher from Lecronau, writhing under the impact of the incoming fire; he went through a macabre dance before collapsing to the ground, his body ripped almost completely in two. Pierre Machin, the boatman from the river Odet, did a double somersault as he was tossed into the branches of a neighbouring tree. Louis Buthol, seventeen years old, lay squirming in the grass, clawing at a gaping hole in his stomach. It was a slaughterhouse, she thought. They were killing her boys, cutting them to ribbons in the full glare of the pilot lights. Tears streaming down her cheeks, she fired into the thicket, laying down three shots, one after the other.

She heard a sound behind her and realized the pilot was opening his throttles for an emergency take-off. If the American didn't leave now, their sacrifice would be wasted. 'Move,' she shouted, waving toward the taxiing aircraft.

The major hesitated. 'What about you?'

'Forget about me. Just get out of here.'

She saw the anguish in his face as he glanced at the decimated corpses and realized with surprise that he was not an emotional cripple after all. His air of aloofness was nothing but an act.

'Go, damn you,' she bellowed.

The major rose to his feet and sprinted across the open ground with Jacqueline laying down as much covering fire as she could, choking back the sobs as she worked her rifle bolt in a frenzy of emotion.

She saw the American scrambling into the cockpit, saw the pilot picking up speed, saw the plane banking gracefully into the darkness, then the truck exploded in a blinding pumpkin of flame and when the debris finally settled, Jacqueline Broussard lay motionless in the dirt and never saw anything ever again.

Greg Anderson looked tired as he entered the office of General Dwight Eisenhower, the Supreme Allied Commander. His eight days in Occupied France had left him emotionally drained and his eyes were rimmed with tension and exhaustion. He couldn't forget the trauma of his departure, the blistering onslaught of machine-gun fire, the hapless *résistants* scattered like garbage around the ravaged meadowland. The horror of the moment was etched into his psyche like a fragment from some half-forgotten nightmare.

Eisenhower's tunic looked bedraggled in the dour London morning as if he had slept in it, which he probably had, Greg reflected, since all-night sessions in the war-room had become a common feature with D-Day approaching.

'Coffee, Major?' the general asked, brandishing a thermos flask.

Greg shook his head. 'I've just had breakfast, sir.'

Eisenhower filled a cup and placed it on the desk in front of him, eyeing Greg appraisingly. 'Take the weight off your feet. Glad to see you got home safely. I understand you ran into a spot of trouble.'

'Trouble's hardly the word for it, sir. We were ambushed by a German patrol. My escort ...' He took a deep breath, seating himself in the armchair opposite. 'Some of them died getting me out.'

'I heard.' The general's features creased in sympathy. 'War's a lousy business, Major.'

It was the first time in their acquaintance that Eisenhower had seen the young major display emotion and he was pleasantly surprised. He liked Anderson but something about the man troubled him deeply; it wasn't his work—Eisenhower had seldom encountered a sharper operator and the major's courage was beyond question—but he was a cold fish in many respects. He rarely smiled, and when he did, it was only his lips which moved. Eisenhower found the paradox disconcerting. 'What was your assessment of our friends in the FFI?' he asked, changing the subject.

The FFI, or *Forces Francaises de l'Intérieur,* was the title given to the combined resistance forces operating in Occupied France.

'They're ready to support our landing forces, General, and slow down the German divisions moving from the south.'

'Good. If the invasion's to be successful, we must have backing behind the enemy's lines. However, the British aren't keen on "Overlord" at all. Churchill wants to hit at what he calls the soft underbelly of the Axis—Yugoslavia and the Balkans.'

'I can understand his thinking. It's a more tempting target than the "Atlantic Wall" where the enemy resources are at their strongest.'

'I think I've finally won him around to our point of view, using "Overlord" as the main assault and supporting it with an operation against the Riviera, but some of the other departments aren't as flexible as Winston. They believe D-Day could prove a costly mistake. I'm dancing on eggshells, trying to appease first one group and then another.'

'They'll have to go with the majority decision, sir.'

'Learn to appreciate their feelings, Major.

They've been fighting Germans since 1939 and they *are* our allies, after all. However, if the French provide a diversionary action on D-Day, I think our success should be assured.'

'They'll do it, General. Recard believes he can cut off the Germans in Bergerac and control the eastern Dordogne until we get our paratroops in. But he must have arms. The British have been dispatching most of their weapons to the Yugoslavian partisans.'

'Churchill's worried about arming the *maquisards*. He feels the French regard "Overlord" as a supportive action, designed to draw the enemy's fire while France is liberated internally by its own people. Maybe he's right.'

'You don't really believe that, General.'

'I'm not sure what I believe any more. Have you considered the problem of getting the arms in? Supposing they fall into enemy hands?'

'I didn't say it would be easy. That's why the decision rests with you, sir.'

'OK,' Eisenhower agreed after a moment. 'Give me a breakdown on what you need and I'll authorize its distribution.'

'Thank you, sir.'

'However, I'm putting my neck on the line with this, and I'm making you personally responsible for ensuring that those weapons get to the right people. Anything goes wrong, anything at all, and we kill the deliveries stone-dead. Churchill will insist upon it.'

'I understand, sir.'

Greg's face was bland as he rose to his feet but inside his senses were racing. He knew the future of his department was at stake and it gave him an uneasy feeling.

Eisenhower examined him thoughtfully for a moment. He regarded Anderson as a brilliant officer but one who stuck out like a sore thumb among the rest of his staff. He wished to God the man would develop a more reasonable attitude.

'You're looking tired, son,' he said. 'Why don't you take the afternoon off? Go to a movie or something.'

'I'm OK, sir. Nothing a few hours' sleep won't cure.'

'I don't want my officers operating like machines. Machines break down, and that's something we can't afford when "Overlord" starts. I need you to take it easy. Enjoy yourself.'

'There *is* a war on, sir.'

Eisenhower pursed his lips, then said, 'Your father's Dilman Anderson, isn't he? Head of the Kholberg conglomerate. I had the pleasure of meeting him once at a seminary in San Diego. I was most impressed by his knowledge of military tactics.'

'Thank you, sir.'

'However ...' The general hesitated. 'Maybe I shouldn't say this, but he struck me as a little on the humourless side.'

'My father raised me in the belief that the most important things in life are duty and achievement.'

'Well, I don't think anyone would dispute that, Major, but it'll be a sad thing indeed if you allow duty and achievement to destroy your youth. Why don't you learn to relax?'

'After D-Day, sir, when we get our men on those beaches, then I'll relax.'

Eisenhower shrugged in defeat. Rarely had he encountered such stubbornness in a junior officer. 'OK, Major,' he said with a dismissive wave. 'Just make sure you don't screw it up.'

'No, sir,' Greg answered. He saluted and left.

Greg was moody as he returned to his own office. The general had him figured to his fingertips, he thought. He *was* a pain in the butt, he just couldn't help himself. His father, who regarded any form of emotion as a dangerous weakness, had raised him with a minimum of affection until in time he had learned to live without it, developing instead the kind of self-reliance his family so admired. At Yale his fellow students had found his manner intolerable and though in physical terms he was far from unhandsome, the local girls had considered him an unqualified write-off. Now, at the age of twenty-seven, tall, rangy, sandy-haired, Major Greg Anderson was a profoundly unhappy man, unable to relate to other people and equally unable to understand why the world was so unready to accept him.

When he reached his office he found his two associates, Lieutenant Warren Seiber of the OSS and Captain Jack Stoker of the Grenadier Guards waiting for him expectantly. He flopped behind his desk and outlined the details of his meeting with the Allied commander. 'This isn't a dress rehearsal,' he said. 'Eisenhower wants Resistance support but he won't risk upsetting Churchill, and Churchill's afraid the French are planning some kind of prima donna act. Any foul-ups and we're dinosaurs, it's as simple as that.'

'Smuggling the arms in won't be easy,' Lieutenant Seiber warned. 'The Heinis'll have that hinterland sealed up tighter than a pickle jar.'

'That's why I need ideas and need them fast.'

Captain Stoker scratched his moustache.

His skin was parchment-like, the result of first degree burns following a direct hit from a Messerschmitt during the desert campaign of 1942. Now he did most of his fighting from behind an office desk. 'Ever play ice hockey, Major?'

'Ice hockey? No.'

'There's a move in ice hockey where you let your opponent think the puck's going one way when in reality it's going someplace else. What we need to make this work is a diversionary tactic. The Jerries know the invasion's just around the corner so they're jumpier than jackrabbits on the opening day of a hunt, but if we can find some method of distracting their attention ...' He let the sentence trail away.

Greg looked interested. 'Maybe you've got a point, Captain,' he said.

'I've always found air raids pretty attention grabbing,' Lieutenant Seiber suggested.

'I wasn't thinking about an air raid,' Stoker told him. 'What we need is something intriguing enough to arouse Jerry's curiosity, but innocuous enough to avoid arousing his suspicions. Maybe I've got the very thing.'

He opened his desk drawer and took out a cardboard folder. His skin looked shiny as he dropped the folder on Greg's desktop. 'These documents came in this morning from the American Legation in Berne. They've picked up an Englishman, an escaped POW named Jonas Caudale. He jumped from a train carrying him to a prison camp at Pizen and managed to cross the border into Switzerland with a whole battalion of *Gebirgsjager* at his heels. This is a translation of a German newspaper report while he was still on the run. It was forwarded by our Research and Analysis Branch.'

Frowning, Greg took the cutting and began to read.

'Excerpt from Nuremburg Gazette, January 7th, 1944.

The biggest manhunt in Austria's history was still under way last night as local authorities continued their search for an escaped prisoner of war. There have been over forty reported sightings and each one is being thoroughly investigated but so far without success. The search is being concentrated in the Cobourg area between Moenke and the Swiss border 79 miles to the west. Military personnel, agents of the *kriminalpolizei* and civilian volunteers are all taking part. Officials have been authorized to pay up to 20 marks to anyone supplying information leading to the man's arrest.'

He looked at Captain Stoker in puzzlement. 'What does this mean?'

'It means the Jerries didn't succeed, Major. Despite their efforts, our man made it across the frontier. He's in Switzerland now, relaxing at a government internment centre.' Stoker perched himself on the edge of the desk, his eyes gleaming with excitement. 'Jonas Caudale is no ordinary POW. He's an ex-shepherd, one of those hard-grained Cumbrians, tough as old boot leather. He grew up in the Lake District among the highest mountains in England. He's also a champion fellrunner.'

'Fellrunner?' Lieutenant Seiber frowned.

'It's sort of a tradition in Lakeland, like log-rolling in Wisconsin. The shepherds and farmers race each other across the mountain peaks. It takes legs of steel and armoured lungs—suicide really unless you've got the stamina for it. Physically speaking, they're probably the fittest men alive. Caudale's the best there is. He's their star turn. Before the war he won practically every hill-racing trophy in Cumberland.'

'Is there some point to this, Jack?'

'The point is, he's asked to be turned loose again. He's appealed to the American Legation to get him to the nearest border. He wants to run home.'

'Run home?'

'Not just to England. To Buttermere in the Lake District.'

Greg sat back in his chair. 'Doesn't he realize there's a war on?'

'I think he's a little eccentric, sir.'

'What's he doing it for?'

'Personal reasons, he claims.'

'Personal reasons? Where the hell does he think he is, Empire Stadium?'

'If you ask my opinion, he's probably a little crazy. They took him prisoner in 1942. Must be pretty tough for a man used to wandering the hills at will finding himself stuck in some stinking stalag.' Captain Stoker's eyes glowed. 'The thing is, on Tuesday night we carry out our first *parachutage* in Section 214, barely twenty miles from the Swiss frontier. Supposing we ask your people to turn this man Caudale loose near the French border then put out a bulletin on the BBC's French Service. We know the Germans monitor the overseas broadcasts.'

'You don't seriously think they're going to concentrate their resources into hunting down one man?'

'It isn't a question of only one man. When they hear the BBC announcement they'll think Caudale has some kind of military significance. Dammit Major, he tied up an entire detachment of SS *Gebirgsjager* during the nine mile journey

31

from Moenke. With luck, he could distract their attention just long enough to help us smuggle our weapons in.'

'It's a million-to-one shot.'

'They're better odds than we're working on now.'

Greg rose to his feet and moved to the open window. He had to admit the idea seemed feasible enough but it was also strangely unsavoury. It required a Judas goat, one who didn't realize he was being set up as a target. God knew, he had never shrunk from responsibility before, but even in wartime a man had a right to his conscience and that wasn't easy when someone else was doing the dying. 'You do realize we'd be handing them this poor bastard on a plate?'

'You want to get those arms to the Resistance or let this crackpot fight his own private war? Somebody has to make the sacrifice. Besides ...' Stoker paused pointedly. 'Have you got a better idea?'

No, Greg thought, of course he hadn't. He was clutching at straws and Stoker knew it. Unless he made sure those arms shipments landed in the appropriate hands, everything they had worked for would be flushed down the sewer.

He came to a quick decision. 'Get onto the American Legation in Berne,' he said. 'Tell them to let Jonas Caudale run.'

The day was unseasonably mild as Theodore Gallagher displayed his identity card at Government Offices in London's Great George Street and made his way up the carpetless stairway to the austere room which housed his small, highly-secret department on the second floor. A half-empty bottle of coffee essence stood on a table by the umbrella stand, surrounded by a clutter of unwashed cups.

Though Gallagher was dressed in civilian clothing he carried the rank of a Royal Naval rear admiral, an unusual distinction for a man so young—he was barely thirty-four—and explicit testimony to the value the War Cabinet placed on his services.

Theodore Gallagher worked for Admiralty Intelligence, collecting and analysing information on enemy naval and mercantile movements. He had joined the Government Code and Cipher School at Bletchley Park and had played a crucial role in the pursuit and destruction of the battleship *Bismark*. In 1943, on the direct instructions of the First Sea Lord, he had assumed command of Department D-14, a small offshoot of British intelligence working in close co-operation with the War Office and responsible for all undercover work relating to the forthcoming invasion of Occupied Europe.

Gallagher knew he was about to enter the most vital phase of his intelligence career, for one of the biggest forces in history, more than a million men, was being assembled across southern England. Though Hitler's troops were being routed in the east, and though the Reich had lost nearly 350,000 men on the Russian front in the past three months, the German leader still believed the Allies could be halted at the Channel and under Directive 51, had begun funnelling powerful divisions into northern France to strengthen his coastal defences. It was part of Gallagher's job to see that his efforts would go unrewarded.

Gallagher was small in stature but he carried himself proudly, as if anxious to utilize every inch of height his body could muster. His hair was black and he wore a thin moustache which gave his features a faintly rakish look. In many ways, Gallagher reminded his assistant Cyril Applethwaite of the Hollywood film actor David Niven—he had the same gentle eyes, the same elegant mannerisms—but there the similarity ended, for Theodore Gallagher was coldly implacable in all matters relating to his job.

'Trouble?' Applethwaite asked as Gallagher flopped into his chair.

'Damn right, Cyril. It's those bloody Yanks again.'

34

'What have they been up to this time?'

'Bloody mindedness, as usual. I've just been to a meeting at Eisenhower's office and I tell you they're going to cock up this whole bloody invasion. They simply refuse to listen to reason. Any damn fool can see the place to hit the Germans is the Balkans. By landing our troops in Yugoslavia, we can knock them out of the war and team up with the Russians for a grand offensive on Berlin. But Eisenhower's got "Overlord" fixed so firmly in his mind it'll take an earthquake to shift it.'

'So "Overlord"'s on then?'

'That's strictly classified, Cyril. No casual remarks in the mess, understand?'

Applethwaite grinned. He was an energetic young man who reminded Gallagher of an overgrown puppy. 'You think the Yanks are trying to push us out of the game?'

'They'd do it if they could. No question of that.'

'Maybe they've already started.'

'What are you talking about?'

Applethwaite took a sheet of paper from his in-tray. 'One of our RAF Lysanders picked up an American major in the Quimper area last night. Had a spot of bother, I understand. Ran into a German patrol and some of the *résistants* got caught in the crossfire. The mechanics found three bullet holes in the aircraft's fuselage. It appears the order for the flight came direct from Ike's office.'

'So now the Yanks are even controlling the RAF. Who was he, this major?'

'His name's Gregory Anderson. He's part of General Coulter's outfit in Berkeley Square.'

'What the hell are Coulter's people doing in French territory?'

'I thought you'd ask that, so I took the liberty of having Anderson's file sent up from Records Branch.'

'Good man, Cyril,' Gallagher said approvingly. 'What did you find?'

'Not much. Anderson's father's some kind of big industrialist who makes armaments for the American War Department. Anderson himself was brought up in a French Canadian community. He's bilingual, speaks the language like a native. He served with Mark Clark in Algeria, acting as a liaison between the French forces and the U.S. Fifth Army.'

Gallagher's eyes began to glitter. 'You think he's been linking up with the Resistance?'

'It's the only possible explanation.'

'The Yanks have no bloody right to be sending men into Occupied France. That's our job.'

'I thought I ought to mention it, Theo.

This business is tricky enough without being hamstrung by our Allies.'

Gallagher began stroking his moustache with his fingertip, a sure sign he was becoming agitated. 'Cyril,' he said at last, 'I want you to get me a full report on this Major Anderson. Don't go through Records Branch, do it under the counter. I'll be damned if I'll sit back and let the Americans run this whole bloody show. If Coulter's people are acting behind our backs, I want to know what the bastards are up to.'

Jonas Caudale felt someone nudging his arm and opened his eyes with a start. For a moment he couldn't remember where he was, then he realized he was sitting in the rear of the embassy car with Lawrence Price, head of the American Legation, leaning over him. Through the windshield, he could see their headlamps picking out the road ahead.

'Almost there,' Price said.

Jonas sat up, shaking his head as if to clear it. He had slept fitfully during the long journey into the mountains and clad in a newfangled sweat suit, he felt just about ready to tackle the day.

A faint nervousness started inside him. For weeks he had harangued the U.S. authorities with little hope of success—in time of war few people listened to the implorings of one man—but by some miracle his prayers had been answered and now, incredibly, he was on his way. The thought filled him with excitement and apprehension.

There were two other men in the car—Hans Tauer, a representative from the Swiss Foreign Office, and the Legation driver, Ernst Muller.

'How are you feeling?' Lawrence Price asked, examining him critically.

'Good, Mr Price.'

'Still sure you want to go through with this?'

'Yes, sir.'

He knew Price thought he was crazy—they all did—but he couldn't expect them to understand. Some things went beyond explanation.

'You do realize that once you cross that frontier, you'll be a prime target? People don't run in the Occupied Territories any more.'

'I'll take my chances,' Jonas said.

Lawrence Price studied him thoughtfully. He scarcely knew what to make of Caudale. The Englishman's face was all angles and lines, and there was a gleam in his eyes similar to the look Price had seen in mountain cats which roamed the hills near his boyhood home. Caudale would be implacable in purpose, there would be no softness in his make-up. He would bludgeon his way through thick and thin. And yet, he had proved an engaging companion during the few weeks they had known each other. Despite his tough exterior he carried a gentleness the American both approved of and admired.

'This is where the road ends,' their driver said as Price lit himself a cigarette. 'We're five miles from the frontier.'

They pulled to a halt and Jonas climbed out, shivering in the crisp air. He breathed deeply, filling his lungs. He saw the starburst of a village in the valley below. It looked so peaceful he found it hard to believe the greatest war in history was being fought barely a stone's throw away.

'Better not hang about, son,' Price warned. 'Don't want some early morning hunter spotting you crossing the border.'

'No, sir. I reckon you're right.'

He launched into his preparatory warm-up and was panting heavily by the time he had finished. Price took out an envelope and pushed it into his hand. 'French francs,' he explained. 'You won't get far without money, even in the mountains. Also ...' He fumbled in his pocket and produced a tiny compass. 'You strap this on like a wrist-watch. It'll tell you which direction you're heading.'

'You've been right good to me, Mr Price.'

'Just doing my job, son.'

'I don't know how I can ever thank 'ee.'

'You can thank me by getting home in one piece. What's the name of that place again?'

'Buttermere, sir.'

'I'll have to visit it after the war.'

'I'll look forward to that, Mr Price.'

Tauer walked up, carrying a rucksack containing spare clothes and iron rations. He handed it to Jonas and motioned beyond the line of firs. 'The border follows the ridge above. There's no fence at this point, but once you're on the downward grade you'll know you're inside French territory. Just keep heading west.'

Jonas shook hands with each of the men in turn and slipped the haversack over his shoulders. A strange excitement stirred inside him. Ahead lay more than a thousand miles of hostile territory. He would be running blind, isolated and alone. He would be relying on his own resources, his chances of survival terrifyingly slim. But he had made up his mind. He would finish the run or die.

He smiled at the others. 'Thanks for all you've done,' he said.

'Good luck, Mr Caudale,' Tauer told him.

They watched him setting off, his wiry body vanishing from sight among the trees and stars.

'He's very brave,' Tauer said.

'Yeah.' Price threw his half-smoked cigarette into the ditch. 'I wonder what the poor bastard would say if he knew we'd already tipped off the krauts that he's coming.'

Chapter Two

Jonas ran with a loose, methodical gait, conserving his energy as dawn came slowly to the western Alps. He disliked running at altitude, and needed to save his strength for the gruelling route ahead. He felt glad to be out, glad to be back in the cool crisp air again, glad of anything which released him from the boredom of inactivity. Those weeks in the internment camp had driven him almost mindless with frustration. This was what he needed—action and freedom. Too long he'd been shut up like a caged animal. It was bad for a man, bad for anything, human or beast alike.

The American Legation people hadn't

been able to understand that. They'd wanted everything defined. Why was he doing such a thing? Couldn't he wait until the fighting was over? Well, Jonas's reasons were strictly his own. He was caught in an obsession of his own making which he wouldn't attempt to rationalize. Sometimes a man had to follow the impulses of his heart, nothing else made any sense.

He remembered a time he had done the Helvellyn ridge in midwinter, the air so cold it had taken his breath away, and on the tip of Dollywaggon Pike he'd come across the body of a man, frozen and gleaming with verglas. The man had been smiling, that was the crazy thing, and something in his face, a deep, inscrutable peacefulness had reminded Jonas of a martyred saint. He'd thought a lot about that smile, wondering if the man had found completeness at the very moment of oblivion. He thought he had a chance to find completeness now. He thought the Americans were giving him that chance.

The incline levelled as he came down the embankment and he examined the route ahead where ribs of shale rose past a clutter of small ravines. It would be uphill all the way, a prospect he did not relish.

He took a rest then checked his pulse, gratified to find it was down to an impressive forty-two beats a minute. He was counting on twenty to thirty miles a day, though he didn't know if he could handle such distances on a sustained basis. His greatest worry was his calorific intake. In such arduous terrain, he knew he would be consuming 6000 calories a day and after two years on POW rations, his surplus fat would be down to five per cent at least; if he lost that, it meant using up precious muscle tissue. Nevertheless, his long years on the Lakeland slopes had imbued him with strong legs and an almost incalculable wind power.

In 1938 on the Buttermere Horseshoe, he had sliced seven minutes off Nelson Mellinger's record in misty conditions and had gone on to complete the Dunnerdale Tower, putting up the fastest time since the legendary Charlie Patterson in 1921. Eighteen months later he had won the Coniston Dod, clocking 37 minutes and 24 seconds after a spectacular descent which had left the other competitors standing. Compared to that, running home from Switzerland should be a doddle.

He sucked in his breath, wiped his palms on his bedraggled sweat suit and set off up the neighbouring hillslope.

At six-thirty in the morning, the garrison commander of the Pelvoux district in the Dauphine Alps, Colonel Otto Sch-neidermann, was awakened in his room by his aide, Lieutenant Karl Keppler. Bleary-eyed, Schneidermann looked at the window where Keppler had already drawn the drapes. 'What time is it?'

'Forgive me, Herr Oberst. It is just after dawn.'

Schneidermann picked up his wrist-watch from the dresser. 'My God, Karl, you know I didn't retire until after midnight.'

Keppler handed the colonel a sheet of paper. 'I think this could be important. It's the *Sicherheitsdienst.*'

The *Sicherheitsdienst* was the weekly information sheet which listed translations of the BBC's French Service broadcasts. Wriggling upright, the colonel fumbled for his spectacle case and scanned the document wordlessly. When he had finished, he looked at Keppler, frowning. 'What does it mean?'

'It must mean something, Herr Oberst. They wouldn't put out a special bulletin for no reason. Perhaps it is some kind of message intended for the local Resistance.'

Schneidermann thought for a moment, the bedside lamp casting ripples of light across his balding skull. He flung back the blankets and reached for the telephone. 'You were right to wake me, Karl. We had better call a Code Red.'

As the morning lengthened the clouds broke up, giving way to a glorious day. Jonas ran steadily, pausing from time to time to drink from the streams pouring down the mountain slopes. He knew regular drinking would be essential, for a fluid loss of more than three per cent of his body weight could seriously dehydrate him.

At first, the route proved easy enough—a long valley, not unlike the Cumbrian vales in which Jonas had been raised; there was a river curling snake-like between the grassy V and craggy outcrops topping the shoulders on both sides. He jogged steadily, glad of the endless days he had spent pounding around his stalag enclosure.

After a short while he set his course directly upward, leaving the main massif behind and entering the snow-cluttered peaks above. Now the ascent became excruciatingly hard and he had to press his palms against his thigh tops to absorb the strain. He had trained too long on the flat, he realized, had lost his appetite for the soul-searing agony of a mountain ascent, but he kept going, ignoring the tears of fatigue moistening his eyes, and bit by bit, foot by foot, scaled the incline and reached the summit of a small plateau.

Here, the land split into a series of

pyramidal outcrops, flanked on one side by a ragged snow-slope. Jonas took the slope at a dizzy run, fighting to see through the ice granules churned up from his shoes. At the bottom, he came to a narrow road threading a tortuous route through sunburnt meadows and tumbling woodlands.

At first he ran in solitary aloneness, but as the morning lengthened he began to pass people. A man at a roadside chalet offered him a tankard of beer which Jonas accepted gratefully, raising the stein in a sweaty salute. A family on a donkey cart addressed him in indecipherable French and after much embarrassed waving of hands, accompanied by peals of laughter from the children, he shrugged an apology and trotted on.

He was feeling better than he'd expected after all those months on POW rations. His wind was sound and his limbs seemed tireless. He felt sure he could run all day if he had a mind to. His spirits lifted as he headed determinedly westward.

Oberleutnant Bruno von Hautle of the 5th *Leibstandarte* SS Adolf Hitler leaned languidly against the leather upholstery and glanced in his staff car's driving mirror. He could see truck convoys trailing down the gradient behind, eight troop-filled Koenigs and a heavy snub-nosed Sturmgeschutz with a scarlet swastika painted on its hull. Motorcycle MPs flanked the column front and rear, sunlight gleaming on their Wehrmacht helmets.

He was intrigued by such an excessive display of force. The Dauphine Alps, despite their proximity to the Swiss frontier, were not as a rule considered a security risk. He could only conclude that something highly unorthodox was taking place.

The road swung into a hairpin bend and he saw more trucks parked on the grassy verge ahead. He tapped his driver on the shoulder and the man drew to a halt, scrambling out hurriedly to open the rear door. Bruno paused as he climbed from the car, examining his reflection in the driving mirror and tilting his cap at a more jaunty angle. He was an athletic young man with merry blue eyes and handsome, suntanned features.

He had chosen a military career not out of any vocational sense but because his reckless, irreverent lifestyle had proved an acute embarrassment to his long-suffering father. He had fought with distinction in Norway and Russia, and more recently had helped stem the enemy advance in the wooded countryside of Tuscany. To his friends, he was an agreeable companion with a full-blooded appetite for living. To his enemies, he was an arrogant and conceited snob.

Troops stood stamping their feet around the stationary vehicles as Bruno von Hautle approached. Some were clad in camouflaged smocks with eidelweiss sleeve badges. Several had twelve-point crampons —'lobster-claws'—dangling from their field packs.

He saw an SS major leaning on a shooting stick, eating fruit from a paper bag. The man was barrel-chested, with a huge beak of a nose which clung to the front of his skull like a canker.

'Strawberries?' Bruno smiled. 'At this time of year?'

The man grimaced. 'They're force-grown. I had them flown in from Italy at enormous expense. I don't suppose you'd have a spot of sugar in your pocket?'

'Never touch the stuff,' Bruno told him. 'Bad for the waistline, the experts say.'

'In that case, I'll have to finish them off raw. Care to try one?'

Bruno shook his head, examining the mountain slope above. Craggy pinnacles, gleaming in the sunlight, were joined by a narrow pine-studded saddle where a miniscule figure was picking its way between the trees; it looked little more than a pinprick framed against the sky.

'What kind of game are you playing here?' he asked.

'Hunting,' the major answered. 'It's rather a passion of mine, though I have to admit it's the first time I've had the privilege of stalking a live human being.'

'Who is he? A deserter on the run?'

'A British POW. His name is Jonas Caudale. Six weeks ago, he escaped from a transport train carrying him to Czechoslovakia. Remarkable though it may seem, the wily beggar actually managed to make it into Switzerland and then for some reason known only to himself decided to continue his run all the way to England.'

'Am I to understand, Herr Major, that you've employed this entire detachment to hunt down one man?'

'You think I'm being extravagant?' Laughing, the major crumpled his paper bag and steered Bruno toward the stationary trucks. 'You're right, of course. In practical terms, catching one miserable POW should be a piece of cake. However, last night the BBC mentioned Caudale in a special bulletin and the local garrison commander, Colonel Otto Schneidermann, decided in his wisdom to call a Code Red. Now the task of bringing Caudale down has fallen to my *Gebirgsjager* and if the man escapes I shall look a complete idiot when the news reaches Berlin.'

49

'Is that why you sent for me?'

'I'm told you were quite an athlete before the war, a champion mountain runner from Garmische in Bavaria.'

'It was a long time ago, Herr Major. I'm no longer in training.'

'It isn't your brawn I'm after, it's your brain. You see, the man above—Caudale—he too is a mountain runner, an ex-shepherd who spent most of his life racing over England's highest summits.'

The major took a map from his tunic pocket and spread it across the hood of the nearest truck. His breath steamed on the mountain air and his bulbous nose looked lumpier than ever. 'You understand my predicament, *oberleutnant?* By calling out the *Gebirgsjager,* Colonel Schneidermann has placed me in a delicate position. My troops are mountain specialists but it's impossible to lay a cordon across the entire country, and if the Englander gets away I'll be a laughing stock in the officers' mess and—even worse—it could seriously damage my career. What I need is someone who can get inside Caudale's mind, understand the way he thinks.'

Bruno appreciated the major's dilemma. 'Very well, let's see what we can do,' he said.

He smoothed out the map, examining

50

the neighbouring terrain. His movements were elegant and graceful. 'That ridge he's on, is it the Kuchler?'

'I believe so.'

'Then if he sticks to the summit, it should take him directly to the Schwabingen Falls?'

'True. On the other hand, he could always drop into the neighbouring valley and vanish into the timber.'

'We'll have to ensure that he doesn't,' Bruno said. 'What we need is a pursuit group to challenge the man on his own terms. That way, he'll keep to the high ground until he reaches the ridge end.'

'And then?'

'I'll take one of the trucks and cut him off at the waterfall.'

The major thought for a moment. 'It's a gamble, but it just might work. It'll be up to the running team to keep him from detouring.' He bellowed at the line of watching men. *'Underfeldwebel?'*

A sergeant came scurrying toward them, running awkwardly under the weight of his heavy fieldpack. 'Yes, Herr Major,' he said, snapping to attention.

'We must have mountain runners among our ranks, men accustomed to racing in the high Alpine peaks?'

'Yes, Herr Major. Breithaupt, Mohr and Weiler are all mountain runners from the

Karnische Alpen, south of Lienz.'

'Tell them to leave their packs behind and pursue the fugitive on foot. They are to overtake the prisoner if possible, force him along the ridge crest if not. They must do everything in their power to prevent him dipping into the timber, is that understood?'

'*Jawol*, Herr Major.' The sergeant saluted and trotted off.

The major looked at Bruno gratefully. 'If this works, you can name your own reward.'

'Make it strawberries,' Bruno told him with a grin. 'And not those sour Italian ones either. I like mine plump and sweet from the southern Rhine.'

'I'll get you a truckload, plus a crate of champagne to wash them down.'

'Consider your Englander already caught.' Bruno laughed as he hurried away to select his men.

It took Bruno almost twenty-five minutes to drive the eleven miles to the Schwabingen Falls. The road dipped as the mountains broke into a series of fractured pyramids, and he saw the river tumbling over the canyon in a breathtaking cascade.

The absurdity of the mission amused him. After months of heavy fighting, he found the idea of pursuing a solitary fugitive too incongruous for words but he had to admit that it offered a blessed respite from the rigours of war.

Parking the truck, he ordered his men to dig themselves in, overlooking the Schwabingen Gorge. He had chosen a good position; hidden by a diagonal snow slope, his troops were virtually invisible to anyone approaching from the ridge above. 'Warn the men not to fire until I give the order,' he told the sergeant. 'Remember we are not barbarians.'

'I understand, Herr *Oberleutnant,*' the sergeant said.

Patiently, Bruno and his men crouched at the foot of the frozen incline while the afternoon sun drew spirals of steam from their sweat-soaked clothing. Waiting was never a problem for Bruno. He seldom minded the passage of time. It had always been his primary virtue, that element of patience, that ability to take each day as he found it, with anticipation and hope. In his mind the future didn't exist. On the Russian front he had watched the enemy T-34s bludgeon their way through the German armour and had stopped believing in the future. He knew that the war was already lost but secretly he cared little about the war; he was a sanguine young man who lived for the excitement of the moment, embracing each contingency with an enthusiasm that confounded everyone who came into his path.

All afternoon they waited, shivering as the high altitude cold bit through their heavy clothing, then as evening drew nigh a flicker of movement on the mountain flank made Bruno's muscles tense. Drawing his Luger, he scanned the snow slope above. A man emerged from the glare, his feet kicking up showers of ice granules as he descended the slippery gradient. Bruno sensed a ripple of excitement pass through the watching troops. The man moved with a curious reluctance as if endless hours of flight had filled him with distaste for mobility of any kind. Suddenly, he slipped on the unstable surface, cartwheeling forward in a flurry of whirling limbs. Startled by the unexpected movement, one of Bruno's troops accidentally squeezed his trigger and Bruno cursed under his breath as a shot reverberated across the open hillslope.

The Englander rolled to a halt, staring down at the soldiers in puzzlement. He made no attempt to rise but lay where he had fallen, framed against the snow. Bruno shaded his gaze against the sinking sun, examining the man curiously. Never in his life had he seen a face quite like it; the features were honed into a series of vertical and horizontal lines and the eyes carried the intractability of a battering ram. There would be no 'give' in such a man, he thought, no hint of submission or compromise. Mind set, he would follow his instincts to the bitter end.

His pulses quickened as the Englander scrambled to his feet and turned back the way he had come. 'Don't shoot,' he shouted, holding up his hand. 'Spread out along the canyon rim and cut him off from the track below.'

A fierce excitement filled him as he tore at his tunic and tossed the garment wildly aside. His hat followed, then his shirt, and clad only in pants and singlet, he started up the slippery snow-slope. He was dimly aware of the river on his left but his eyes remained fixed on the fugitive in front who was scaling the rise with commendable ease. Bruno's own legs felt awkward and unstable and his soles slithered on the crusted neve. After seven months at the front and another four on garrison duty he was out of condition, that was painfully clear. His limbs were stiff, his muscles sluggish and a terrible sickness swept his stomach as he gulped oxygen into his tortured lungs.

The snowfield ended and the ridge divided, forming a tributary spur which curled toward the river gorge and Bruno's pace quickened as his feet found more stable purchase. The spur narrowed into a slender knife edge, the rock broken by a series of vertical pinnacles following one upon the other like the teeth of an upturned comb. Bruno's skin chilled as Caudale, without breaking step, began leaping from pinnacle to pinnacle. He moved with the precision of a dancer, his wiry frame floating through the air as if suspended on invisible wires.

Bruno had no time to consider the wisdom of such a tactic. A gap opened at his feet and he hurled himself forward, his foot landing on the first of the rocky pinnacles. Carried on by his own momentum, he soared into the air again, struggling to measure distance and velocity. He saw the chasm yawning beneath him as he danced fearfully from pillar to pillar, his knees jarring with each successive step. Caudale, in front, was bounding along with the casualness of a trapeze artist and Bruno guessed that leading him here had been a deliberate strategy. The Englander was trying to force him to quit or kill him into the bargain. Straining to remain alert he went on jumping until the pinnacles ended and they were running across good solid ground again.

Directly in front the spur curled down toward the river's edge and here, a great blanket of foliage formed a canopy along the rim of the Schwabingen Gorge. Bruno realized that if Caudale reached the cover of the pines, it would take an army to winkle him out. He tried to step up his pace but already his stride was beginning to falter. Once, he would have handled the pinnacles with ease, secure in the knowledge of his own strength and staying power. Now, he was running on stubbornness and little else.

On one side, the ridge dropped in an almost perpendicular ramp to the river bluffs beneath. If he managed to negotiate the incline, he calculated he might reach the river first and cut off the Englander in full flight. It looked a perilous descent route but he switched direction without a thought and shot down the precipitous embankment, his legs working like pistons to keep his body aloft.

He followed a crisscross pattern in an attempt to control his wild momentum but the faster he moved, the more hazardous the incline became. He somersaulted forward, tumbling helplessly over and over, and hit the ground with a sickening thud. For several moments he lay in a daze, staring blankly at the fleecy sky, then he dragged himself to his feet and squinted up at the mountain slope above. Where the hell was Caudale?

He spotted a wiry figure sprinting down the ridge crest and clawed his Luger from its holster, clasping it with both arms outstretched. 'Halt,' he shouted in English.

Caudale, running like a man demented, scarcely faltered. He hurled himself forward in a spectacular leap and Bruno, dry-mouthed, followed his progress with the Luger, his finger frozen inside the trigger guard. He watched the Englander plunge into the river gorge and vanish beneath the foaming water. The act was so unexpected, so suicidal in intent, that for a moment he could scarcely believe his senses. The river swept Caudale up, carrying him with an inexorable force toward the cataract edge; for a moment he teetered on the brink, struggling against the current's pull, then in a flurry of whirling limbs he corkscrewed over and plummeted into the cauldron beneath.

Panting, Bruno fixed his gaze on the billowing spray but there was no sign of Caudale's body. Either it had been dragged to the bottom or the sheer force of the water had ripped it to shreds. He was filled with an inexplicable sense of regret. It seemed cruel that the man should die after such a spirited performance.

He felt strangely despondent as he pushed his Luger back into its holster and stumbled back wearily to rejoin his men.

The sound of the telephone brought Greg Anderson abruptly awake. He was lying on a camp bed in the corner of his office, awaiting news from Occupied France. Throwing back the blankets, he glanced at his wrist-watch. It was four-thirty in the morning.

On the opposite side of the room, Captain Stoker and Lieutenant Seiber stirred in their bunks as he reached for the receiver. 'Anderson here.'

'Lieutenant Kusack, sir. "F" Squadron.'

'Yes, lieutenant?'

'Bingo,' the lieutenant said.

'The arms got through?'

'They sure did, Major. Our boys are on their way home now. Delivery complete.'

'Any casualties?'

'No, sir. The run went clean as a whistle. According to reports, the Heinis had most of their forces concentrated where they expected Caudale to be. There wasn't a German in sight. We made it on the button, sir.'

'Thank you, lieutenant,' Greg said calmly.

He put down the receiver and sat grinning at it in silence for a moment. Then with a mighty whoop, he leapt into the air and hurled his pillow exhuberantly at the ceiling. Captain Stoker and Lieutenant Seiber stared at each other in amazement. It was the first time in their acquaintance they had ever seen Greg Anderson laugh.

On the first Tuesday of every month Prime Minister Winston Churchill made a habit of entertaining His Majesty, King George VI, in the ground floor dining room at Number 10 Downing Street. It was a private affair in which the two men would talk over the war and the latest Allied developments.

Three nights after Jonas's entry into France, having enjoyed an excellent meal of trout and venison supplied by the King's Balmoral estate, they sat in front of the fire while Churchill lit his customary cigar.

'Curious report on the BBC French Service the other night,' the King remarked. 'Couldn't make sense of it at all.'

Churchill blew smoke toward the ceiling. 'I had no idea you listened to the French Service.'

'Whenever I can. It's my favourite language.'

'Did the report concern a Lakeland

shepherd trying to run across the Occupied territories?'

The King looked at him sharply. The Prime Minister could be infuriatingly evasive on issues he did not wish to discuss but tonight he appeared to be in an expansive mood. 'The man's name is Caudale,' Churchill said. 'He's some kind of eccentric who's got it into his head that despite the war, he can conduct his own private marathon. No one quite knows why, but he does have a facility for stirring up the enemy.'

'So the radio broadcast was genuine?'

'Up to a point. The Americans needed to drop supplies to the *Maquisards* near the French border and they used Caudale as a decoy. I understand the plan worked like a dream.'

The King was thoughtful for a moment. In the firelight, his pinched face looked strangely morose. 'I hate war,' he breathed at last.

Churchill said, 'I know what you're thinking. We betrayed Caudale, used him as a sacrificial goat. Well, it's true. That's what war is all about—exploiting resources, playing games with other people's lives. If the loss of one demented shepherd can save us men on D-Day, I'd call it a pretty fair exchange. However ...' The Prime Minister's eyes gleamed. 'As

61

things turned out, Caudale managed to survive. He was picked up by members of a local Resistance group who found him floating in a river, more dead than alive. They radioed the news to our SOE Headquarters at Bletchley. He's recovering now at a remote farmhouse somewhere in the Alpine foothills.'

'So our Lakeland shepherd could still make it home after all?'

Rolling his brandy in his glass, Churchill stared into the fireplace. 'Wouldn't it be pleasant to think so.'

The morning sunlight cast wavering patterns through the brown paper strips covering the *Daily Express* windows as Anne Huntley, blonde, slim, twenty-two years old, made her way toward the Editor's office, her high heels clicking on the linoleum floor. She was an attractive girl—not startlingly so but certainly enough to pass muster—and she carried a freshness which charmed everyone she met. She had started her career on the *Newcastle Journal* but thanks to the war and the dearth of male reporters had graduated to Fleet Street after only eight months.

She tapped lightly on the Editor's door before entering. 'You wanted to see me?' she said, doing her best to appear bright and intelligent.

Huddled over a bundle of cuttings, Editor Hugh Miller waved her to a chair. Thickset and heavy-jowled, Miller was a prize-winning journalist in his own right; in 1939, he had been the first to reveal Germany's intentions in the Danzig Corridor and he was a recognized authority on international politics, having covered wars and revolutions all over the world.

He picked up a sheet of paper from his desktop. 'Listen to this. It's a translation of a news bulletin which went out a few nights ago on the BBC's French Service.' Slipping his spectacles over his nose, he began to read: ' "Jonas Caudale, the celebrated Lakeland fellrunner who outstripped a detachment of Hitler's elite SS after escaping from a train in the Austrian Alps has announced his intention of running all the way home to Buttermere. Six weeks ago, he crossed seventy-nine miles of German countryside, pursued by enemy forces with tracker dogs and members of the local police, reaching the safety of Switzerland in a flying finish that would have delighted the great Jesse Owen. Not content with humbling the Fuhrer's supermen, Caudale sets out tonight on his latest marathon by entering Nazi Occupied France by the Swiss border. If Herr Adolf's strutting gamecocks care to renew their acquaintance, we feel sure Jonas will be happy to show them another clean pair of heels." '

Anne frowned. 'What does it mean?'

'I don't know what it means but it must mean something.'

'Did you check with the BBC?'

'They refuse to comment.'

'Then oughtn't we to leave it alone? Could be military.'

'There's been no D-notice issued. And supposing the story's genuine?'

'Running home to Buttermere across enemy-occupied Europe?' Anne thought for a moment. 'Sounds like something out of mythology, but it might be worth looking into.'

'My feelings exactly.' Miller took off his spectacles. 'People are tired of reading about the war. The Lake District in spring should be just the thing to pull them out of the doldrums. I want you to go up there and check this Caudale out. Visit his home, talk to some of his friends. Dig out a little background on his sporting achievements. He's a local athlete, a champion fellrunner. A nice personality profile is what I'm looking for.'

'Hugh, has it occurred to you that this whole thing could be a hoax?'

'Only one way to find out. Investigate.'

He fixed her with a beady stare and she sighed resignedly. She had worked at the *Express* long enough to recognize the look. When Miller got an idea into his head, it would take a blitzkreig to shift it. Still, the prospect of getting out of London was a pleasant one and she was humming happily as she tidied her desk and took a taxi to the railway station. The train journey north however proved lengthy and uncomfortable; the passenger cars were packed with troops and she found herself stuck in the corridor until a gallant sailor offered her his seat.

She arrived at the little Lakeland town after innumerable delays, feeling drained and irritable. The green slate buildings looked picturesque in the lap of the surrounding mountains and the central square with its old-fashioned clock tower reminded her of an Alpine calendar.

She made her way straight to the local newspaper office and met the editor, a balding man with a blue-veined face. He seemed delighted when she showed him her press card.

'It isn't often we get reporters from London in this day and age,' he said. 'Nobody's interested in what happens up north any more. All the attention's focused on the south. Understandable, I suppose. After all, that's where the Channel is, and across the Channel lies the enemy.'

'Well, we're about to put you back

on the map.' Anne smiled. 'I'm looking for information on one of your local fellrunners, a man named Jonas Caudale.'

The editor stared at the ceiling. 'Caudale, Caudale. It's a common enough name hereabouts but I have to confess I've never heard of a Jonas.'

'That's strange. According to our information, this particular Caudale should be something of a local celebrity. He won practically every major hill-racing event prior to the war. He also set up a number of records—records which haven't yet been broken.'

'I doubt that,' the editor said. 'It would be impossible for him to have done such things without my being aware of it. Fellrunners in the Lake District are like movie stars. I don't like to question your sources, Miss Huntley, but I think somebody's been feeding you duff information.'

She frowned. 'Would you mind if I looked at your records? I'd like to check the fell-race results for the late Thirties.'

'By all means. However, speaking as an *aficianado*, I can assure you that if Jonas Caudale existed I would most certainly know about it.'

Anne sat in the tiny office and went through the sporting files as the editor's secretary brought them in. They were detailed and prolific and dated right back to the turn of the century. Nowhere could she find a reference to Jonas Caudale.

Disappointed, she returned the folders and thanked the editor for his help.

'This isn't London, you know,' he said. 'We're a close knit community here in Cumberland. Everyone knows everyone else. If there really *was* a Jonas Caudale, you'd only have to ask once.'

'Can you tell me how I get to Buttermere?' she enquired. 'That's where Caudale's supposed to come from, isn't it?'

He chuckled. 'Still following your nose, hey?'

'If I go back to London without checking, my editor will have my hide.'

'Well, there are no buses at this time of year. Your best bet is a taxi. Bit expensive, I should think, driving all the way over Newlands Pass to look for a phantom who doesn't exist.'

'Put it down to feminine curiosity,' she told him with a wry smile. 'The first time I heard about Santa Claus, I sat up all night watching the fireplace.'

The house was large and rambling with a quaint, old-fashioned porch. It stood in its own grounds, surrounded by a high stone wall. At its rear, craggy mountains soared into the March sky.

Anne told the driver to wait on the forecourt and pulled at the old-fashioned bell. After a moment, a voice called from a patch of rhododendrons. 'Can I help you, young lady?'

A man walked toward her across the daffodil-studded lawn, pulling off a pair of gardening gloves. He was white-haired and narrow-chested. She estimated him to be in his early seventies.

'Mr Sanders?'

'That's me.'

'I'm Anne Huntley from the *Daily Express*. The taxi driver tells me you're the largest landowner in the valley, is that true?'

The man smiled. 'Only partly. I run a few farms, but most of the land is in my wife's name. For legal reasons, we keep our properties separate.'

'You will, however, know most of the smallholders working in the area?'

'I know everyone working in the area. This is Buttermere, not New York. We're like one big family here.' He opened the door, ushering her in. 'Let me get you some coffee. It's still a little cool outside, even if spring's in the air.'

She sat in the study while Sanders pottered about noisily in the kitchen. The room, cluttered with antiques, carried an air of slightly archaic elegance. Its walls were covered with pictures, some of Saunders himself clad in the uniform of an army colonel. Through the window, mountains reared against a faultless sky. She thought she had seldom seen anything so beautiful.

Sanders came into the room, carrying the coffee on a silver tray. 'It's bottled essence, I'm afraid. The genuine stuff's impossible to get these days. Also, my wife's gone to Windermere for the afternoon, so you'll have to excuse the rough and ready approach. I admit I've never been properly domesticated.'

'You're very kind,' she smiled. 'And I must say, I do envy you living in such an exquisite corner of the world.'

'Yes, indeed. I spent a few years in India serving with the Northumberland Fusiliers but apart from that, Buttermere has always been my home.' He settled himself in the armchair opposite, his eyes twinkling. 'Until now, I've never regretted a minute of it, but looking at you I'm beginning to wonder if London might not have had its attractions after all. Shut up here in the middle of nowhere, it isn't often I'm visited by such an attractive young lady.'

'Are you sure it isn't Ireland you came from? I can always recognize a man who's kissed the Blarney Stone.'

He laughed and sat back in his chair, pressing his fingertips together. 'What exactly are you seeking, Miss Huntley? I can't imagine the Sanders having done anything to warrant the attention of the *Daily Express*.'

'Mr Sanders, I'm trying to track down a Buttermere fellrunner who, according to our information, was quite a champion in this area just before the war—a local shepherd named Jonas Caudale.'

Sanders thought for a moment, then shook his head. 'There's no shepherd named Caudale in this valley. No fellrunner either. Never has been.'

'You're sure? Please think, Mr Sanders. Is there any chance you could be mistaken?'

'Young lady, I've known everyone who's lived in Buttermere during the past sixty years, male or female. Caudale's a common enough name but I can assure you there are no Jonases.'

She felt her spirits sink. She'd been right all along, the story had been a hoax. Probably some kind of coded message intended for the Resistance. She'd guessed as much, but that didn't make it any easier.

He examined her sympathetically. 'It looks as though your journey's been for nothing.'

She managed a disappointed smile.

'Well, if I hadn't come, I'd never have met you and tried your excellent coffee.'

'That's what I like about the modern generation.' He chuckled. 'They say the nicest things.'

Sanders stood at the window, watching Anne leave. He waited until her taxi had pulled through the gate before walking upstairs and letting himself into a tiny attic. The room was cluttered with junk and assorted pieces of bric-à-brac. He dragged a large chest out of the corner and rummaged around until he found what he was looking for, an old photograph with a gilt-edged frame. Tucking it under his arm, he made his way back to the drawing room downstairs.

He stood at the window, studying the photograph thoughtfully. It had been taken at Buttermere one bright morning in early July. It showed Jonas Caudale clad in running gear and wearing a victor's sash across his shoulder.

Sanders tore off the back of the frame and carried the photograph to the fire grate. He struck a match and lit it in one corner, watching impassively as the picture burst into flame. He waited until there was nothing left but a small heap of blackened ash then he picked up his gloves and returned to the garden outside.

Chapter Three

The wind bathed Bruno's face as his scout car sped through the Alpine pastures. High mountains towered on every side and hoarfrost glistened on the nearby pines. They skirted a lake, its surface still as polished glass. Thirteen days had passed since Bruno's pursuit of the Englander Jonas Caudale and already he had consigned the incident to memory. He felt sorry for the man of course, but he had little time for sentiment; Caudale had been the enemy and though his death had been regrettable, dying, in time of war, was an essential part of existence.

Bruno's Division was being transferred west to occupy the Alpine village of Viatte and as a mountain specialist he had been ordered ahead of the main column to scout the surrounding terrain. It was a task he welcomed since it offered a blessed escape from the dreary monotony of convoy travel.

Seated beside him in the vehicle rear was Willi Fredier, a reporter from the *Nuremburg Gazette*. Fredier was a dry little man with a mischievous sense of

72

humour which Bruno found admirably complemented his own. Throughout the morning, he had kept up an amusing dialogue on all aspects of German political life (including the Führer's legendary testicular deficiency, on which Fredier appeared to be something of an expert) interspersing his remarks with frequent nips from a schnapps flask he carried in his jacket pocket.

Bruno had been reluctant to accept Fredier's company at first but the major had insisted, pointing out that Goebbels himself had requested the reporter be afforded every facility. Now he was delighted to have the man along, for Fredier provided a much needed diversion from Lieutenant Rolf Kurtner seated in front. The grey-haired Kurtner had appeared intelligent at first glance but had turned out to be as thick as a post, and to make matters worse, he insisted on carrying out a running commentary on the local culture as they rattled through the rugged landscape.

'The Romans built this road,' he told them. 'At least, they laid the foundations. It was an important junction during the early Roman Empire. They created Augusta Praetoria to control the rights of passage. You'll find their monuments all over the place.'

'We're not the first conquerors then,' Bruno observed.

'Not by a long shot.'

Willi Fredier smiled. 'Maybe it wasn't the skill of our flying columns which defeated the French after all, but the simple desire of the people to be dominated. Like a woman.'

Kurtner said, 'It's easy to be frivolous, but do you remember what happened to the Romans in the end?'

'Indeed. Instead of fighting, they spent all their time screwing.'

'A noble enterprise.' Bruno chuckled. 'The outcome of this war could be decided not by artillery shells, but by ricocheting fly buttons.'

Lieutenant Kurtner frowned at the ribald flippancy. 'Herr *Oberleutnant* wouldn't be so complacent if he'd come up against the local Resistance. Their terrorist units give our people quite a headache one way and another.'

'I find that hard to believe,' Fredier said. 'A Division like the *Leibstandarte* must seem invincible to tattered bands of *maquisards.*'

'Quite the opposite. In fact, they're growing more audacious by the minute.'

'A sure sign that there's an invasion in the offing,' Bruno commented.

The conversation was beginning to bore

him. Kurtner's lack of humour cast a pall of gloom over the entire company and he lay back in his seat, closing his eyes as the country dipped and undulated.

The sound of a shot brought him abruptly awake. For a moment he thought he had been dreaming, then a second shot, louder than the first, echoed through the adjacent pine trees and he sat up, blinking. Their driver was weaving all over the place, struggling to bring the scout car under control. Ahead, Bruno saw a hay cart blocking their way and behind it, a group of men firing in ragged volleys, the flame from their rifles flashing in the sunlight.

The scout car spun to a halt, its front wheels propped precariously over a ditch, and Bruno yelled, 'Everybody out.'

Scrambling over the side, they burrowed into the dirt, Fredier wincing as he dropped awkwardly to the ground.

'All right?' Bruno asked.

'Twisted my ankle. Just like the bloody thing.'

'Let's hope that's all you have to worry about.'

Bullets were ricocheting off the blacktop roadway, making metallic clanging noises as they ripped through the vehicle body-work above. Bruno saw the others staring at him expectantly and realized with a start that he was the officer in command.

He removed the pistol from his holster and began surveying the surrounding terrain. On one side, a narrow watercourse spread across a jagged gully. On the other, the land dropped to a prominent rock hovering above the pastures below.

Bruno detected an immediate flaw in the enemy's strategy. The spot they had chosen was perfect for ambush, except for one crucial point; behind the ditch, and directly to the rear of where he was lying, the earth provided an incline along which a man might crawl undetected, if he kept his body close to the ground.

'Lay down as much covering fire as you can,' he ordered the driver. 'I'm going to try and outflank the bastards by sneaking along the slope at their rear.'

'You're crazy, *Oberleutnant*. They'll pick you off like a clay pigeon.'

'Not the way they're shooting, they won't. Those idiots couldn't hit a stationary tank at four paces.' He looked at Lieutenant Kurtner. 'I think you'd better come too.'

Kurtner's face was several shades paler than usual but he nodded grimly and picked up his machine pistol. The two men rolled over the ditch rim and eased cautiously across the grassy hillslope. The ground was wet from the intermittent rain and coated in places with a thin covering of slime. Bruno dragged himself forward by the elbows, the odour of damp vegetation lingering in his nostrils. If he'd judged this wrongly, they'd be in a fine old mess and no mistake. Cut off behind, and a perfect target for the *résistants* above. No wonder Kurtner looked so sickly.

He slithered belly-flat through a small hollow and a marmot, startled by his intrusion, shot like a bullet into a cluster of rocks. Pausing, he tried to calculate their position. From the firing, he guessed they had reached a point almost level with the spot where their ambushers were hiding. He glanced back at Kurtner whose face was now flushed with exertion. 'Give me your machine gun.'

Kurtner seemed glad to get rid of it. Bruno passed him his revolver and the lieutenant stared down at its ribbed butt as if half afraid the thing might go off in his hand. Holding the weapon in front of him, Bruno wriggled to the top of the slope. There was a lull in the firing as attackers and defenders alike paused to reload and he took advantage of the moment to lift his head above the rise. He saw the partisans almost within touching distance, three men and a boy, dressed in battered caps and work clothes.

He slipped off his safety catch and shouted in French, 'Stand where you are.

Throw down your weapons, and place your hands on your heads.'

For a moment the *résistants* froze, caught in a silent tableau. Then one, the nearest, a raw-boned man with a bulbous nose, swung his rifle in a desperate arc, and Bruno gently squeezed his trigger. The man plummeted backwards into the roadway and lay twitching convulsively. The three remaining *résistants* stared in bewilderment at their dying comrade then dropped their rifles and raised their arms in surrender.

Bruno smiled to himself as he waved to his companions and examined the prisoners curiously. If this was the standard of the French Resistance, he thought, his Division would be as safe as if it had remained in Bavaria.

In the pale light of dawn, Bruno watched the truck pull to a halt beneath the steel-framed railroad bridge. Crouched in the rear, the hostages, fifteen men and women, looked sullen and defiant. A terrible foreboding gathered inside him as he stared at the scene with sickly reluctance. The SS commander, after studying Bruno's report, had decided to revenge the guerrilla attack by executing a group of local villagers as a warning to the inhabitants. To Bruno, the measure seemed barbarous in the extreme and a hollow emptiness settled in his stomach as SS stormtroopers climbed over the tailboard and kicked the hostages to their feet. 'This is a dreadful mistake,' he whispered.

Major Gruber, standing at his side, nodded in agreement. 'I know, *Oberleutnant*, but some things must be done in the name of duty. Our *résistant* friends broke the cardinal rule—thou shalt not shoot at the *Leibstandarte*. Someone has to pay.' Gruber was the local Wehrmacht commander, the man responsible for controlling the surrounding area. He was medium-sized and balding, with an olive skin and soulful brown eyes.

'These people had nothing to do with the attack on my scout car,' Bruno said.

'I'm afraid the matter is out of my hands. The colonel hopes that by taking reprisals, he can dissuade the locals from further defiance.'

Bruno saw the SS colonel striding toward them, accompanied by a group of subordinates. He drew to a halt in front of the truck, his death's head cap badge gleaming in the darkness. His eyes were cold, his lips bloodless. 'Is everything ready?'

'Yes, *Standartenfuhrer*.'

'Then let the executions commence.'

79

Bruno cleared his throat. '*Standarten-fuhrer,* taking reprisals against these villagers will achieve nothing. The job of the Wehrmacht is difficult enough without alienating the local population.'

The colonel frowned, examining him intently. 'Aren't you the officer who captured the terrorists?'

'Yes, *Standartenfuhrer.*'

'Then you, of all people, should understand the purpose of this punishment?'

'Hanging fifteen hostages can hardly be called a punishment. In a community like this, families will be related. Friends, uncles, cousins. Kill them and no one will remain untouched.'

'Good. Perhaps their dying will have the intended effect.'

'*Standartenfuhrer,* in the name of humanity, I beg you to at least reduce the number.'

The colonel's sharp eyes scoured Bruno's features. 'I see you feel compassion toward the enemy.'

'They are ordinary people, *Standartenfuhrer.*'

'Compassion is an admirable thing, *Oberleutnant,* but do not let it cloud your judgement.'

'My first allegiance is always to the Reich,' Bruno said.

The colonel nodded, satisfied. 'Very

well, I am not an unreasonable man. I will reduce the number to eight. Not one person less.' He raised his voice, addressing the sergeant on the truck. 'Release seven hostages, then proceed with the executions.'

Bruno felt numb. His appeal hadn't worked. The colonel was intent on his eye-for-an-eye philosophy.

A line of ropes dangled from the bridge girders and he saw the prisoners shivering as the troops slipped nooses over their heads. Somehow the shivering seemed to emphasize their helplessness.

Major Gruber squeezed his arm. 'I know how you feel, *Oberleutnant,* believe me. I am a human being also.'

Footsteps echoed behind them and Bruno saw a woman approaching from the direction of the village. She wore a headscarf and a belted raincoat which did little to conceal her explicit figure. Her face was grave but her eyes carried a hint of hidden fire. She drew to a halt, staring at the scene in front.

Major Gruber left Bruno's side and walked toward her. 'Madame Le Gras, you shouldn't have come here.'

'These people are my friends.'

'But you are torturing yourself unnecessarily.'

'If they can die, the least I can do is

watch their suffering. Someone has to bear witness to your infamy.'

Major Gruber muffled a cough with his glove. 'Madame Le Gras, you must learn to be a little more discreet. One of these days someone will report you to the Gestapo and when that happens I shall no longer be in a position to protect you.'

The woman ignored him. She stared at the grisly preparations, her headscarf fluttering in the wind. Gruber strolled back to Bruno, meeting his gaze with a casual shrug. 'She's known these people all her life. She doesn't realize what she's saying.'

Bruno examined the woman curiously. She carried a strong sensual air which somehow accentuated the vehemence of her anger. Her eyes were glacial and her mouth was moulded into a thin firm line as if she was holding her emotions in check with an effort.

He heard a shout from the railroad bridge and turned unwillingly. The preparations were complete, the executions ready to begin. The truck eased forward and eight hostages swung like puppets in the early morning rain.

He averted his head in disgust. It was a savage charade they were playing and he wanted no part of it. The woman, he noticed, stood frozen to the spot, staring resolutely in front. He watched her in wonderment, amazed at her strength. Not until the last hostage had finished struggling did she turn and walk away.

A young corporal met Greg at the railway station as he climbed from the crowded train. 'Major Anderson? Welcome to the Lake District, sir.'

Greg glared at the man, tossing his holdall into the waiting jeep. 'I'd like to know what this is all about,' he said.

'Didn't London explain, sir?'

'London explained nothing, as usual.'

'Then I'm sure Colonel Greenewalt will be able to fill in the details.'

Greg kept his composure with an effort as they headed south into the rolling hillslopes. It had been a long, uncomfortable journey from London but there was little point in taking out his anger on the unfortunate driver.

He leaned back in the passenger seat and watched the scenery flitting by. It was the first real day of spring and the Cumberland countryside looked breathtaking. A lake lay on his right, its placid surface picking up slivers of refracted sunlight. Whitewashed cottages nestled among the pasture folds. In different circumstances, he felt he could easily have appreciated this ride but with D-Day approaching, he resented any distraction from his work. He hadn't believed the order at first, had insisted on checking the details with Eisenhower's secretary, but there had been no further clarification. In the end, he'd had little choice but to drop everything and head north. Now he was filled with impatience and frustration.

The road began to climb and he spied twin lakes ahead, cradled in the lap of majestic mountains. After a while they jerked to halt at a tiny inn and he saw a man strolling toward them. The man was tall and athletic-looking, dressed in the uniform of an army colonel. He shook Greg's hand, smiling. 'Art Greenewalt. Glad you could make it, Major. I hope you'll find your visit worthwhile.'

Brushing dust from his tunic, Greg climbed from the jeep and followed Greenewalt to a pony and trap waiting at the inn rear. The colonel patted the animal's rump. 'Ever driven one of these things?'

'No, sir.'

'City man, I take it?'

'Not exactly. I was brought up in Maine. But ...' He shrugged. 'I guess I was more interested in automobiles than horseflesh.'

'That's OK. I'm an old hand at buggy-handling. Back in Montana, we used them all the time. Some of those dirt roads can knock hell out of a weak suspension.'

Greg climbed into the buggy seat and Colonel Greenewalt flicked the reins, guiding their mount into the empty lane. 'I guess you're wondering what this is all about?'

'Yes, sir, I am. I'm up to my eyeballs in work at the moment.'

'They warned me you were an obsessive man. Don't you ever feel the need to unbend a little?'

'This isn't exactly my idea of "unbending", sir.'

'We're human beings, Major. We have to ease up once in a while, otherwise we disintegrate. However, as it happens, I'm something of an obsessive man myself and I thought you might stand a better chance of appreciating what I have to say if you looked at this valley from the locals' viewpoint.' He paused for a moment then added, 'That was a pretty good idea using the decoy in Section 14.'

'The idea belonged to Captain Stoker,' Greg told him.

'Just the same, it paid off beautifully. I understand the *parachutage* went without a hitch.'

'Yes, sir.'

'Ever wonder about the man you sent in?'

'Caudale? Never.'

'No qualmy feelings afterwards?'

'The qualms came at the beginning. It isn't pleasant sending somebody to his death. But once the *parachutage* paid off, I decided the sacrifice had been justified.'

'Well, let me set your mind at ease. Your man was neither killed nor captured. As a matter of fact, by some miracle, he fell into the hands of a French resistance unit near the Alpine village of Viatte. He's got a slight chill, the result of a drenching while hiding from the SS, but otherwise he's A-okay.' The colonel gave the reins a flick, and said, 'As a matter of interest, this is the place Caudale was making for. Buttermere.'

Greg glanced around him. 'It's a beautiful spot,' he admitted.

'Yes. There's a kind of timelessness here. The modern world scarcely intrudes at all. That's why I hired the buggy. I wanted you to understand something of the feeling Caudale has for this place. You might find it hard to believe but every rock, every slope, every summit has its own special name.' He waved at the peaks in front. 'That's Low Bank over there and Whiteless Pike above. Wanlope's the crag along the hillcrest and Lad Hows is the bulge on the far side of Rannerdale Beck. Sourmilk Gill's the waterfall across the lake. You can also see Ling Crags and Mellbreak, Scale Knott and Ling Comb. That's Red Pike sticking above the outcrops there, and Chapel Crags and Starling Dodd. It shows you how the people feel about this land. They're part of each other, interchangeable.'

'Colonel, is there some point to all this?'

Greenewalt was silent for a moment as wind rippled the lake surface, carrying with it the scent of moorgrass and heather. 'Do you think Caudale could actually do it? Run back to Buttermere?'

Greg frowned. 'Is that some kind of joke?'

'It's no joke, Major, believe me.'

'Across Occupied Europe? Are you kidding?'

'The other night, he tied up the entire countryside for damn near fifteen hours. Every soldier in a thirty-mile radius was after his hide but he still got away.'

'Are you seriously suggesting we use him again?'

'For the arms drops, no. I had something more elaborate in mind.'

The colonel took out a packet of cigarettes and offered them to Greg. Greg shook his head and the colonel lit one himself, blowing smoke through his lips and nostrils. 'With the invasion on our doorstep, our intelligence people are facing a dilemma. The Germans know we're coming and they're already preparing to meet our landing forces. We have to divert their attention elsewhere but that's a tricky business. A sudden upsurge in guerrilla activity, for example, would confirm the imminence of an Allied offensive. What we need are small, simple distractions, innocent on the outside, but intriguing enough to occupy the enemy's mind and tie up his resources.

'We already have a number of projects under way. We've set up phony camps to confuse the Germans about our jumping-off point. We're putting out counterfeit radio traffic and General Patton is heading a bogus army group in the south-east of England to strengthen the impression that the invasion will come from that quarter. We're accommodating our bombing patterns and the British SAS have parachuted dummies into the Cherbourg peninsular. But what we need are more isolated incidents to cement the overall effect. Our OSS people feel that your idea of using Caudale as a decoy was an inspiration.'

'Colonel, you're not trying to tell me that if Caudale goes on running, he could tie up the German war machine? One man?'

'No, I'm not. But he could prove a useful component. By transmitting progress reports via the BBC we just might, with luck, convince the Germans that his run has some kind of military significance.'

'You're crazy.'

'Why? It worked before.'

'That was pure luck. They'll never fall for it a second time.'

'London thinks they will. They think it's worth a try.'

'It's no go, Colonel.'

'Give me one good reason.'

'Because Caudale's mad, that's why.'

'But it's the kind of madness that produces results. If we can keep Caudale running, he'll help to bolster our bodyguard of deceit.'

Somewhere nearby, they heard a dog barking. A faint uneasiness gathered in Greg. He knew what was coming, sensed it with a fatal intuition, knew in his heart there was no other way. He looked down at his hands. 'What is it you're asking me to do, sir?'

'The arms drops can be handled by other officers. We need somebody to go into Occupied France. I realize you've already done more than can be reasonably expected of a man but you know the people, you know the terrain. The important thing is to get Caudale on the move.'

'Are you offering me a choice?'

'I can't order you to go, son. Christ knows, you'll be setting yourself up as a perfect Aunt Sally. When those broadcasts hit the air, Jonas Caudale will be a marked man and keeping him at large will be a hazardous enterprise. All I can tell you is, by helping to build up our smoke screen, you could save a great many lives come D-Day.'

Greg stared at the hills ahead, a terrible tension tightening in his stomach. 'I'll be happy to give it a try, sir.'

The roar of the Halifax thundered in Greg's ears. Braced against the bulkhead, he tried to ignore the chill night air slicing through his padded flying suit. Strapped into a bucket seat on the opposite side of the hull, the sergeant gunner watched him sympathetically. The sergeant understood the terror of dropping into enemy territory and his dark eyes commiserated, but Greg reflected that the sergeant had one major advantage. No one was asking him to go.

The light in the forward section switched to red and giving the thumbs up signal, the sergeant reached forward to release the catches on the jump-hole hatch. Greg felt his pulses quickening as he fastened his parachute to the quick-release clip under his knees and watched the sergeant ease back the metal cover. He seated himself in the opening, both legs dangling over the edge. The wind battered his face, scattering his hair in all directions. Below, the land lay in a sprawl of total blackness.

The sergeant checked the static line which would spring his parachute loose, and winked encouragingly. Then the light in the forward section switched to green and he tapped Greg lightly on the shoulder.

Greg took a deep breath and leapt out and down, the icy slipstream scouring his cheeks and throat. He felt himself turning helplessly in the wind, the aircraft engine still ringing in his ears. He heard a fluttering noise, saw the great white canopy spreading above his head and a wave of relief flooded him as his momentum gradually slackened.

Floating earthwards, suspended beneath the billowing parachute, he watched the land solidifying amid the gloom and braced his legs for the impact. The ground rushed up, his heels hit the crunchy topsoil, then he was rolling over and uncoupling his harness before the silk had a chance to settle. Gathering the parachute together, he wrapped it into a bundle and buried it beneath a cluster of rocks. He was panting by the time he'd finished.

The sound of a truck echoed in the darkness and his muscles tightened as he saw a vehicle rattling toward him along the bumpy road. The vehicle slithered to a halt and he heard the rough cadence of men's voices.

The ground sloped to the left and he saw the ripple of a shallow river. He splashed across it and climbed up the other side, feeling sick and disorientated.

A figure emerged out of the gloom and he froze in his tracks as a voice uttered a sentence in husky French. 'The mountain flood shall thunder as before.'

'And ocean bellow from his rocky shore,' Greg said.

The figure gestured with its arm. 'This way, quickly.'

He panted as he stumbled along in the spectre's wake, burrowing under a wire fence. He saw the outline of a road then the figure straightened and Greg discerned a woman with an ashen-pale face, her hair hidden beneath a silken headscarf.

'You're two fields off target,' she said. 'Another hundred yards, and you'd have landed in the middle of the German SS.'

'We've had no news of any SS here.'

'They arrived last night, an entire Division.' A note of bitterness entered her voice. 'They celebrated the event by hanging eight villagers.'

She led him to a nearby hedge and dragged a bicycle out of the ditch. It was a tandem two-seater. 'You know how to ride?'

He nodded and swung deftly into the saddle, his sweaty palms gripping the handlebars. The woman settled herself in front and his nostrils caught the fragrance of her perfume as they pedalled swiftly along the narrow lane. 'Where are we going?'

'To the village. I have an apartment there.'

'Are you Suzanne Le Gras?'

'Yes. And for the moment you're my brother from Limoges, Auguste Odru, remember that. I've told practically the whole village that you're coming so no one should seem surprised. Did they issue you with ration books and identity papers?'

'They're in my pocket.'

'The Wehrmacht will expect you to report for a document check in the morning. Don't be alarmed, it's just a formality. All newcomers have to go through the same routine.'

'When do I get to see Caudale?'

'In a day or two. He's at a farmhouse about fourteen miles outside of town. I'll take you there as soon as it's safe.'

He eyed her scarf curiously in the darkness. He could see the curve of her skull and the indentation of her slender neck. 'Does your husband know you're doing this?'

'My husband is dead. Killed by the Boche.'

'I'm sorry.'

'I don't believe in sympathy,' she said. 'I believe in retribution.'

The road dipped, and he saw lights moving in the village ahead. They heard the roar of truck engines and men shouting. The woman cursed under her breath. 'They're searching the houses. Someone must have seen you floating down. We must reach my apartment before the Germans get there. Otherwise, they'll know we violated the curfew.'

They hid the tandem in a copse of trees and entered the village from the rear, picking their way through a row of darkened gardens. Dogs barked, and Greg heard rifle butts hammering on the cottage doors.

'Does this happen often?'

'They do it from time to time to keep us on our toes. It's all part of the subjugation process. Come this way.'

He followed her into an alley and up a wooden stairway. She opened a door and he ducked inside, leaning against the plastered wall. Drawing the drapes, she switched on the electric light then undid her headscarf and tugged it loose, running her fingers through her auburn hair.

He stared at her in surprise. In the field,

he had taken her for a woman of middle age. Close, he saw she was barely thirty, and her face carried an elusive vitality that was difficult to define.

He froze as boots clattered on the stairway outside. The woman's eyes flashed. 'Take off your coat and sit at the table. Quickly.'

She poured him a glass of wine and he cupped it between his palms as someone hammered on the apartment door. The woman slipped up the latch, tugging it open. A German officer stood on the threshold, flanked by two Wehrmacht infantrymen. 'Madame Le Gras?'

'That's correct.'

'We have come to search your apartment.'

He gestured to the soldiers who thrust Suzanne rudely aside and began rummaging around the cluttered parlour.

The officer looked at Greg haughtily. He was young and spotty-cheeked with a narrow, receding chin. 'Who is this?' he demanded.

'My brother. He's just arrived from Limoges. He's going to work at the Kurfestamm plant.'

'Let me see your papers,' the officer snapped.

Greg fumbled in his pocket and took out his forged documents. The officer checked them briefly before placing them back on

95

the table. 'Have you lived in Limoges long?'

'Most of my life,' Greg said.

'A native then?'

'I moved there when I was three. From Marseilles.'

The officer slapped his gloves lightly against his thigh. It was an unconscious gesture, yet one clearly intended to intimidate. He was watching Greg closely. 'How is Sainte-Phall these days?'

Greg looked blank. 'Sainte-Phall?'

'You do not listen to the evening broadcasts?'

'We ... have no wireless at my parents' home.'

'But I understood Sainte-Phall is a big celebrity in Limoges. You must at least have heard the name?'

Sweat broke out between Greg's shoulder blades, running in a trickle down his spine. He breathed deeply, filling his lungs with air. His voice sounded husky and strained. 'I do not believe such a person exists.'

The officer studied him in silence for a moment, then his lips twisted into a wintry smile. 'How fortunate for you, M'sieur Odru. You are quite correct. I chose the name Sainte-Phall at random to see how you would react.'

Greg heard a movement on the landing and a second officer entered the apartment.

This one was older, smaller, gentler-looking. Glancing at Suzanne Le Gras, he politely removed his hat. 'What is going on here?'

'I am questioning the residents, *Sturmbannfuhrer*,' the first officer said.

'That will not be necessary, *lieutnant*. I am personally acquainted with Madame Le Gras.'

'*Sturmbannfuhrer*, my orders—'

'I know your orders. I was the one who issued them. You may take my word you will find nothing unusual in this apartment.'

The officer stiffened, glancing down at Greg. Then clicking his heels, he jerked his head at his two subordinates and stormed out through the door.

The second officer turned to Suzanne. 'I'm sorry you've been disturbed tonight. One of my men thought he spotted something in the sky. It was probably a bird, but in times like these it pays to be cautious.'

'We have nothing to hide here, Major Gruber.'

The major hesitated, rubbing the side of his nose with his thumb. 'I meant to apologize about that little unpleasantness yesterday. You do understand it was out of my hands? The SS are a law unto themselves and ambushing one of their

97

scout cars was an act of suicidal lunacy. When the colonel called for reprisals, there was nothing I could do.'

'I'm sure that will be a familiar cry when the time comes for the settling of accounts.'

The major looked at Greg. His eyes were large, brown, inherently gentle. 'You're a stranger here, aren't you? I know almost everyone in this village.'

'This is my brother from Limoges,' Suzanne said. 'I told you he was coming.'

'Ah yes, the new worker for the Kurfestamm plant.'

The major picked up Greg's documents and examined them idly. 'What brings you to Viatte, M'sieur Odru? City life becoming a little dull for you?'

'My wife died,' Greg said. 'There's nothing to keep me there any more.'

'So you thought you'd try a little country air, eh?' The major smiled as he dropped the documents back on the table. 'Well, you'll find us one big happy family here. I like to run things in a civilized manner. Keep away from subversive elements and your life should be both pleasant and agreeable.'

The officer clicked his heels and bowed to Suzanne. 'Till we meet again, Madame Le Gras.'

He strode from the room, closing the

door gently behind him and Greg ran his fingers through his sandy hair. 'Close,' he breathed.

Suzanne nodded, hugging herself impulsively.

'Thank God the major trusts you.'

'The major trusts no one. He pretends to be more enlightened than the others but underneath he's just as ruthless, just as tyrannical.'

'At least he's more polite about it.' He looked around the tiny room. 'Where do I sleep?'

Suzanne nodded at a curtained alcove. 'In there.'

'And you?'

'In the room next door.' She regarded him coolly. 'I'm responsible for your safety, nothing else.'

His lips twisted into a rueful grin. 'Well, as long as we've got that settled, how about getting me something to eat?'

Chapter Four

Lotte Monsard put down the food tray and examined herself anxiously in the mirror. She looked pale, she decided, and her cheeks carried a transparency that seemed to accentuate the hollowness under her eyes. She wore no make-up, but the flowered dress was the best she had and it flattered the lines of her angular body.

She knew she wasn't beautiful, not in the accepted sense. She'd always been a plain child, a little on the scrawny side, but she'd blossomed magically when she'd reached adolescence. Men found her comely now, she could tell by the way they looked at her. She saw the hunger in their eyes, the secret, furtive longing. She wondered if the Englishman found her comely.

Ever since the *résistants* had brought him to her farm, Lotte's emotions had been thrown into disarray. It was not so much the visitor's looks—he was no oil painting, to be sure—but two years had passed since the Germans had taken away her husband and God knew, it wasn't easy for a healthy young woman living alone in such an isolated setting. The man reminded her of a puma on the prowl; he was fluid and graceful, wiry and muscular, moody and self-contained. He was also very attractive.

Her hands were trembling as she picked up the food tray and carried it out to the barn. A pile of straw, feed for the few scrawny cows which still grazed Lotte Monsard's pastures, cushioned the bare stone wall. Jonas lay in the straw, listening

100

to the rain. He looked up as she entered but when he saw who it was he let his body relax.

'I've brought you something to eat,' she told him in English.

He ran his fingers through his tangled hair. 'What time is it?'

'Almost eight.'

She placed the food tray at his side and watched silently as he began to eat. Beard stubble had begun to form around his cheeks, adding to his grizzled appearance. 'How long do I have to stay here?' he asked.

'Until the others decide what to do with you.'

'I'm not a spy, if that's what they're thinking.'

'They know that. They're waiting for news from London, that's all.'

She leaned forward and placed her palm against his forehead. 'Temperature's down at last. You should be feeling better now.'

'I feel fine,' he told her.

Why on earth did she find him so attractive, she wondered. She was behaving like a fool and she knew it. In a day or two, the Englishman would be gone—out of her life for ever. Then only the Germans would remain—the Germans and the awful bloody war.

The door creaked open and Lotte's

daughter, Yvette appeared on the threshold, clutching a bottle of wine. Yvette was six years old with slender pigtails tied in a crown above her head. 'I've brought you something to drink,' she said in heavily-accented English.

His eyes softened as he looked at the child. 'That's right good English you speak, Yvette. Learn it at school, did thee?'

'My father teach me.'

'Aye? Where's your father now?'

'In Germany.'

'They took him for the labour camps,' Lotte said, opening the wine and filling Jonas's glass. 'Most of our young men—the able-bodied ones—have been conscripted for German war work.'

His eyes sobered. 'You know what'll happen if the Germans find me here?'

'They won't find you. Put your mind at rest.'

'Just the same, it's time I was moving on. The longer I stay the more dangerous it is for thee and the bairn. Besides, I have to be getting home.'

'To England?' the little girl asked, toying absently with her braids.

'Not just England, Yvette. Buttermere.'

'What kind of a place is that?'

'A place where nothing ever changes.'

'Things go stagnant when they don't change,' Lotte said.

'You're wrong. They give us a link with the past and it's the past that tells us what we really are.'

She was silent for a moment then she said, 'You have a wife waiting in Buttermere?'

'No. No wife.'

'Then why can't you leave it until the fighting's over?'

'I'm trying to run myself clean again.'

'Even if it kills you?'

Jonas's eyes were flat and curiously detached. 'In a funny sort of way,' he said, 'I almost hope it will.'

Night was falling and Bruno shivered as his car sped along the mountain road. It would be dark soon—another dinner in the officer's mess, a far from tempting prospect. Major Gruber was hardly the world's most scintillating conversationalist and he had already beaten most of his fellow officers at chess.

What he needed was feminine company, he decided, but the hostage hanging the other morning had done little to improve relations with the local populace. He dreamed blissfully of amorous adventures in Berlin. He'd been quite a success there, a regular Lothario. His address book had been crammed with names—and small wonder, he thought. The ladies had liked his sense of style, his handsome looks, his regal bearing. He was a remarkable figure of a man and no mistake, athletic, well-proportioned, intelligent. He was also witty, charming and resplendent in his army uniform. He searched for a word to describe his appeal and settled at last upon 'panache'.

The mountains closed about him, their contours fading as shadows crept across their craggy folds. He watched the road's surface forming a metallic ribbon over the rippling pastureland. Then a terrible iciness gripped his heart as he saw a child framed in the headlights ahead. It was a little girl, he realized, seven or eight years old; she was talking to a doll and seemed oblivious to the vehicle's approach.

'Look out,' he shouted, slapping his driver on the shoulder.

The man jammed his foot on the brake and the scout car skidded out of control. Sensing the danger at last, the child froze like a stricken doe and Bruno counted the seconds as he waited for the impact.

Something moved on the hillslope above and he saw a man tearing down the embankment. Lean as a scarecrow, he was running like the wind, twenty yards, fifteen, ten ...

Bruno felt the scout car shudder as his

driver wrestled with the wheel. The little girl's face, pale as alabaster, seemed to fill the entire windshield. He held his breath, watching the stranger eating up the distance and a sob of relief burst from his lips as the man hurled himself forward and swept up the child, carrying her clear with his own momentum.

The vehicle shrieked to a halt and Bruno glanced over his shoulder, shivering with shock. 'You damn fool,' he snapped at the driver. 'You almost killed that child back there.'

'Forgive me, *Oberleutnant*. In such a remote area, I expected the road to be empty.'

'Wait here,' Bruno ordered.

He climbed from the car and strode toward the dishevelled figures who were dragging themselves dazedly to their feet.

'Are you all right?' he asked in French, touching his cap in a polite salute.

The man fixed him with a surly stare and deep inside he felt a faint tremor of recognition. He was sure he had seen the face somewhere before.

He knelt down and gently smoothed the girl's pigtailed hair. 'You are not hurt, *chérie?*'

She shook her head, tears streaming down her freckled cheeks.

'My driver gave you a scare there, hey?

He should be whipped soundly for his stupidity.'

Rising, he said to the man, 'I ask you to accept my apology. There's no excuse for such irresponsible behaviour. My driver will be severely reprimanded.'

The stranger looked at him, his eyes as cold as verglas. Again Bruno was struck by his familiar appearance. 'We've met before, am I right?'

Silence.

Bruno said, 'I never forget a face and I've seen yours' before, I'd be willing to bet on it.'

No answer. No reaction at all apart from that implacable stare. Bruno felt his anger rising. There was a limit to his patience, a limit to his goodwill. The man was deliberately mocking him.

'I warn you, my friend, if you are trying to provoke me, you are treading on dangerous ground.'

Someone shouted from the hilltop and he saw a woman framed against the sky. She stood for a moment, her cheeks tinged by the setting sun, then she came running down the slope toward them, her flowered dress billowing in the wind. He watched, embarrassed, as she clasped the little girl into her arms. 'You are the child's mother?'

She looked up at him out of tear-stained

106

eyes and Bruno took off his cap. 'Forgive me, Madame. My driver had no idea there were inhabitants in the area. He was driving too fast for the mountain roads. If it hadn't been for your husband here, I regret to say your daughter could easily have been killed.'

'He's not my husband,' the woman whispered. 'He's a Polish voluntary worker assigned by the local Wehrmacht.'

'Ah.' Bruno's face cleared. 'So that's why he wouldn't answer my questions. The fellow doesn't speak French.'

The woman cupped the little girl's head in her palm and he felt his embarrassment growing. He replaced his hat and saluted crisply. 'Please accept my apologies, Madame. I am relieved your daughter suffered little more than an unpleasant shaking. You have my word it will not happen again.'

But as he strode back to his car he was filled with a gnawing sense of curiosity. He knew he had seen the man before and sooner or later he knew he would remember where.

Jonas heard the door open as Lotte came into the room. She had stopped crying now but the blackness of her hair seemed to accentuate the paleness of her skin.

'She's sleeping,' she said. 'I think the

107

shock has knocked her out.'

'Reaction, probably.'

'She owes you her life.'

'The bairn owes me nothing.'

'If you hadn't grabbed her ...' She shivered. 'You were very brave out there. I want you to know how grateful I am.' She hesitated a moment, a tiny pulse throbbing in her throat. 'Please wait.'

She vanished into the bedroom, leaving the door slightly ajar, and Jonas heard the floorboards creaking. After a moment, she called his name. He saw her clothes folded neatly over a chair as he entered. The oil lamp cast ripples of light across her naked breasts and the crisp triangle nestling between her thighs.

Her eyes were calm, her face expressionless. 'It isn't much,' she told him softly, 'but it's the only way I have of saying thank you.'

At his training camp in Somerset they had taught Greg Anderson that patience was a virtue to a man operating behind the lines. Impetuousness led to sloppy groundwork, they said; there was no excuse for it. It was important to establish his presence in the village, important to assuage the suspicions of the occupying forces, important to melt into the paintwork. So for six days he wandered around the streets of Viatte

with Suzanne Le Gras introducing him
to everyone in sight and soon most of
the local residents had accepted him as
her brother from Limoges. As long as the
Gestapo didn't check out his background,
he reasoned he stood a good chance of
surviving. Meanwhile, he had to forget
Jonas Caudale and concentrate on the
myriad subtleties of day-to-day living.

It was not an easy task and sometimes
he wondered if he was capable of pulling
it off, but he enjoyed the novelty of being
part of a community and he enjoyed the
company of Suzanne Le Gras. Suzanne
was unlike anyone he had ever met
before; she was fine-boned and graceful,
and she possessed a quiet dignity he found
enchanting. Thirteen months earlier, her
husband, a Resistance fighter, had been
shot by the Germans in the grounds of
the local schoolhouse.

'You must hate them an awful lot,' he
said when she told him the story.

She looked surprised. 'I never think
about hate. The *Boche* are the *Boche*.
They have to be destroyed, that's all.'

On another occasion, he asked, 'Aren't
you ever frightened?'

'I'm frightened all the time.'

'Yet you look so strong, so sure of
yourself.'

'I'm acting, didn't you realize that?'

He was not a man who unbent easily in the company of women but Suzanne Le Gras seemed to touch some hidden chord within him. She was frank, direct and fearless. She was also, despite her abrasive nature, intuitively responsive to his feelings, and he was soon telling her things he had never mentioned to a living soul. It was the first time in his life he had unburdened to another human being and he found the experience purifying.

'You're not a bit like an American,' she said one night.

'What are Americans supposed to be like?'

'Fresh. A little on the boastful side. You're quiet and self-contained and really very shy.'

'Could you learn to like me a little?'

'That's a funny question.'

'I mean in the human sense. Not because we're allies, not because we work together, but because you like me as a person?'

'I'm not capable of such feelings any more. The *Boche* took care of that, along with everything else.'

'You'll change,' he promised. Then surprised at his own temerity, he reached out and gently squeezed her hand. 'Everything changes with time.'

He liked her, there was no denying that fact. More than liked. In the few days they had spent together, he noticed a subtle change in himself; some of his reserve had gone, some of the icy composure he so abhorred and hated. Despite the trauma of his arrival, he had never felt so peaceful in his life.

On the morning of the seventh day, Suzanne decided it was safe enough to leave the village. She borrowed a *gazogene,* a charcoal-burning truck from the local baker, and drove Greg over the steep mountain passes.

The farmhouse stood on an elevated saddle, commanding a spectacular view of the valley below. No one could approach from any direction without being spotted at least a mile away.

A dog barked as Suzanne drew to a halt and Greg saw a number of men walking toward them, carrying carbines.

'The leader's name is Marcel,' Suzanne told him. 'He runs the local *résistants.'*

Marcel wore a thick bandit moustache and gave no sign of welcome. He regarded Greg sullenly, as if all strangers were to be treated with suspicion as a matter of course. Greg asked him about Jonas and he led the way to the old-fashioned farmhouse, motioning Greg inside. He made no attempt to enter himself.

Greg had to stoop to get through the low-beamed doorway. The parlour was dimly lit and had a stone-flagged floor. A metal stove stood in the corner and shanks of meat hung from the rough-hewn ceiling. Narrowing his eyes, he saw someone waiting in the semi-darkness. 'Jonas Caudale?'

'Aye.'

The voice was soft and melodic, soothing to the ear.

'I'm Major Anderson,' Greg said.

'They told me you were coming.'

Greg moved forward to examine the Englishman curiously. Caudale was lean, that was his first impression. He carried the rangy musculature of a mountain goat and his face was all angles and lines with blunt panels where the cheeks should be. The features were agreeable—to a certain extent sensitive—but they conveyed the adamantine resilience of tempered steel. And yet, Greg had to admit it was a pleasant face. A face that was genuine and unaffected.

'I've heard a lot about you, Caudale.'

'I've heard about you too, Major. Some of the Frenchies aren't too happy at having you around.'

'I gathered that.' He hesitated. 'You're running home to Buttermere, I understand? That's quite a concept. What's the idea?'

'It's personal, Major,' Jonas said.

'Think you can make it?'

112

'I know I can make it.'

'Good. That's good. Because you see, Caudale, we want you to make it too. By "we", I mean London. SHAEF. The Allied High Command. My job is to get you through undetected.'

'You came all this way for that?' Jonas sounded amused.

Greg said, 'War isn't simply a question of bombing your enemy into submission. Morale's important too. Our people need someone to show them the way, someone they can relate to, and you've been elected, coach.'

He waited for Caudale's reaction but there was no reply. He began to feel slightly embarrassed. Something about the man unnerved him. 'Well,' he added awkwardly, 'why don't you wait here while I talk to our friends outside and see what kind of support they can drum up?'

The guy was nuttier than a fruitcake, he thought as he emerged into the sunlight. He hadn't wanted this assignment in the first place and now having met the bastard he wanted it even less, but there was little point in bellyaching. After all, nobody said they had to be bosom pals.

The *maquisards* stared at him sullenly as he crossed the cobbled yard toward them. 'He's feeling good,' he said.

Marcel spat on the ground. 'Who cares how he's feeling? We came to fight the *Boche*, not play nursemaid to a crazy Englishman.'

'That's just it. London wants to keep Caudale on the move, which is why I need your help.'

'What kind of help?'

He paused for a moment. He wasn't sure that his plan was viable but he had given it considerable thought and it seemed the most reasonable one around. 'I guess Caudale's most direct route would be north through Burgundy,' he said, 'but that would take him across flat, rural farm country where he'd be easy to spot, easy to track down. Caudale's a mountain runner, he feels at home in Alpine terrain. I want him to head south across the Central Massif and into the Pyrenees. He can then swing west toward the coast. The two main danger points are the Rhone basin and the Carcassonne Valley. The landscape's leveller there, he'll be vulnerable and exposed. However, right now I want a network of "safe houses" where he can rest between stints. I want water stops at strategic distances. I want solid food—and that means protein. I know how tough it is with the rationing and all but Caudale must have meat to keep him going.'

Marcel asked wryly, 'Anything else you'd like, Major?'

'Yes. Guides to accompany Caudale in stages—men who know the countryside inside out. And runners, lots of runners. I want everyone who can stay on his feet for longer than twenty minutes to get out and create an elaborate diversion. I want the countryside so flooded with runners, the Krauts will think it's the biggest sporting revival since the Munich Olympics.' He smiled. 'And hidden somewhere among them will be our elusive protégé, Jonas Caudale.'

Lotte lifted the coffee pot from the stove and filled Jonas's mug. In the first flush of dawn her cheeks looked pale and sickly.

'We always knew it would come to this,' he said. 'We always knew it was only a matter of time.'

'I realize that.'

'I'd stay if I could. It just isn't practical, that's all.'

He looked down at the hearth. God knew, he'd give his heart and soul to spend the rest of the war in Lotte Monsard's bed, he thought, but it was time to go.

'There was never any point to it,' he added. 'When the fighting's over your husband will be coming home.'

'I don't even know if he's still alive.'

'Don't talk that way. You have to believe he's still alive.'

Somewhere outside, they heard a cock crowing. Men were moving about in the chill mountain morning, the drone of their voices muffled and indistinct. He drained his coffee and rose to his feet. 'I don't want you coming into the yard,' he said. 'I want you to stay here. It's easier that way.'

Tears from her cheeks ran into his mouth as they kissed and he felt the softness of her body pressing against his chest. Keeping his face averted, he moved to the door, shivering as the pre-dawn air bit through his flimsy sweat suit. He hadn't wanted this, had tried to avoid it if the truth were known—Lotte had risked her life to hide him from the Germans and didn't deserve to be treated so shabbily—but he hadn't been able to help himself. Besides, he couldn't stay even if he wanted to. It wasn't a private affair any longer.

He saw Major Anderson, the American officer, walking toward him across the yard. Anderson looked pale in the dusky morning and his sandy hair was rumpled and dishevelled. 'How are you feeling?' he asked.

'Fine, Major. I'm fine.'

'Legs OK?'

'Haven't let me down yet.'

116

'Good.' Greg waved to a youth standing apart from the others. 'That's Lucas. He'll be your guide for the first five miles. He speaks a little English but not too much, so avoid drawing him into lengthy conversation. We've got water stops and rest points arranged along the way.'

'You've thought of everything,' Jonas said.

'Just doing my job, Caudale. That's what I'm here for, seeing that you get to Buttermere. Now if you're feeling up to it, how about getting this show on the road?'

Eight minutes later, after warming up in the rising daylight, the two runners set off into the mountain morning.

The April sun cast a golden mantle across the rooftops as Bruno strolled through the streets of Viatte with Major Gruber, the local garrison commander. A handful of people scurried by, women mostly, clad in dowdy, threadbare clothing, scouring the shops for scraps of food. Four years of war had left their mark on the battered village. The houses were run-down and falling to bits. Several had crumbled into dereliction. Bruno examined a shop where charred timbers dangled from the shattered masonry, leaving the upper floor supported by a gridwork of twisted girders. 'What happened here?' he asked. 'Air raid?'

'There are no air raids in Viatte,' Major Gruber told him. 'The store was demolished in a spontaneous demonstration. This is a business owned by a Jew.'

'Spontaneous?' Bruno raised one eyebrow.

'The people were quick to embrace the truth once it had been explained to them.'

Bruno chuckled, slipping his arm around Gruber's shoulder. '*Sturmbannfuhrer*, do you really believe the Jews are an inferior species?'

Gruber hesitated as if he suspected Bruno might be luring him into a trap. His lips twitched into an uncomfortable smile. 'Of course not.'

'Good. I can't stand stupidity.'

'You're a strange one for the *Leibstandarte*. I thought all you death's head heroes were Nazi fanatics.'

'Let me tell you something. Have you any idea of what the SS eat for breakfast?'

'Breakfast?' Gruber looked puzzled.

'They eat porridge. That's because our Führer, in his wisdom, decided that porridge must contain some secret character-building ingredient since it provided the major diet of the people who built the British Empire.'

'You're teasing me.'

'Sadly, the story is true. But how can one respect a man who produces such twaddle?'

Gruber whistled under his breath. 'Are you always so forthright? Supposing—I'm speaking hypothetically, you understand, but supposing I were to report you? It would look very bad on your record, would it not?'

'Let me explain something, my impetuous friend. I have taken part in three major military campaigns. I have been decorated twice, and have been commended on four occasions by SS Reichsfuhrer Himmler himself. You, on the other hand, if my memory serves me correctly, have seen no action at all. If we were each to submit a report on the other, which do you imagine they would believe?'

The major's face paled. 'Your's naturally, *Oberleutnant.*'

'I think we understand each other,' Bruno smiled.

He was about to move on when he noticed a woman through the store window in front. She was standing at the clothing counter, the sunlight illuminating her long hair and sculpted features. His breath caught in his throat. 'Isn't that the lady you spoke to at the hostage hanging?'

119

The major followed his gaze. 'Ah yes, that is Madame Le Gras.'

'You must introduce me, *Sturmbannfuhrer.*'

'That might be unwise. Madame Le Gras can be a little difficult at times. She has an unfortunate habit of speaking her mind.'

Bruno chuckled, taking the major's arm. 'When will you learn that there are some creatures in this world a man simply cannot ignore.'

Suzanne had taken a scarf from the counter and was examining it in the mirror as Bruno and Gruber entered the store. 'How charming,' Bruno declared.

Close, she was even more beautiful than he'd first imagined. The emphatic line of her nose and chin, rather than detract from her femininity, seemed somehow to emphasize it.

'In the interests of discerning men everywhere, madame, you must allow me to buy this for you.'

Her dark eyes examined his uniform, his SS insignia, his medal ribbons. 'Who is this clown?' she asked Major Gruber.

Gruber's cheeks flushed but Bruno laughed out loud. She was a woman in a million, he thought. Who else would have dared confront a German officer so outrageously? 'Allow me to introduce myself, madame. I am *Oberleutnant* Bruno von Hautle of the *Leibstandarte* SS Adolf Hitler.'

'Am I supposed to curtsy?'

'I hope I'm not as terrifying as that. But since our countries are constitutionally linked, shouldn't we at least make an effort to be friends?'

'Our countries are not linked, *Oberleutnant.* Yours has temporarily conquered mine but that is a situation we hope to rectify.'

'Madame Le Gras,' Gruber said hastily. 'I have warned you before to watch your tongue.'

Bruno waved the objection aside. 'We are civilized people, Gruber, and I understand the lady's sentiments. Does your husband live in the village, madame?'

'My husband is dead. Killed by the *Boche.*'

'Ah, this terrible war.' He shook his head. 'Such memories are difficult to erase. However, I assure you that I am neither your conqueror nor your enemy—simply a man who would like, if possible, to make your acquaintance.'

Her eyes examined him fearlessly. She said, '*Oberleutnant* von Hautle, like the others here I have learned to live with German soldiers on our streets. I have learned to tolerate their boorishness, their

121

arrogance, even their cruelty, but the one thing I have never been able to accommodate is a fool.'

My God, she's magnificent, he thought, watching with admiration as she stormed out of the store, her eyes flashing.

Gruber shook his head in embarrassment. 'I must apologize, *Oberleutnant*. I did warn you the woman was noted for her insolence.'

'Nonsense, Major, I am hopelessly in love.' Bruno laughed. 'At last, I have found a monster worthy of myself.'

Suzanne heard a knock at the apartment door and found Major Gruber waiting on the threshold.

'Will you invite me in for a moment, Madame Le Gras?'

He took off his cap as he entered, standing uncertainly in the centre of the room. 'I am acting as an emissary. The new SS *Oberleutnant*, Bruno von Hautle, would like you to have supper with him this evening.'

'He must be an extraordinary man to have a major acting as his pimp.'

Gruber flinched. 'Please. I dislike this even more than you do. I came because I was afraid that had the message been delivered by someone else, you might have reacted irrationally.'

'Am I to understand that this is an official command?'

'Let me say simply that it would be imprudent to anger this man. One does not refuse an officer of the *Leibstandarte*. In the past I have done my best to overlook your behaviour on the grounds that the loss of your husband had prejudiced your judgement. But von Hautle is dangerous. Though his rank is inferior to my own, his influence is extensive. Should he choose to regard you as an enemy, there will, I'm afraid, be little I can do to help you.'

She leaned back against the wine cupboard, chuckling with amusement. 'He's quite a fellow, your SS lieutenant. Since he considers himself such a great lover, it does seem a pity to disappoint him. Go back and tell von Hautle I'll be delighted to have supper with him this evening.' A faint smile creased her lips as she added softly, 'I do hope the idiot is up to it.'

Jonas sat on the bed, massaging his aching limbs. The hiss of an oil lamp filled the room, its desultory light casting eerie shadows beneath the low-slung ceiling beams. The farmhouse was an isolated one chosen by the *résistants* as a comfortable sanctuary where he could replenish his strength for the following morning.

Greg watched him in silence, leaning

123

against the doorpost. It had been a satisfactory start all things considered, better than he'd expected. His relay teams had kept Caudale on the move and so far, at any rate, the Nazis seemed unaware of what was happening.

'You ran well today,' he said. 'More than half a marathon.'

'Thanks to your decoys. You're some operator, Major.'

'Greg. Call me Greg. If we're going to work together, we might as well drop the formalities.'

He'd been wrong about Jonas, he decided. The Englishman wasn't screwballed after all. In fact, he was one of the sanest men Greg had ever met. He was also one of the most likeable. So why was he putting his neck on the line in such a crazy fashion? There had to be a reason. People didn't run across enemy-occupied territory, not in Greg Anderson's book. Jonas Caudale was an intelligent man, he was bound to have some specific purpose in mind. But if the guy didn't want to explain, who was he to insist?

The smell of cooking reached them from the other room and his stomach rumbled as he recognized the aroma of rabbit stew. He slapped Jonas's shoulder. 'Come on and eat. We've managed to drum up enough protein to replenish some of the carbohydrates you sweated out today.'

'I feel like a racehorse, the way I'm being pampered.'

Greg escorted him into the kitchen then wandered outside to light a cigarette. It was a cool night with a touch of rain in the air and he felt tired and achingly lonely. He stood in the shadows, breathing out smoke through his lips and nostrils.

The rigours of command he could handle any day, but having no one to talk to was beginning to get him down. Which was strange, he reflected, since he had never talked—really talked—to any human being before Suzanne. It just showed what a little biology could do. She'd affected him more than anyone in his entire life, partly because she was the only person he had ever managed to get close to and partly because she'd aroused within him feelings he had never dreamed possible. He had only to close his eyes to see those sculpted cheekbones, those proud features, that maddeningly enigmatic smile. One day out and already he was missing her. He longed desperately to see her again.

He eyed the farmer's bicycle leaning against the barn wall. It was over seventeen miles to the village of Viatte—hardly an easy haul in such rugged terrain, particularly for a man who had never claimed to be in top physical condition, but as he pictured Suzanne's expressive body the yearning inside him developed into a physical ache.

He threw away his cigarette, picked up the bicycle and set off determinedly into the darkness.

Chapter Five

Suzanne noticed the sidelong glances of the Nazi officers as a grinning sentry showed her to Bruno von Hautle's quarters. They were all the same, these cocky young supermen, she thought. They acted out their fantasies by numbers, each believing he was behaving in some way that was totally unique. Well, tonight she was going to redress the balance. Tonight, she would make von Hautle suffer for his arrogance.

She felt no sense of unease at their coming encounter. Since her earliest girlhood, she had been conscious of her power over men. She had wielded it assiduously, confident of her ability to manipulate and intrigue. Von Hautle would pay for summoning her here so imperiously.

The sentry was still smiling as he tapped on Bruno's door. It was opened a moment later by Bruno himself. 'You came,' he

126

said, injecting a note of surprise into his voice as if he'd half suspected—or pretended to—that she might have refused. She wanted to laugh out loud. A man like this would be putty in her fingers.

'I was led to believe it was a royal command.'

'Major Gruber has an unfortunate sense of occasion. He should have been an actor instead of a soldier. Please come in.'

He dismissed the sentry and took the raincoat from Suzanne's shoulders, stooping with an air of gallantry to kiss her hand. Oh God, he thinks he's Rudolf Valentino, she thought.

'I wish to apologize for the other morning,' he said. 'The execution of the hostages was an unpleasant experience for us both.'

'Not quite. The ones who died were not your friends.'

'I find no pleasure in such events, particularly when I believe the victims to be innocent.'

'You could have stopped it happening.'

'A simple lieutenant hardly argues with an SS *Standartenfuhrer*. If I had, there may have been an extra hostage dangling from that bridge. However, I thought—for this evening at least—we might try to forget the war.'

'The only way we can do that is when

you and your friends go home.'

He chuckled. 'Gruber warned me you'd be forthright. I am not responsible for the occupation of your country, Madame Le Gras, so do please try and meet me half-way. My only concern is to enjoy life while I am still able.'

He waved her into the room where the table had been decorated with candles. The meal itself was laid on silver platters. There was venison, potato salad, fresh trout, mushrooms and artichokes.

'It's a cold offering, I'm afraid, but I'm sure you'll find it to your liking. We SS officers still enjoy a few privileges including the best food available, and I'm delighted to have someone to share it with for a change, particularly a companion of such extraordinary beauty. I know how stringent the rationing has been of late.'

A bottle of wine stood chilling in the ice bucket and he opened it with a practised flourish. Everything he did seemed part of some ludicrous seduction charade. 'You'll find this rather good,' he promised, handing her a glass. 'I know you French lead the world in wines, but some of our German vintages deserve to be tried.'

They sat at the table and she sipped absently, scarcely noticing the flavour. For the first time, she realized that Bruno von

Hautle was extraordinarily good-looking.

'I've been finding out about you,' he said, his eyes filled with a disarming merriment.

'From Major Gruber?'

'Who else? The major's a splendid fellow, but he has one basic flaw. He wants desperately to be liked. That can be something of a handicap in a garrison commander.'

'Not the sort of weakness you yourself would display.'

'It isn't necessary. I am already well-liked.'

'It's probably your modesty.'

'Are you always so prickly, Madame Le Gras?'

'I find uniforms bring out the worst in me.'

'It's not the uniform that counts. It's what's underneath. I hope you don't mind my mentioning this, but I'm surprised you've managed to survive so long. In such unsettled times, speaking one's mind can often prove terminal.'

'We do have a high mortality rate,' Suzanne admitted.

'And a very short Christmas card list, I have no doubt. However, in the interests of a convivial evening, I shall remove my tunic at once.'

She watched as he rose to his feet

and draped his jacket over the back of the chair. 'That's better,' he said, sitting down.

'You really believe it makes a difference? You carry the swastika wherever you go. It's engraved in your soul, like a symbol of guilt.'

'Guilt—along with modesty—is not one of my shortcomings. Who cares anyway? We're young, we're alive, we're together. We're also about to eat so for the sake of digestion may I suggest we call a truce, at least for the next twenty minutes?'

Despite Suzanne's resentment, dinner proved a pleasant meal. The venison was succulent and covered with a spicy sauce which Bruno assured her contained a secret ingredient known only in certain parts of his native Bavaria. She let him do most of the talking, and he expounded happily on his early manhood as a mountain runner and his training days in the notorious SS. Without the hated uniform, he seemed different somehow, and although he was undoubtedly conceited, he was also warm, pleasant and convivial.

'Why have you come to Viatte?' she asked after a while.

'Orders from Berlin.'

'Is it because of the coming invasion?' She saw him hesitate, and laughed shortly. 'For God's sake, you think we don't know the Allies are massing across the Channel?'

'Massing's one thing, getting here's another.'

'You know they're bound to, sooner or later.'

'They'll find us waiting if they do.'

'In the middle of the Alps? Surely the most sensible course would be to strengthen your defences on the coast?'

'A wise general takes out insurance against a second front.'

It was a casual remark and one which, in normal circumstances, she wouldn't have given a second thought, but she put down her wine glass and sat for a moment motionless in her chair. She'd been so engrossed with the young American she hadn't considered the reason for the SS detachment's arrival. What a fool she had been, what a stupid, amateurish, inexcusable fool. She'd forgotten her training, allowed her mind to become distracted. Of course the Nazis would take precautions to prevent a *Maquis* uprising. They had come to subdue the local Resistance.

She eyed Bruno thoughtfully across the table. The situation had subtly changed, she realized. No longer was he an arrogant seducer to be put in his place. Now he was a quarry, an objective. He was the only one who could tell her what she needed to know. She had to win his trust. She had to get inside his head.

She seized his hand, squeezing it hard, and his eyes widened in mock surprise. 'I thought you hated me.'

'I thought so too,' she said with a smile, 'but the extraordinary thing is, I find you grow more attractive as the evening goes on.'

It rained as Greg cycled wearily into the village. His body felt stiff, and his limbs ached. It had been a long ride over the mountain passes.

He made his way to Suzanne's apartment and tapped lightly on the door. When there was no reply, he tried again, hammering more loudly. A latch creaked as someone peeked out of a neighbouring window. He recognized Madame Latour, a trim little woman with skin like stretched parchment.

'Oh, it's you, M'sieur Odru. I wondered who could be calling at this time of night, especially now that the curfew's in force.'

'Where is Madame Le Gras?' Greg asked.

'I thought you'd know. She's having supper with the new SS lieutenant at the Wehrmacht billeting house in the high street. It's an old hotel the Germans converted at the beginning of the war.'

He clenched his teeth and, heart thumping, rattled down the staircase.

'M'sieur Odru, you musn't go there,' she called, staring after him anxiously. 'You'll be breaking the curfew.'

But Greg scarcely heard her. A terrible breathlessness gathered in his chest as he picked up his bicycle and pedalled furiously into the darkness.

Bruno's kiss was tender and unhurried. Sitting on the sofa, he seemed determined to savour every moment and Suzanne responded dutifully, her nostrils catching the fragrance of his shaving soap.

There was no question in Suzanne's mind about where her duty lay. From the beginning, she'd set herself to do anything, however demeaning, to rid her country of the hated invader. She had to win Bruno's confidence, inflame his senses by whatever means available.

The last two hours had been carefully orchestrated. She had forced herself to be warmer, softer, more amenable, and Bruno, unaware that he was being manipulated, had pursued his conquest with enthusiastic fervour. She had played her role with practised ease, exuding a subtle blend of ardour and hesitation as she'd led him delicately through the seduction ritual.

Now it was time for a fractional application of brakes.

'This has gone far enough,' she said, as his mouth lifted from hers. 'I didn't come here to romp in the hay like a simple farmgirl.'

'You make it sound like some kind of crime.'

'I scarcely know you, remember.'

'A situation I am doing my damndest to rectify.'

Soft as thistledown, his hand moved beneath her dress, lightly caressing her breast. She let her head fall on the sofa rest as his fingers sent a tingling sensation throughout her body.

'Please. I am asking you to stop.'

'And if I don't?'

'You must,' she insisted.

But she was lying, and she knew it. She was using him, coldly and deliberately, ensnaring her trap with the oldest bait of all. And Bruno responded just as she'd known he would, following his instincts with the blindness of a lemming.

There were no preliminaries. The consummation was swift and direct and he hurt as he entered her, she was still dry. Then she felt the cool touch of his skin, the warm moistness of his mouth, and her body shuddered as a wave of heat concentrated in her lower limbs. She heard a noise, faint at first, growing louder, and with a sense of wonder, realized it was the sound of her voice whimpering helplessly in the night.

Thirty yards away, drenched by the relentless downpour, Greg Anderson stared up at the window in an agony of anguish, misery, jealousy and despair.

Few men could have been as ignorant in matters relating to the opposite sex as Greg Anderson in the spring of 1944. Though he was worldly enough in many respects, his authoritarian upbringing had turned him into a vegetable most women chose to ignore. At the age of twenty-seven, the extent of his amatory experiences had been limited to sordid couplings with paid prostitutes when his bodily needs had become too pressing so it was scarcely surprising that Suzanne Le Gras had had a profound and intoxicating effect upon him.

It was not that he loved her, he assured himself (love was an emotion he found difficult to define) but her presence seemed to imbue him with a feeling of wholeness, a sense of wellbeing. Not that Greg trusted his feelings—indeed, he had been so long immune from them, he was bound to find any awakening destabilizing—but he warmed to Suzanne's fixity of purpose, her staunchness and resolve, and the realization that she had given herself to an enemy officer—even though he appreciated her motives—wounded him more than he cared to admit. He reacted, as he reacted to most of the crises in his life, by throwing himself into his work.

It wasn't easy tearing his mind away but for the next three weeks his sole concern became the simple task of getting Jonas Caudale across Occupied France. To his surprise, he discovered a strange affiliation with Jonas, one he found difficult to explain. He was not a gregarious man but there was something in Jonas's character he recognized and related to. Though it made no sense and followed no rational pattern, the torment driving the Englishman seemed somehow to match Greg's own.

If Jonas himself recognized this, he gave no sign. He lived in a kind of limbo, approaching each day with an air of philosophical detachment. In the beginning, he had seen his run as a solitary affair, a personal covenant between himself and the mercurial components of fate. Now, flanked by a multitude of pacers, he began to feel his obsession getting out of hand. He was grateful however for the company, and grateful too for the regular refreshment stops which Greg organized at strategic rest-points, and though his

French companions spoke little English he had to admit he found their presence comforting.

At first, the road picked a tortuous route through the low-level hill country of the Alpine provinces but gradually the character of the landscape began to change, the craggy hummocks giving way to dry, yellow plains and long straight roads. Here, Jonas slowed his pace, conserving his energy for the peaks ahead. He ran usually in the early mornings, accompanied by relays of companions who guided him through the baffling labyrinth of roads linking the Alpine foothills to the Central Massif.

He spent the nights in scattered barns and farmhouses where, fed and pampered, he felt his confidence gradually growing. At the Rhone, his progress was halted for a time when they found the bridges unexpectedly guarded, and installing Jonas in a sheltering barn, Greg and his *résistants* scoured the countryside until they located an enterprising boatman willing to ferry them across the river.

Near Annonay a woman rode up on a bicycle to warn them of a *Milice* patrol and they hid in the hedgerows as the trucks roared by. At Mont-de-Bourge, approaching the Central Massif, the local mayor greeted Jonas on the village outskirts, welcoming him with a formal, if incomprehensible speech, and inviting him to spend the night at his family cottage.

In the morning, Jonas swung south toward Longagne, encountering few serious obstacles. He skirted the small, attractive town of Mansac, built on a crossroads of eleven canals, and passed the monastery of St Maurice which commanded spectacular views of the Aubrac Mountains.

Though it seems extraordinary in retrospect, he completed this early section of his run with little or no interference from the Germans. One explanation could be the sparse distribution of the occupying forces in Vichy during the spring of 1944, and another undoubtedly lies in Greg Anderson's ingenuity in flooding the countryside with decoys. Field hands who had never worn a pair of running shoes in their lives took to the roads in droves, jogging, trotting, loping, sprinting, confounding French and German authorities alike. Jonas himself was unaware of this, just as he was unaware that every night, as he sat in the seclusion of some isolated farmhouse, news of his progress was being relayed via the BBC to millions of people all over Europe.

Josef Goebbels walked onto the terrace overlooking the Berghof grounds. The

April sun was dazzling, carrying with it the scent of rising pine sap and on all sides the Untersberg peaks rose against an azure sky. The Führer's residence towered above the little town of Berchtesgaden like a medieval fortress—and a fortress it was, Goebbels reflected, for Hitler had bought the house as a country retreat during his early rise to prominence and had used it as a blessed escape from the pressures and tribulations of the political rough-and-tumble. Here he had built a complex defence system which could, if necessary, be turned into a formidable redoubt.

Hearing a movement on the terrace behind him, Goebbels turned to see Eva Braun, the Führer's mistress, emerging through the open French window carrying a tray of coffee. Blonde and suntanned, Eva Braun's face exuded an ingenuousness Goebbels heartily approved of. He knew many of his colleagues resented her relationship with their country's leader but Goebbels had discovered long ago that Eva was a simple girl who was bound to the Führer by love rather than personal ambition.

'That was quick,' he said as, smiling, Eva placed the tray on the terrace parapet.

Taking out a handkerchief, he fastidiously dusted the stone wall before seating himself, watching as Eva poured the coffee from a silver pot. Secretly, Goebbels felt sorry for Eva. He knew the Führer had never forgotten his first love, Geli Raubal, who had shot herself in a fit of pique after Hitler had refused her permission to study singing in Vienna.

'You are looking well,' he said as Eva handed him his cup.

'It's the mountain air. You know how it agrees with me.'

'And the Führer?'

She grimaced, sitting on the wall at Goebbel's side. 'He gets so moody these days. He knows the Allied invasion is coming but no-one seems able to predict where it will happen or when. I'd hoped these few days in the mountains would perk him up a bit but he carries the war wherever he goes.'

Goebbels spotted Hitler himself approaching up the drive. Dressed in Wehrmacht grey, the Führer looked, at first glance, small and nondescript, despite his aggressive moustache. He was reading as he walked, his bland face creased in thought.

Goebbels rose to his feet and thrust out his hand in an energetic salute. Hitler seemed puzzled to see him. 'Josef, no one told me you were coming.'

'Forgive me, my Führer, I meant it as

a surprise. You have heard the news from Montargis?'

Hitler nodded, brandishing the sheaf of papers in his hand. 'I have it here.'

'An excellent achievement on the part of the Gestapo. They have rounded up nearly all the terrorist ringleaders. I think we can look forward to a period of tranquillity and progress in the Loire.'

Hitler was silent for a moment as he stood at the terrace parapet, gazing over the valley below. In the harsh sunlight, his moustache looked curiously unreal.

'Josef,' he said softly, 'who is Jonas Caudale?'

Goebbels blinked, glancing at Eva Braun. 'Caudale, my Führer? I have never heard such a name.'

Hitler waved a sheaf of papers in front of his nose. 'These are transcripts of BBC broadcasts recorded over the past few weeks. Read them.'

Silently, Goebbels's eyes scanned the typewritten pages. Boots crunched on the gravel drive as a squadron of SS guards marched past. When he had finished reading, he handed the sheet back to Hitler.

'Remarkable.'

'Is that all you can say?'

Goebbels shrugged. 'The man is an escaped prisoner of war. He's been luckier than most, but in such unsettled times these things are bound to happen. He has the advantage of being at large in a country sympathetic to his own. The French underground is notorious for helping escaping POW's.'

'But why did he leave the safety of Switzerland, and why is the British government taking such an extraordinary interest?'

'Obviously they're trying to tie up our resources in the hinterland.'

'Josef, I think you fail to appreciate the significance of these reports. Caudale is making a mockery of German manhood.'

'My Führer, he is only one man.'

'A man who is giving our enemies an invaluable propaganda platform. These broadcasts are damaging our prestige. You, of all people, should recognize that. Wars are not won solely by force of arms. When you control minds, you control nations.'

Goebbels remained silent. He knew from experience that once Hitler became obsessed with an idea, arguing was point-less. The wind picked up, bringing with it the odour of freshly-cut grass. Absently, Hitler brushed the hair from his eyes. 'Get me a full report on the circumstances surrounding this affair,' he ordered.

'*Jawohl*, my Fuhrer,' Josef Goebbels replied.

Winston Churchill sat on the lawn at Chartwell, eating lunch beneath the canopy of a beach umbrella. It was the first warm day of spring and he was determined to make the most of the April sunshine. He had spent the morning building a wall at the lower end of the vegetable garden and his blue coveralls were coated with dust and smeared with cement. Churchill found bricklaying absorbing and therapeutic, a blessed respite from the problems of war. A newspaper lay propped against the teapot in front of him, and his eyes narrowed as they focused on a column heading.

His wife Clementine crossed the lawn, clutching his gas mask in a canvas case. 'You're supposed to be setting an example,' she chided. 'How can you persuade people to carry gas masks if their own prime minister isn't doing it? Really Winston, you are the limit. What if somebody spots you from the river?'

Churchill ignored the reprimand, stabbing the tabloid with his finger. 'Have you read this?'

'Don't be silly. You know nobody touches the papers until you've finished with them. You get so angry when the pages are creased.' She leaned over his shoulders, reading aloud. 'British shepherd

143

throws enemy forces into chaos.'

'It's Caudale. He's still on the run.'

'Who on earth is Caudale?'

'He's a Lakeland fellrunner. He escaped from a German POW train a couple of months ago and managed to make it into Switzerland. Now he's on the move again.'

'Well, that's splendid, darling, but look how long you yourself remained at large when you escaped from the Boers during the South African War.'

'You don't understand. This man is running home.'

'To England?'

'To Buttermere.'

Clementine looked blank. 'Doesn't he realize there's a war on?'

'He doesn't care about the war. He's got half the German army scuttling around in circles looking for him.'

He rose to his feet, tugging at his coverall fastenings. His cheeks were flushed, his eyes elated. 'We've got to use him, Clemmie. He's too good to ignore. Get Eisenhower on the telephone and ask him to meet me at the War Office at three o'clock. Tell him I have something important I'd like to discuss.'

Gallagher looked jubilant as he strode into his office and dropped the folder he was carrying onto his desktop. He pulled open a drawer, and began rummaging through the papers inside.

His aide, Cyril Applethwaite, watched him curiously. 'You seem pleased with yourself this morning.'

'Not pleased, Cyril. Gratified. I'm feeling gratified this morning because at long last I have discovered what the bloody Yanks are up to.'

'What's that then?'

He opened the folder he had just brought in and scattered its contents across his blotting pad. 'Some maniac called Jonas Caudale is running home to Buttermere across Nazi Occupied France and the Americans have been taunting the Jerries by broadcasting his progress over the BBC.'

'What's he doing it for?'

'Because he's a nutcase, I assume. His motives aren't important. The point is, Churchill thinks his run could be a great morale booster when D-Day comes along. He wants Caudale kept on the move as long as possible.'

'But surely it's the Yanks' show. They found him, they put him into motion.'

'Sometimes I despair of you, Cyril. You're always so ready to accept the status quo. If Churchill says he wants Caudale kept running, it's up to us to

145

keep him running.'

'What are you planning to do?' Applethwaite asked warily.

Gallagher smiled, and straightened the papers in front of him. 'Take over the initiative from the Americans, of course.'

Bruno heard someone hammering at the door and reached for his wrist-watch on the bedside dresser. It was barely eight o'clock. His voice was irritable as he called, 'Who is it?'

'Forgive me, *oberleutnant,* but I carry a message from *Sturmbannfuhrer* Zieff. You are to report to Gestapo headquarters at once.'

He groaned under his breath. Beside him on the pillow, Suzanne stirred restlessly. 'What's happening?'

'Nothing for you to worry about,' he said, kissing her on the nose. 'Duty calls.'

A hint of humour nestled in Suzanne's eyes as he quickly showered and pulled on his uniform. 'Jump, Fido,' she whispered.

'I'm a German officer. You know I have to obey orders.'

'I'm sure the army won't grind to a halt if you turn up a few minutes late. Why don't you come back to bed?'

'Ah, *chérie,* if only I could, but an order from the Gestapo is like a summons from the Almighty Himself.'

146

'I had no idea you were such a timid man.'

He kissed his fingertip and pressed it lightly against her naked breast. 'I know you are teasing me. And the idea is tempting, I have to admit. But some things transcend even the pleasures of love, my dear. I'll make it up to you, I promise, as soon as I return.'

'What makes you think I'll still be here when you return?'

'Where, in heaven's name, could you go?'

She stuck out her tongue at him as he hurried, grinning, to the door.

Driving through the village, he reflected on his relationship with Suzanne Le Gras. She was a strange one, he had to admit. Affectionate one minute, provocative the next. There was little doubt his life had taken on a new vitality during the last few weeks. She was a constant challenge, baffling as a puzzle to which he could find no solution. Did she love him or hate him? He neither knew nor cared. He was a buoyant young man who lived for the moment and despite her capriciousness, Suzanne Le Gras offered a blessed respite from the squalor of war.

When he reached Gestapo Headquarters, he found the forecourt crammed with people. Everywhere, men in running gear

147

were being shepherded from trucks by heavily-armed troops. He watched the activity in puzzlement.

The ancient stone building had once served as the village school and the reception area was crowded with athletes of every age and description. He gave his name to the officer on duty and was escorted to a basement at the foot of the stairway. The smell of excrement filled his nostrils as he stepped through the door and he drew to a halt in surprise. Tied to a chair was a man in soiled running shorts. He had been beaten so badly that his face was no longer recognizable as human. His eyes were closed and his mouth was a bloody cavern, sucking desperately at the air. In the corner, the man's interrogator was washing his hands at a tiny sink.

Bruno felt a tightness in his diaphragm. Everywhere he went he was confronted with evidence of Nazi brutality. A major came toward him, carrying a short leather riding crop which he slapped absently against his thigh. Bruno noticed the crop was stained with blood.

'*Oberleutnant* von Hautle?'

He nodded coldly.

'I understand you were once a mountain runner, is that true?'

Again he nodded. He couldn't trust himself to speak. He wanted to punch the smugness out of the major's face. The major noticed the contempt in his eyes and glanced at the captive, smiling understandingly.

'I do not blame you, *Oberleutnant*. It's an unsavoury business we are conducting here. No man in his right mind enjoys inflicting pain on another human being, but some things are necessary in the name of duty.'

'Is this your idea of duty? Beating a helpless Frenchman to death?'

'The man is a subversive. He's been helping to cover the tracks of an escaping Englander, a POW named Jonas Caudale.'

When he heard the name, Bruno caught his breath. He thought for a moment that his memory must be playing tricks. The brain did that on occasions, distorted, equivocated. 'Did you say Caudale?'

'You know this fugitive?'

He rubbed his temple with a fingertip. It couldn't be the same man. Jonas Caudale was dead. Bruno knew he was dead. He had seen him tumble over the Schwabingen Falls. True, they had found no body but the sheer force of the water would have pounded him to a pulp.

The major frowned, noting his discomfort. 'I think you had better explain yourself, *Oberleutnant*.'

As briefly as he could, Bruno described how he had intercepted Jonas on the Kuchler Ridge and how Jonas, in a desperate attempt at escape, had hurled himself into the river gorge.

When he had finished the major whistled in astonishment. 'So you know what this Englander looks like?'

'It was hardly a protracted meeting, *Sturmbannfuhrer.*'

'Nevertheless, you've established contact with the man. That makes you an invaluable asset indeed. Reichsfuhrer Himmler has ordered that no efforts are to be spared until Jonas Caudale is in custody. Our units are combing the area now, searching every village, every barn, every farmhouse. As an experienced mountain runner and someone who has actually encountered the fellow, I would welcome your advice.'

Bruno dragged himself out of his reverie. He forgot his anger as he forced his brain to think. 'Have you considered the possibility of a spearhead group—perhaps twenty trained athletes familiar with the terrain—acting as a flying column ahead of your main search force? In a sense, you would be the beaters and they the hunters. Once the quarry's forced to bolt, they would be in an admirable position to challenge him on his own terms.'

'An interesting idea,' the major said.

'They'd be far more flexible than the rest of your command and they'd also be in top physical condition so if the fugitive escaped into the mountains, they'd be perfectly capable of trailing him.'

'Good thinking, *Oberleutnant.*'

Bruno seemed unable to stop. 'They would need a liaison, of course, someone who could deal with the local populace. There is a Frenchwoman here in the village whom I trust implicitly. Her name is Suzanne Le Gras.'

'Wouldn't she slow the team's progress?'

'Naturally, *Sturmbannfuhrer,* she would not be part of the chase itself. And bearing in mind the value our Reichsfuhrer places on publicity, it might be a good idea to invite along the reporter from the *Nuremburg Gazette,* Willi Fredier. A little trumpet blowing never did anyone any harm.'

The major chuckled. 'Take any measures you see fit, *Oberleutnant.* After your last encounter it would be churlish not to offer you a chance to redress the balance.'

'I do not understand, *Sturmbannfuhrer,*' Bruno said, puzzled.

'Under the authority invested in me by *Reichsfuhrer* Himmler, I am placing you in complete command.'

Chapter Six

For the hundredth time that morning Lotte Monsard examined the note she had received from Jonas. It had been brought to her by one of the local *résistants*, scribbled on the back of an old tourist postcard showing the Gorges du Tarn. In English, Jonas had written: *'Joints aching but legs holding up well. Marcel says I'll be able to write properly from Gavarnie. Give my love to Yvette. J.'*

It wasn't exactly a romantic message, she thought. Hardly calculated to set her senses racing. But then, Jonas had pledged nothing, promised nothing, and she was grateful for any communication, no matter how slight.

She was reading it for the umpteenth time when the roar of engines reached her from the yard outside. Quickly, she tucked the card into her apron pocket and pulled back the window drapes. Three trucks stood in the cobbled forecourt, their camouflaged awnings fluttering in the wind. Her heart jumped as she saw German soldiers running around the house to guard the windows at the rear.

As SS officer stood talking to a man in civilian clothing and when he turned toward her she recognized his face. It was the officer whose staff car had almost killed Yvette several weeks earlier.

He knocked sharply before entering, lowering his head beneath the ceiling beam. 'Good-morning, Madame,' he said, taking off his hat. 'I wonder if you remember me? Some time ago, my driver—an ignorant brute—almost ran down your little girl on the Viatte road.'

'I remember,' she said warily.

'I came back to see if everything's all right.'

'Everything's fine. Why shouldn't it be?'

'Your daughter. She's recovered?'

Lotte nodded, a terrible dread settling in her stomach.

'She got quite a shock back there. It was a very close thing.'

'Well, she's fine now.'

'I'm glad. Upstairs, is she? In her room?'

'Yes.'

'I wonder if you would call her down? I'd like to satisfy myself the child has not beep harmed.'

Weakly, she raised her voice. 'Yvette?'

Footsteps clattered on the stairway and Yvette emerged, eating an apple. When she saw the SS officer, her features froze.

'Hello, *chérie,*' he said. 'You remember me?'

'Yes, m'sieur.'

'Are you feeling all right?'

'Yes, m'sieur.'

'No qualmy feelings after what happened?'

'No, m'sieur.'

'And your Polish farmhand? He is fine also?'

'He is no longer here,' Lotte said hastily.

'Ah. Transferred away, has he? Where to this time?'

'I don't know. Ask the Wehrmacht. They do all the labour allocations.'

'And they've left you alone to run the farm? Not very sporting of them, I must say.'

The officer knelt down, staring directly into Yvette's eyes. Gently, he straightened her hair. 'Where you do think your farmhand is now, *chérie?*'

'I do not know, m'sieur.'

'You're sure of that?'

'Yes, m'sieur.'

'I would not like you to lie to me, Yvette. It makes me very angry when people lie to me.'

'I am not lying, m'sieur.'

'Leave the child alone,' Lotte said.

The officer straightened, shaking his head. 'I wish I could, Madame. But I have the strangest feeling that your Polish labourer isn't a Polish labourer at all. I think he's an escaped English POW named Jonas Caudale.'

High in Lotte's throat, a pulse began to throb. The officer regarded her mildly. 'Well?'

'I suppose you've come to arrest me.'

'It is not you we are taking, Madame, but the girl.'

She felt a sudden constriction in her chest. 'No.'

Kneeling, she seized Yvette in her arms, hugging the thin body tightly against her.

The officer sighed. 'Please stand back. It will make things unpleasant if you try to resist.'

'Leave my daughter alone.'

'Madame, I have no wish to harm your daughter, but my superiors are adamant that the Englander must be caught. Now, if you were able to help me in some small way ...'

She gazed at him in silence. She could feel Yvette shivering in her grasp.

The officer waited a moment, then sighed again. 'Very well,' he said. 'Come, Yvette.'

He reached out, taking the girl's arm.

'No!' Lotte exclaimed, tightening her grip.

With a pained expression, the officer

seized her wrists and tore them brusquely free. He dragged her to her feet and she sucked in her breath as the note from Jonas fell from her apron pocket. The officer's eyes gleamed. He stared at her for a moment, then knelt down, picked up the note and read it quickly. A sob of dismay lodged in her throat as he saluted jubilantly and hurried to the door. A sergeant came running forward to meet him as he crossed the yard.

'Tell the men to get back on the trucks,' Bruno ordered. 'The woman is not to be harmed but detail someone to watch the farm. Under no circumstances must she be allowed to communicate with the local populace.'

Willi Fredier, fanning himself with his hat, said, 'Getting soft-hearted, old friend?'

'Just being practical. I haven't time to fill in the paperwork.'

'So where are we going now?'

'Gavarnie.'

'My God, that's half-way across France.' Fredier's eyes shone with sudden interest. 'You've got something on the Englander's whereabouts?'

'Not exactly, but I know where he's heading,' Bruno said, and helped Suzanne into the passenger cab.

The search operation which took place in

156

the middle of April 1944 was one of the most extensive rural France had ever seen. On Himmler's orders, a vast horde of troops, not only Germans but members of the French GMR, came swarming into Vichy in droves. Villages were combed, peasants interrogated and anything which might offer a fugitive refuge, including several barns, were systematically destroyed. More worrying still from Greg Anderson's point of view, the decoys who had provided Jonas with such admirable cover during the early stages of his run were rounded up and carted away. It was clear the Germans were playing no longer.

The first indication Jonas had of this dangerous new development came as he was picking his way through woodlands near the Sylvans River. It was a mild day, the sky filled with fleecy white clouds. His companion, a young Frenchman named Alexander, panted hoarsely as he trotted at Jonas's side. They had been jogging all morning and their bodies were limp and tired. A sound like rolling thunder reached them through the trees and they paused, frowning, in their tracks. 'Hear that?' Jonas said.

Alexander's hair stuck up in unruly clumps. 'Probably geese.'

'Not geese. Dogs.'

'Dogs?' The Frenchman's cheeks paled. 'Are you sure?'

'I'd recognize a dog pack anywhere. We'll never outrun them.'

'Perhaps we could climb a tree. We'd be out of their reach up there.'

'What if the Goons come along?'

'The river then. Dogs can't follow us through running water.'

'How far's the river?'

'A mile. Maybe less.'

'OK, let's give it a try.'

They changed direction, following a labyrinthine route through the heavy timber, their bodies imbued with a new intensity. There were no footpaths and several times they had to retrace their steps as the landscape repeated itself. Jonas tried to shut his mind to the baying at his rear, but like a maddening tune that wouldn't go away the sound taunted his senses.

The trees faltered, forming a natural break where the forest had been cut back to accommodate a power line, and they turned along it, tripping and stumbling over the rough, uneven ground. 'Sure we're heading in the right direction?' Jonas panted.

'Almost there. Another few minutes should do it.'

They charged desperately through the scrub, the howling of the dogs clamouring in their ears. Suddenly, Alexander squealed. 'Dear God, I can see them.'

Jonas spotted the leaders of the pack emerging from the timber. With the scent of victory in their nostrils they were running flat out, their nostrils flared, their muscles rippling. He picked up a rock and hurled it as hard as he could. The first one missed and he tried another, scoring a direct hit on the pack leader's nose. The animal gave a piteous yelp but its speed barely faltered.

'Head for the river,' Jonas yelled at Alexander.

'What about you?'

'Forget about me. Separating's our only chance.'

Almost delirious with fear, Alexander plunged into the underbrush and Jonas set off in the opposite direction, drawing away the dogs. He was running flat out, ignoring the branches tearing at his sweat suit, ignoring the grass tufts scuffling at his shoes, ignoring everything except the desperate need to keep moving and the baying of the hounds at his rear.

The trees fell back and he saw a derelict hut ahead, flanked by a twisted tangle of barbed wire. An abandoned axe handle lay in the grass and he seized the shaft in both hands and turned to face his pursuers. They were almost upon him, strung out in a ragged line, their sinewy bodies quivering with triumph. Without faltering, the first of the hounds launched itself in a murderous leap. Jonas saw the eyes blazing, the teeth gleaming, and judging his timing to a fractional second, swung the axe handle like a baseball bat. Clunk—a shiver rippled along his arms as the blow took the animal on the side of the skull, hurling it into a cluster of nettles.

A second dog streaked in and Jonas switched aim, driving the shaft forward like a spear. He caught the Doberman high on the chest, flinging it into a dizzy somersault.

Then the animals were all over him and he smelled the foetid odour of their breathing, felt the heat of their snapping jaws. He reeled under the weight but the harder he struggled the wilder they became. Half-crazed, he lurched toward the barbed wire, crying out as teeth clamped on his upper shoulder, slicing through the layers of muscle tissue. There was no thought in him now, only a desperate yearning for survival.

He dropped to the ground and burrowed into the barbed wire coils. The prickles ripped his skin, tearing his sweat suit to shreds, but gritting his teeth, he squirmed deeper and deeper, the dogs squealing as the savage spikes gouged their unprotected hides. Several let go of their quarry; wriggling free of the needle-sharp tips, and lashing out with his feet, Jonas drove the others furiously back.

He could see them milling about, crazy with frustration, their lithe bodies leaping and pivoting as he burrowed deeper, shivering helplessly like a man in the throes of a seizure. His skin was bleeding in at least a dozen places and through the tattered remnants of his sweat suit he saw ugly gashes on his thighs and forearms. Ignoring the damage—God knew, it was impossible to tell if there was anything left of his body worth saving—he concentrated on creating a space between himself and his attackers.

When he reached the centre of the coils, he paused and checked his shoulder. Wiping away the blood, he examined the puncture marks forming a vivid triangle across the inflamed flesh. The holes were rimmed with blue and a purplish bruise was spreading rapidly across his deltoid muscle. He kneaded his fist, gratified to see that the limb was still functioning at least. His other lacerations were more bloody than anything else—scratches caused by the wire barbs—painful but not debilitating.

He saw the derelict building at his rear and steeling himself against the spikes, hooked his fists over its ravaged rain gutter and dragged his body aloft. He paused for a moment, summoning his strength, then tore himself free of the wire tendrils and wriggled onto the roof. He was in the middle of a disused logging camp, he saw—or what was left of it. A few rusting implements lay scattered in the grass and beyond the clearing stood a metal chute, the type used to slide timber down the mountainside. The chute dropped through the trees in an almost perpendicular arc and a flicker of hope stirred inside him as he saw sunlight gleaming on a lake below. If he could reach the log chute he might be able to get out of here.

He moistened his lips, trying to stop his body trembling. Everything depended on timing, on judging his move to the exact split-second. He looked at the dogs who were leaping into the air, striving to catch a glimpse of their beleaguered quarry. Easing the haversack from his shoulders, he hurled it as far as he could, grunting with satisfaction as the animals followed it into the underbrush.

He didn't wait to watch the battle as the hounds fought savagely for the pack's possession but leapt from the roof and sprinted across the open ground, his eyes fixed on the log chute in front. It shuddered closer, its slender runnel dipping down the hillslope supported on metal rods, twenty yards, fifteen, ten ...

162

Something rustled in the grass behind him and he saw a Doberman pounding along in his wake. He launched himself into a desperate leap gasping in gratitude as his fingers closed on the funnel rim, then he scrambled breathlessly into the curvature and shot like a rocket down the plummeting hillside.

The Doberman, still in full stride, soared into the air and landed in the chute at Jonas's rear, clattering downwards at the same stupefying rate. Haunches braced, teeth bared, it took the gradient with scarcely a tremor, its eyes fixed hungrily on Jonas's neck.

Jonas could scarcely believe the speed he was going. The world whipped by in a dizzy blur, the trees blending, the sky shimmering. His stomach tightened as he saw the lake directly below and realized he was coming to the conduit's end. He gritted his teeth as his body shot from the narrow tube. For a moment he seemed to be floating on air then the water came rushing up to meet him and he clamped his heels together, bracing himself for the impact.

Splooosh, he vanished beneath the surface, coldness enveloping him like a shroud. The water was luminous in places but as he plunged downward it began to darken, taking on different textures, different densities. He felt a heavy weight thrusting him deeper and realized with a sense of alarm that the Doberman had landed directly on top of his shoulders. He swivelled sideways, fingers grasping the matted hide. The animal thrashed wildly, its claws raking his lacerated skin. His hands locked on its windpipe and he felt the dog's powerful muscles as it tore and twisted, trying to get at his throat.

Something rose from the darkness to meet them, the lake bed. The Doberman's strength was awesome as it wriggled and squirmed, confused by the water, confused by the stranglehold on its throat, confused by the tenaciousness of the creature who, until only a few seconds ago, had been its helpless and terrified quarry. Jonas increased the pressure, his muscles bulging through the tattered sweat suit and the dog gave one last despairing shudder as it felt death approaching and its struggles dissolved into a series of feeble spasms.

He thrust it away and headed for the surface, sucking air into his tortured lungs. For a moment he lay bobbing on the waves like a piece of discarded flotsam, then he heard a whistle and saw a figure scrambling through the nearby trees. The figure drew to a halt at the water's edge and gestured at him wildly. The figure was Greg Anderson.

Jonas wiped the blood from his face, rolled onto his stomach and struck out tiredly for the shoreline.

Bruno heard music playing as he waved the column to a halt in front of the little inn. He climbed from the staff car, stretching his body wearily. For more than six hours they had driven across rural France, heading west toward Languedoc-Roussillon.

'We'll rest for an hour,' he told the sergeant. 'Warn the men no drunkenness. I don't want to alienate the local population.'

The inn was crowded as he entered with Willi Fredier and Suzanne. There was a bluish haze in the air and the acrid-sweet smell of French cigarette smoke. The customers were singing lustily, accompanied by the proprietor on a battered old accordion. At the sight of Bruno's SS uniform, their voices faded into silence.

He took off his cap. 'Please do not stop on our account. We enjoy good singing, particularly in such amiable company.'

The proprietor hesitated for a moment then resumed playing, the strains of his accordion filling the room. Bruno steered Fredier and Suzanne toward the serving counter.

'Do you imagine we will be welcome

here?' Suzanne asked.

'Our money's as good as anyone else's. Besides, we need refreshment. We still have a long way to go.'

'Why do I get the feeling the customers would be much happier slitting our throats?' Willi Fredier glanced around the interior uneasily.

Bruno laughed. 'You're such a pessimist. You look for hostility wherever you go. When human beings make contact—real contact—political differences fly out of the window.'

A serving girl moved toward them, wiping her hands on a towel. 'Bring us some of the local wine,' Bruno said.

The door opened and the rest of the troops began pouring into the bar, gathering around a group of tables at the rear.

'I think your men are a little embarrassed,' Willi Fredier observed.

'They want to be accepted. Soldiers are human beings too. Fighting and dying are easy. It's making friends that matters.'

The girl returned with the wine and Bruno raised his glass. 'To our noble fellrunner, wherever he is. May he enjoy his last hours of freedom.'

'You have a plan?' Fredier asked.

'I have a strategy. Since Caudale

did most of his training on English peaks—three thousand footers—my hunch is he'll try to avoid the higher altitudes. By following the BBC bulletins, I should be able to anticipate his approach and cut him off on the lower ridges as he nears Gavarnie.'

'You're very confident,' Suzanne said.

'In myself, no. In human nature, yes. That's why I'm able to manipulate people so easily.'

'Does that include me?' she asked.

'I would never attribute human failings to such an exquisite animal,' he told her with a smile.

The inn's customers were beginning to relax now that the shock of the Germans' arrival had subsided. Their voices rose on the warm smoky air.

'These are good people,' Willi Fredier said. 'Even in war, they know how to enjoy themselves.'

'One day you and your friends will be gone,' Suzanne told him. 'Then they'll celebrate in earnest.'

'Do you really hate us so much?'

'You may occupy our land, but never our hearts.'

Bruno laughed. 'How differently you talk in bed.'

'And how typical of male conceit to imagine that because of a biological function, we share some common empathy.'

The music drew to a close and the customers applauded. Some of the Germans rose to their feet and began moving among the assembled throng, filling their glasses with wine. Suddenly, there was an air of good-humoured bonhomie in the crowded inn. One of the soldiers toasted the glory of France and the customers cheered in acknowledgement.

'Is this your idea of tyranny?' Fredier said to Suzanne. 'Why can't you admit that you've built up barriers which don't really exist? It isn't war which comes naturally to the human spirit but the timeworn desire for companionship.'

Suzanne said, 'What you're witnessing is the intoxicating quality of French wine, that's all.'

The German troops seemed anxious to keep the party spirit going. A young corporal climbed onto a chair and began to sing. His voice was gentle and melodic. *'Die Fahne hoch, die Reihen fest geschlossen ...'*

The words echoed faintly on the afternoon air, and the customers listened as the other Germans joined in. Their voices lifted under the smoky rafters, the song gathering in strength and momentum.

'S.S. marschiert in ruhing festen Schritt ...'

Now the tune was no longer gentle. The singers roared lustily, their cheeks flushed, their eyes sparkling. Bruno saw veins throbbing in their throats and temples.

'*Marschieren mit uns in ihrem Geiste. mit ...*'

A hush filled the room as the singers drew to a close. Then a chair scraped as a man rose to his feet. He poured his wine contemptuously on the floor and strode from the inn without a word, slamming the door behind him. Another followed, tilting his glass in the same disdainful fashion, then another and another. All over the inn, chairs clattered as the customers went through their silent ritual of defiance. Within minutes, the room was empty.

Bruno shook his head in bafflement. 'If I live to be a hundred I will never understand these people.'

Suzanne chuckled dryly. 'No *chérie*, I don't believe you ever will.'

Chapter Seven

The forest was like a monstrous canopy, leading nowhere. Greg had lost track of the passage of time just as he had lost track of the endless thicket engulfing them. He felt sure they had been stumbling about for at least a month.

A fine old mess he'd got himself into, he reflected. He wasn't even supposed to be here. He should have kept his wits about him instead of losing his cool when the French kid had come crashing out of the underbrush and announced that Jonas was being hunted by wild dogs. He hadn't stopped to think, that was the stupid thing, had gone charging blindly into the brush without waiting for any kind of back-up, and could easily have been lost in here if he hadn't, by some miracle, spotted Jonas bobbing on the lake surface.

Jonas had looked in a pretty bad way at first, his sweat suit in tatters and his shoulder punctured by an ugly dog bite, but Greg had fixed the wound with a dressing from his first aid kit and after a few minutes' rest and a sip of cognac from his spirit flask, the wiry Englishman had been good as new. It was he, Greg Anderson, who was coming apart at the seams. His stomach crawled as he listened to the baying of the dog pack at their rear.

'How much longer can we keep this up?' he demanded. 'I'm no athlete, never professed to be. I'm a desk man. I plan things.'

'You're doing fine, Major. We'll make

a fellrunner of you yet.'

'Don't patronize me,' he snapped. 'I'm the one who's supposed to give the morale-boosting speeches.'

'Just trying to lift your spirits.'

'There's nothing wrong with my spirits. My spirits are terrific. Speaking dispassionately, my spirits have never been better. It's my body that's falling to bits.'

He was being unreasonable and he knew it but Jonas seemed impervious to fatigue. Nothing slowed him, even for a moment. He was inexhaustible, a regular dynamo. Greg supposed he ought to feel grateful at having such an redoubtable companion, but all he could think of was the sound, chilling in its intensity, of the packhounds homing in for the kill. He heard a new sound drifting through the trees and paused, holding his breath. 'Listen.'

'Aye, Major, I hear it.'

'Wind coming.'

'Not wind. It's a river.'

The leaves parted and Greg saw, directly in their path, a surging torrent forging through the forest in a silver arc. His heart sank as he calculated its width. It was at least forty feet from bank to bank.

'You might as well know, Jonas, that when it comes to water I have a tendency to sink like a stone.'

'I thought Americans never said die, Major.'

'Appealing to my sense of patriotism will not do a damn bit of good. How the hell are we supposed to cross this thing?'

'We'll anchor each other and work our way over step by step. At least it should stop the dogs.'

Greg watched Jonas ease himself into the thigh-deep water, bracing his legs against the current. He edged away from the riverbank and locked his arm around a rocky projection, waving at Greg to follow.

Greg winced as the icy rapids rose around his trembling knees. He could scarcely believe the river's momentum as it drove solidly against him. Slowly, gingerly, he shifted sideways, holding onto Jonas's shoulders for support. His feet felt numb on the shaley bottom and spray danced into his face, chilling his cheeks and throat.

He took Jonas's hand and began to inch toward the next boulder, fighting for balance every step of the way. The river was an indomitable force bent on his destruction. He reached the boulder, gripped it tightly and nodded at Jonas to follow. With infinite care, Jonas began to pick his way through the gurgling current.

They moved pendulum-like, beating a

slow methodical route from rock to rock, the water pummelling them step by precarious step. It was a slow and agonizing process, Greg battling the current, his clothing soaked, spray from the waves lashing into his cheeks as he positioned his feet against the silted bottom, trying not to slip on its unstable surface. At the river's centre the water rose above their waists and he gasped in disbelief as he felt the fury of the undertow tearing at his lower limbs. The boulders were nearly all submerged now, their surfaces slippery to the touch, and he felt a surge of panic as he realized the rock was sliding from his grasp. 'Jonas,' he yelled. 'I'm losing my grip.'

A salmon leapt out of the water, its silvery body forming a perfect loop in the bright spring sunshine, then his fingers peeled helplessly from their perch and he gasped out loud as the current whizzed them dizzily downstream.

He had little time to assimilate what was happening for the water filled his nostrils, choking off his lungs. The current seethed and boiled, hammering his body from every direction. There was no question of fighting it, he was being buffeted along like a piece of cotton in the wind, and though he was still clinging remorselessly to Jonas's arm, he was unable to slow his progress even for a moment. His head broke the surface and he thrashed out with his legs, struggling to see through the dancing spray. There were boulders everywhere, forming a treacherous obstacle course through which he desperately tried to steer.

A fallen tree lay wedged against the riverbank and he reached out, seizing a splintered bough. The impact almost ripped his body in two but he held on tight, wriggling into the shallows and dragging Jonas painfully behind him. Like soggy water rats the two men floundered out of the water and collapsed exhausted beneath the trees.

Major von Kummerl of the Third Mountain Corps watched the dogs gambolling confusedly along the riverbank. He saw a sergeant hurrying toward him as his troops tried to bring the bewildered animals under control. The sergeant was carrying a piece of sodden clothing. Von Kummerl examined it briefly for a moment, holding it at arm's length as if half afraid the dripping material might contaminate him in some way. It was a raincoat, he realized.

'You think it belonged to one of the fugitives, *Sturmbannfuhrer?*' the sergeant asked.

'I imagine so. They probably crossed the river here.'

'Perhaps they drowned.'

'And then again, perhaps not.'

The major studied the water thoughtfully. Its fast-moving current would make it difficult to negotiate but by braving the undertow, the fugitives had driven an effective wedge between themselves and the pursuing dogs. If he attempted a similar manoeuvre, however, he risked having a disaster on his hands. 'Bring the Frenchman here,' he ordered.

The Frenchman was a local woodcutter commandeered to act as guide. Von Kummerl asked him if there was a bridge nearby.

'*Oui*, M'sieur le *Sturmbannfuhrer*. There is a small footbridge only a mile or two upstream.'

The major calculated swiftly. He knew the nature of the surrounding terrain. It formed a natural amphitheatre, hemmed in on three sides by forbidding cliffs. A daring thought occurred to him. He licked his finger and tested the wind. 'We will cross the river and set fire to the foliage.'

The sergeant was surprised. 'Is that wise, *Sturmbannfuhrer*? In such a stiff breeze, the flames will quickly get out of control.'

'That is what I am counting on. The high cliffs will contain the blaze and prevent it

175

spreading southward, but anything lying in its path will be burned to a cinder.' He smiled as he waved his men upstream. 'I think our elusive friends are about to find life a little hotter than they'd bargained for.'

Greg's nostrils caught the odour as they paused to rest near a bramble thatch. Acrid and pungent, it was not immediately identifiable. He sniffed hard, filling his lungs with air. For the first time, he noticed fog-like wisps drifting among the branches.

Smoke.

Suddenly, the forest seemed alive. He spotted a stag, fully antlered, bounding through the brush in a madcap gallop. He saw rabbits and squirrels, marmots and weasels, all heading in the same direction. 'What the hell's going on?' he exclaimed.

Jonas hurried to the top of a tiny rise and Greg followed, pushing the bushes aside to peer across the leafy canopy. In places, the symmetry of the trees was broken by denser clumps of hardwoods which rose above the mattress of foliage like isolated islands. A monstrous barrier of swirling smoke, dense at the bottom, lighter near the top, was rippling into the sky, breaking into individual columns like the tendrils of some macabre sea anemone. Even at that distance, they could see crimson flashes darting among the undergrowth.

'Jesus,' Greg breathed. 'The krauts have set the forest on fire.' He could scarcely believe it. He glanced at the amphitheatre of rocks behind. 'They've got us neatly cornered. We'll have to turn back.'

'Screw that,' Jonas said.

'For Christ's sake, we're in a blind alley with no way out.'

'There's always up.'

'Up? Are you kidding?' Greg blinked at the precipice. 'I never climbed anything higher than the bedroom stairs in my life.'

'It'll be a piece of cake, Major. Trust me.'

Greg followed him through the trees, filled with a terrible foreboding, and by the time they reached the cliff-base the air was so heavy with smoke it was almost impossible to breathe. Spiralling wind currents whipped the branches above their heads and Greg's genitals moved in an involuntary spasm as he examined the perpendicular buttresses of rock. 'Jonas, it's straight up.'

'Don't worry, it looks steeper because of the angle.'

'Listen sport, I think I'll take my chances with the fire.'

'Forget it, Major. This is our only way out of here.'

Greg watched dry-mouthed as Jonas clambered up the shale and without hesitating, began to climb. He was like a monkey on the uneven rock, picking his way with an expert eye. Filled with a sickly uneasiness, Greg followed. There was a deep cleft in the limestone surface and he jammed his foot into it, reaching up with his right hand. His fingers located a tiny projection and he switched balance, fumbling for hand-holds.

He was careful not to look down, concentrating instead on the few square feet through which they moved. He had no concept of time. Time appeared to lose its meaning as he went on picking his way from cleft to cleft, from shelf to shelf. To his surprise, he found the going relatively easy; there were plenty of holds to choose from and he might almost have enjoyed the experience if it hadn't been for the suffocating smoke flurries swirling around his cheeks. He heard the sound of Jonas's shoes scraping against the rock above.

'How're you doing?' Jonas called through the drifting fumes.

'Can't catch my goddammed breath.'

'Just relax. And don't move until you can see the route ahead.'

'How come you know so much about this anyhow?'

'Been climbing all my life. When sheep

get cragfast, there's no other way to get them down.'

For over an hour, they moved up the precipitous incline, picking an uneven path around featureless slabs and jutting overhangs. Despite the steepness of the gradient, Greg marvelled at the way the mountain, which had seemed unscalable from below, offered an abundant variety of hand and footholds. Eventually however, they found themselves confronted by a slender groove which slithered upward for twenty or thirty feet, flanked on each side by huge slabs of unbroken rock.

Fiery brands danced on the wind currents and when Greg glanced down, he felt his stomach cringe. The entire valley was a sea of flame, and at the blaze's rear a great globule of soot-blackened earth formed a macabre 'no man's land' in which nothing lived except flickering cinders.

He saw Jonas working his way up the groove above, spread like a crab across the shiny surface. The move looked dangerous in the extreme. Straddled across the cliff, it would be all a man could do to keep himself in position. One hesitation, one fractional error of judgement would send him hurtling into the abyss below.

Bit by bit, panting and straining, Jonas scaled the crack and peered down sweatily from the ledge. 'OK, Major?'

'I'll never make it.'

'Spread your legs. See those bumps to the left and right? Use them as footholds.'

Greg's body felt limp as he pressed his toe against a miniscule nodule and leaned into the groove, straddling the rock-face like an acrobat.

'Stretch, Major, stretch. Get those legs wider.'

Biting his lip, Greg tried to inch upwards. His body was spread across the limestone wall, his weight suspended delicately on his outstretched feet. He felt his thigh muscles beginning to tremble. 'I can't move,' he yelled.

'Try.'

He scoured the rock with his fingertips, a terrible sickness gathering inside him. 'There's nothing here.'

'Squeeze your palms against the rock and move up to the next crack.'

'I can't, goddammit. I'm not built for this. I get dizzy on Brooklyn Bridge, for Chrissake.'

'Major, that fire's coming up fast. You've got to move.'

Sweat streaming into his eyes, Greg willed his legs to operate. He inched higher, his body shuddering, and gave a gasp of relief as his toe found a tiny purchase. He pressed it gratefully, bringing up his other leg, but to his horror there was no corresponding projection on the opposite side.

'It won't go,' he croaked.

'Make it go. Lean back so you can see where you're heading.'

Clenching his teeth, Greg forced himself away from the cliff-face and despite the precariousness of his position, realized at once that Jonas was right. With his head free of the rock he could discern tiny cracks at each side of the slippery slab. He jammed his foot against the nearest and wormed his way tremulously upward.

'Good man,' Jonas yelled. 'Now follow the groove.'

Greg obeyed, keeping his legs as wide as possible, shifting his balance inch by laborious inch. The strain on his joints was stultifying and he struggled to quell the terror in his stomach as he willed strength into his aching limbs. Somehow, wriggling and slithering, he managed to worm his way up and join Jonas on the shelf above.

'What did I tell you?' Jonas said. 'Easy, eh?'

Greg blinked. 'Did I make it? I figured I fell of at least ten minutes ago.'

Blazing brands sailed through the air and he felt the hot updraught from the fire below. Numbly, he stared at the cliff ahead. 'What happens now?'

'Now it starts to get tricky. We can't go up, because there's an overhang. We'll have to traverse into yonder chimney.'

Greg's heart sank as he eyed the narrow flake of rock which ran for almost forty feet to a deep cleft in the precipice face. 'Jonas, there aren't any footholds.'

'That's OK. We can use the flake like a banister.'

'What about our feet, coach?'

'Press them against the cliff. It's simply a matter of nerve.'

The thought of traversing the buttress filled Greg with trepidation and his throat was dry as he watched Jonas seize the flake and begin edging delicately sideways. Swallowing hard, he followed nervously, trying to ignore the great immensity below. It took almost twenty minutes to cover the forty feet to the chimney base and Greg was struggling every inch of the way. By the time they reached the cleft, his muscles were shivering all over. Through the swirling smoke, he caught glimpses of the gridiron on the forest floor and whistled softly through his teeth. 'Look at those flames. It's like the whole world took fire.'

'At least it'll keep the Goons away.'

The heat was almost intolerable now. Greg touched his clothing and realized with surprise that despite their ducking in the river, his garments were almost bone-dry. His cheeks smarted where blazing twigs, tossed upwards by the wind, had scorched his unprotected skin.

Jonas, huddled in the chimney, was practically unrecognizable. His face was blackened with soot and his hair was singed into a brushwork of crisp brown strands. He looked grotesque as he studied the gap above. The gully meandered for sixty feet or more but half-way up, an errant boulder had fallen from the summit and wedged itself between the rough-hewn walls, forming a formidable chockstone. Caught like a cork in a bottleneck, the boulder protruded several feet beyond the precipice wall, presenting a difficult obstacle.

'Jonas, we'll never get over that.'

'Aye, we will, Major. All it takes is a bit of puff.'

Jonas worked his way deftly up the fissure until he had reached a point directly beneath the wedged chockstone, then easing outward he began to wriggle around the jutting rim. It looked a strenuous and clumsy move but Jonas managed it without too much difficulty, panting as he dragged himself onto its upper surface.

'Come on, Major. It's a doddle.'

Greg jammed his spine against one side

of the chimney and his feet against the other, working his way upward with small shuffling movements until he had reached the underside of the chockstone. Here, he paused and examined the obstacle critically.

'Get your arms around it,' Jonas told him from above.

'I'll bring the bloody thing down on my head.'

'No way. It's been wedged in this chimney for the past thousand years. It'll take a damn sight more than your weight to dislodge it.'

Greg sucked in his breath and hugged the chockstone against him. Squeezing out of the chimney mouth, he wriggled awkwardly around it. He caught a glimpse of the flames below and his heart hammered as, wheezing and choking, he wrestled his body upwards, joining Jonas on the roof above.

'What did I tell you?' Jonas said. 'Easier than it looks, isn't it?'

Greg didn't answer. He was panting hard with strain and exertion.

'The next bit's simple,' Jonas added. 'Just straddle the gap with your feet—the way you did as a kid, remember?'

He began to inch up the narrow crack, using his palms as a stabilizer, not bothering to look for hand-holds but letting the pressure of his limbs create an effective wedge, holding him buoyantly aloft. Muscles trembling, Greg followed, gaining height in short erratic bursts. To his relief, it proved a simple procedure, but the constant wafts of arid hot air drifting up from the furnace below filled him with a dangerous sense of instability.

Suddenly, he realized that Jonas had stopped. He was leaning back in the chimney's belly, carefully examining the route ahead.

'Crack's opening out. There's a whacking great slab above our heads.'

'Can't we get around it?'

'No chance. We'll have to move out.'

'How, for Pete's sake?'

'Only one way. Through the front door.'

'Are you nuts? There's a sheer drop out there.'

'Let's hope you're wrong, Major,' Jonas said and with barely a pause, swung his body out of the narrow opening.

There was a moment in which time seemed to stand still and Greg, crouched in the slender crack, listened to the howling of the wind, the roaring of the flames. 'Jonas?' he shouted, 'Jonas?'

Jonas's voice reached him from around the corner. 'I'm OK. There's a good solid ledge here.'

'Christ Jonas, that was a crazy move.'

'Your turn now, Major. Work your way

up to my position and step out.'

Greg breathed deeply, edging upwards. He could see the tiny nodule of rock which Jonas had used as a stepping stone. It looked minute framed against the fissure rim, but ignoring the charcoal pit below, he measured the distance and swung himself out of the chimney opening. He saw the cliff-face etched against the sky, its buttresses picking up ripples of refracted light. He saw Jonas poised above him, bending forward to seize his hand. He saw the cleft in the rock which formed a bridging point to the mantelshelf itself Then with a sinking heart, he realized he had stepped too low. Desperately, he tried to switch direction but he was already too late. He felt himself sliding down the rock wall, Jonas receding swiftly above.

He reached the base of the slab and dropped over the edge, the cliff flitting past in a dizzy blur. His body was framed like a laundry mark against the hanging buttresses of rock, locked in a paroxysm of helplessness and terror.

Something caught his left side, checking his drop for a fractional moment, and he reached out instinctively, hanging on for all he was worth. It was a tiny bush growing out of a rocky fissure and his stomach cringed as he realized he was dangling bodily from the precipice with the flames twisting and roaring beneath him. 'Jonas,' he shouted. 'Jonas, for God's sake.'

Jonas's voice drifted eerily down the cliff-face. 'Hang on, Major. I'll try and get to you.'

He heard the scraping of feet as Jonas made his perilous descent. Tiny stones came clattering down the cliff, peppering Greg's hair and shoulders. His legs pedalled the air as he felt the incredible heat of the furnace below. 'Jonas, I'm burning up.'

'I'm coming as fast as I can.'

Slack-mouthed, Greg watched the bush working its way out of the fissure. The pull of his body was tearing the roots from their fragile nest. Blazing foliage danced around his head, carried on the buffeting wind, and to his horror one of the brands settled among the shrub leaves, setting the flimsy branches alight. 'Jonas, the bush is on fire.'

Through the smoke, he saw Jonas perched on a narrow mantelshelf. Jonas had taken off his jacket and was tying the sleeves tightly around his ankle. Lowering himself over the rim, he slid the fluttering garment carefully across the cliff-face. 'Grab hold.'

Greg swallowed. The bush was blazing merrily now. In a matter of seconds its foliage would be a solid ball of flame. He reached out, his fingers closing on the jacket's hem. Switching his weight, he let go of the blazing sapling and transferred both hands to the bedraggled garment. Even through the fumes he could see Jonas's knuckles gleaming whitely as he struggled to maintain a grip on the platform above.

'I can't lift you from this position,' Jonas panted. 'You'll have to climb.'

Greg reached up the taut folds of the straining jacket and began hauling himself toward Jonas's ankles. A terrible tearing sound reached his ears. 'The material's giving way.'

'Move, Major. Hurry.'

Hauling and wriggling, he worked his way up Jonas's calves.

'Keep going,' Jonas told him.

'What if I pull you loose?'

'Just do it.'

Greg felt the tension in Jonas's body as he inched awkwardly up the lean, muscular frame. Jonas was hanging onto the mantelshelf for all he was worth, struggling to stay in position. 'Can you reach the ledge?'

Hooking one arm around Jonas's shoulder, Greg groped up and felt a wave of relief as his fingers settled over a rocky jughold. Swinging free, he hauled himself over the last few remaining feet and collapsed breathlessly onto the mantelshelf.

'Give me a hand here,' Jonas gasped.

Greg seized him by the back of the shirt and with Jonas kicking and scrabbling from below, dragged him onto his slender perch. For several seconds, the two men lay panting like landed salmon then Jonas wearily raised his head. 'There's a crack at the end. Looks like a small cave.'

He shuffled along the platform to examine the jagged opening. 'It's a tight squeeze,' he said, 'but it'll give us a bit of protection against the smoke.'

Greg followed him into the cavity. It was like an upturned soup bowl, its roof laced with cracks, its floor cluttered with rubble.

Jonas began picking up rocks and stacking them in the cave mouth. 'If we block the gap, it'll keep the fumes out,' he said.

'How will we breathe?'

'There's air coming through the roof. We must be closer to the summit than I thought.'

Working feverishly, they built a makeshift wall, sealing the tiny chinks with pebbles from the cavity floor. When they had finished, Greg sank to the ground exhausted, examining his hands in wonder. 'God, I look like a piece of meat on a butcher's slab.'

'But with one small difference, Major.'

'Yeah? What's that?'

Jonas chuckled. 'You're still alive.'

'Jonas?'

'Aye?'

'Think it's night yet?'

'Can't be. We've been lying here less'n three hours.'

The cave interior was like an oven, its arid heat tempered by the myriad air currents which came filtering through the cracks above. Outside, the roar of the flames rose and fell in a constant symphony. Greg saw sharp flashes darting between the cracks of their makeshift barrier.

He ran his fingertips over his damaged cheeks. His skin carried the texture of papier mâché. 'My whole body's burning up.'

'Aye, mine too.'

He stared at Jonas through the gloom. He could see only the faint contours of his body. 'You saved my life today, hauling me up that cliff.'

'Nay, Major. You scaled that rock-face like a regular pro.'

'Think so?'

'Wouldn't say it if I didn't. When this war's over, you'll be putting up routes all over the United States.'

Greg lay back, sighing softly. He could

hear the wind battering their refuge like a tidal wave. 'Sometimes I think the war will never end.'

'Got to finish sometime.'

'Who says? Wasn't there one in Europe that lasted for a hundred years?'

'That's history. This one can't go on much longer.'

Greg said, 'What'll you do, Jonas, when we all go home?'

'What else would I do, Major? Being a shepherd's the only thing I know.'

'Must be an idyllic existence roaming the hills all day.'

'Well, I suppose for a city man it wouldn't seem much of a life. But it's the only one I ever wanted.'

'Lonely though. Take a bit of getting used to, I'll bet.'

'The hills are like people, they have their moods, their ups and downs. Sometimes they're friendly and sunny-like, but catch them on a bad day and they'll likely bite your head off.'

'I know what you mean. I come from a little town called Camden in northern Maine. It used to get pretty rugged in winter.'

He was silent for a moment then he said, 'Jonas, you don't have to be a shepherd. You're an intelligent guy, you could really make something of your life. I mean, every

191

man has a Godgiven duty to explore his full potential.'

'Is that your personal philosophy, Major?' Jonas sounded amused.

'It's the way the world is run, coach.'

'Your world, not mine.'

Greg rubbed his chest, massaging the skin as if infusing it with warmth. He hesitated to ask the question that was uppermost on his mind. He had tried to bury it, tried to purge it from his consciousness, but like a bad penny it kept stubbornly returning. 'Jonas, will you tell me something?'

'If I can,' Jonas said.

'Why are you doing this?'

'Doing what?'

'Running home?'

There was a slight pause. 'It's personal, Major.'

'What does that mean, personal?'

'Means it's nowt to do wi' anyone else.'

'But Jonas, I'm your friend.'

Jonas rolled awkwardly onto his side, his body picking up flickers of light from the wall cavities. 'If you really are my friend,' he said, 'you'll never ask that question again.'

Greg awoke and lay for a moment, trying to regulate his breathing. Something was different, he knew it. Jonas had disappeared.

'Jonas?' he shouted, blinking rapidly. 'Jonas?'

'It's OK, Major.'

Jonas appeared in the cave-mouth, ducking his head beneath the splintered ceiling.

Greg shivered with relief. 'I thought you'd vanished.'

'It's nearly midnight. Fire's almost burnt itself out. We've only a few more feet to the summit.'

'Can we see well enough to climb?'

'Aye, I think so.'

The blackened landscape lay like crumpled carbon paper as Greg crawled onto the mantelshelf. He gazed awestruck over the scene of devastation. Even in the darkness, he could see woodcoals smouldering amid the monstrous mattress of ash. 'God, what a mess.'

'Think you can follow me in the dark?'

'I can try.'

They headed toward the clifftop, their pace quickening as the gradient slackened. Suddenly, Jonas ducked behind a boulder, dragging Greg to a halt. 'Somebody's up there.'

Faintly, almost indiscernibly, they heard a series of scrapings along the precipice rim and a figure appeared, blotting out the stars. Greg saw a long Gallic nose, a bristling moustache.

'It's Marcel!' Jonas exclaimed excitedly.

'Marcel?'

'Bloody Frenchman must be looking for us.'

Greg felt a wave of overwhelming relief. 'Thank God, thank God.'

Whimpering with joy, they scrambled up the remaining few feet and joined the astonished *résistant* leader on the summit.

Chapter Eight

Something changed in Jonas after the cliff-face episode. It was nothing identifiable, but his body seemed to lose momentum. Not that his wounds were debilitating in themselves—most were superficial, especially the burns, and even the gash in his shoulder presented little discomfort beyond intermittent bouts of bleeding when he ran too purposefully, but an accumulative tiredness began to gather inside him.

He suffered from 'shin-splints'—needle-sharp pains which lanced the fronts of his lower legs. Skin rashes formed on the sweaty parts of his body. He endured cramps, blisters and inflamed tendons.

There was never a time, it seemed, when his organism was wholly free from pain. The iron resolve which had borne him so admirably through the early stages of the run began to disintegrate as he plodded doggedly westward.

He saw little evidence of German activity during this period; Greg and his *résistants,* forced to abandon their teams of decoy runners, had taken to distracting the enemy's attention with lightning sabotage attacks which, though worthless in a strategic sense, helped keep the Germans occupied. Every night, groups of volunteers trailed aniseed sacks over the surrounding countryside, blotting out Jonas's scent to impede the use of tracker dogs.

At St Leyre, he climbed the abandoned mulberry terraces which rose like disjointed stairways toward the crystalline plateau bordered by the Cevennes. The bleak pastures of the Aubrac chilled his blood but he skirted the village of Buron, with its massive chestnut trees, and entered the Midi-Pyrenees where the stark limestone mesas of the Causses rose to the north and east.

Joints aching, muscles throbbing, drained with fatigue and exertion, he was unaware, as he swung north toward the Cirque de Gavarnie, that daily bulletins on his progress continued to be broadcast to clandestine listeners all over Europe.

At six forty-five a.m. on May 3rd, 1944, in the tiny Pyrenean village of Chelon, *Underfeldwebel* Otto Kemmerich of the German 5th *Gebirgsjager* rose early, having spent the night with a certain lady of the town, and made his way downstairs to find the parlour bristling with armed men. Their grim faces left the sergeant in little doubt that he was in the presence of mountain *maquisards* and though he was not a cowardly man, sweat gathered between his shoulder blades as he raised his hands in a gesture of surrender.

The intruders confiscated the sergeant's pistol and marched him out to his car, which he had parked the previous evening beneath a line of plane trees. Seated behind the driving wheel was a young man with short-cut sandy hair. 'Good-morning,' the stranger said in English and Sergeant Kemmerich gave a start, for to his surprise the man spoke with an American accent.

Kemmerich was bundled into the vehicle rear with two partisans and for the next twenty minutes they drove through the snowcapped mountains. After a while, he saw the awesome chasm of the St Dozier Gorge ahead and the solitary suspension bridge spanning its banks. On a rocky promontory, surrounded on three sides by sheer cliff walls, stood his command post, a German artillery emplacement. Virtually unapproachable except through one meticulously-guarded gate, the concrete pillbox commanded an excellent view of the bridge itself; no one could cross in either direction without passing under the sights of the gun crew inside.

The American pulled to a halt in a little copse of trees and swivelled around in his seat. 'We are going to take a little walk,' he said in German. 'We are going to get out of the car, and without any sign of tension, stroll across to the blockhouse. It will be your job to placate the sentry. Should he fail to be placated, or should he, for any reason, refuse to open the security gate, you will be shot dead on the spot, is that understood?'

Kemmerich nodded, his heart thumping.

'Act sensibly and you may yet come out of this alive. Fail, and you will certainly be killed. Can I count on your co-operation?'

Sergeant Kemmerich had few illusions about the danger of his predicament. He nodded again.

The two Frenchmen vanished into the underbrush and the American propelled him roughly toward the bunker entrance. The young sentry was reluctant at first to open the gate but after Kemmerich convinced him that his companion was, in fact, the local Gestapo agent, he stepped back to allow the visitors through.

The moment the American was inside the barrier, he seized the sentry by the throat and pressed a pistol against his temple. 'You have one hope of living through the morning,' he said, his voice surprisingly mild. 'Do exactly as I tell you and you will be drinking beer with your friends in the café tonight. Resist and you will be shot where you stand, is that clear?'

The sentry's eyes looked glassy as he too nodded.

The American motioned with the pistol. 'Walk in front of me,' he ordered.

Kemmerich and the sentry moved along the narrow tunnel leading to the chamber's interior. The walls had been hewn out of solid rock and the ceiling was studded with wire-bracketed lightbulbs. The sentry paused to unlock a second door, its massive panels even heavier than the first, and Kemmerich saw the circular bunker with its twin Geb H40 artillery pieces covering the suspension bridge below. The gun crew, four men in *Waffenrock* smocks, were in the process of eating breakfast. A fifth stood watch at the observation slit.

What happened next was instilled for ever into the sergeant's memory. The sentry came to a halt and to Kemmerich's alarm, began bellowing a discordant warning. Moving so fast that his arm was a blur, the American hit the guard over the back of the skull. Corporal Hopper, still poised at the observation window, swung his rifle in a rapid arc and the American, without taking aim, loosed off a single shot that caused Hopper's face to crumple inwards like a battered tin can.

One of the men at the table lunged toward a line of carbines, bringing down the breakfast table with a resounding crash. Again, the American fired and the man's spine arched as the bullet tore between his shoulder blades, carrying him forward by its own momentum. He hit the wall and hung there for a moment before collapsing to the ground, leaving a crimson smear in his wake.

The remaining survivors raised their hands.

Footsteps echoed in the tunnel outside and the two Frenchmen burst in, pistols at the ready.

'Keep an eye on them,' the American ordered, jerking his head at the motionless prisoners.

He took out a small hand mirror and moved to the observation slit, using the sun's reflection to flash a signal to the opposite side of the gorge. A similar signal answered, then something moved on the road below. Kemmerich saw two figures trotting slowly over the suspension bridge.

The American smiled at his bafflement. On a shelf above the equipment cupboard stood a half-empty bottle of schnapps. He took it down and pulled out the cork with his teeth, then handed the bottle to Kemmerich. 'Drink, good buddy,' he said in English. 'It isn't every day of the week a man gets to see history being made.'

Oberst Albert Schirmer of the 4th Battalion *Hochgebirgs* gave his name to the sentry on duty and entered the 'Long Hall' of the German Reich Chancellery leading to Adolf Hitler's private study. Nearly five hundred feet long with walls of marble stucco, the gallery had been carefully designed to impress visiting diplomats and Schirmer could never help feeling intimidated when he strode between the gilded bronze sconces, the exquisite gobelins and the beautifully shaped tables.

As he approached the twenty-foot high door which marked the entrance to Hitler's office, the Führer's aide-de-camp, *Generalleutant* Volkmar Brauer, former commander of the 3rd *Fallschirmkorps*, came out of a tiny ante-room and strolled toward him, smiling. 'Schirmer, when did you get back from Italy?'

'Just arrived,' Schirmer said. 'I haven't had time to shave yet.'

Brauer examined him shrewdly. 'You're looking tired, old friend.'

'I've had no sleep for three days.'

'That bad, eh?'

Schirmer grimaced. 'The French have broken through to the Itri-Pico road. They're threatening to cut off the 1st Parachute Division.'

'You've come to report that?'

'Naturally.'

Brauer slipped his arm around Schirmer's shoulder and drew him gently aside. 'As one who cares about your welfare, let me give you a piece of advice. Go home and get some rest. See your wife, play with your children. Come back tomorrow. This isn't the day to be bringing bad news, believe me.'

He looked meaningfully at the door to the Führer's study, where two SS men clad in black uniforms with white leather strappings stood to attention. Through the mahogany panels, decorated with the initials 'A.H.' Schirmer heard Hitler's voice raised in an hysterical tirade. Harsh, distorted with emotion, it was scarcely recognizable as human.

Never in his life had Schirmer heard such a display of fury. He looked at Brauer with astonishment. 'Is he often like this?'

'These days, it's becoming more regular. French terrorists have managed to smuggle an English POW across the St Dozier Gorge in Occupied France and for personal reasons the Führer is deeply upset.'

Schirmer was incredulous. 'Volkmar, you are talking about one man. The news from Italy represents a major strategic defeat.'

'That is why, as your former comrade-in-arms, I heartily recommend that you postpone delivering your message for another twenty-four hours. It will do wonders for your career, I assure you.'

Schirmer studied him in silence for a moment, then put on his cap. 'You're a good friend, Volkmar. You have always been honest with me. I will come back in the morning.'

'I think you are being very wise,' Brauer said.

'Speed and boldness,' Churchill declared in his emphatic tone, 'those are the factors which will determine our success on D-Day. Once the initial landings have succeeded, we must ensure that our main forces are never so stretched that they're unable to hold out against a determined counterattack.'

In the Smoking Room at the House of Commons, the small group of cabinet members listened in silence as the British Prime Minister outlined his thoughts on the forthcoming invasion. Having fortified himself with several pre-luncheon *aperitifs,* Churchill's plump face was unusually exuberant. 'Armoured units will make determined thrusts inland and establish bases to protect the advance of our main body of troops. It's important to insure against the enemy withdrawing from Italy and concentrating his resources in Occupied France.' He paused as a House of Commons usher appeared at his elbow, carrying a note on a silver platter. 'A message from the intelligence service, sir. It concerns the man Caudale.'

Churchill frowned as he took the note and read it quickly, narrowing his eyes in the haze of tobacco smoke. His cherubic features broke into a delighted smile.

'Good news, Prime Minister?' one of the MPs asked in a respectful tone.

'Excellent, gentlemen,' Churchill said as he snipped the end off a fresh cigar.

Bristling with curiosity, the man leaned forward, straining to read the handwritten note. To his disappointment, the message was brief and maddeningly enigmatic.

It said simply: *'The shepherd is coming home.'*

At the London offices of the *Daily Express*, Anne Huntley looked up startled as her editor, Hugh Miller, stormed into the room and dropped a sheaf of papers on her desk. 'If there's one thing I can't stand, it's a reporter who doesn't do her homework.'

'What are you talking about, Hugh?'

'This is what I'm talking about.' Snatching up one of the sheets, he began to read. ' "Jonas Caudale, the Lakeland shepherd who set out from Switzerland to run home to Buttermere across enemy-occupied territory, has now reached Muret, twenty miles south-west of Toulouse, according to French Resistance reports. Caudale, now within striking distance of the Spanish frontier, has sworn to remain on the French side of the borderline, challenging the German authorities to intercept him. Holder of six Lakeland mountain records, Caudale has already survived forty-one days behind enemy lines." '

Miller scowled at her. 'That was a bulletin from the BBC's French Service. Here's another. "News has just reached us that Jonas Caudale, the Lakeland shepherd who is running home to Buttermere across

204

Nazi-occupied France, has now entered the foothills of the Pyrenees. Informed sources say he will turn west toward the coast. Caudale, who has successfully eluded enemy patrols for more than a month now, has sworn to make his way to England single-handed. A War Office spokesman described his progress this evening as 'heroic'." ' Miller's eyes blazed.

He picked up a third sheet. 'This one's a little more informal. "They seek him here, they seek him there, those Nazis seek him everywhere. Word on the Kanstrasse is that poor old Adolf has gone into a seizure, and who can blame him? After years of proclaiming their unconquerability, the Führer's nordic goliaths have been tumbled by Jonas Caudale, a diminutive David from the Lakeland fells. Can this be the nation which strutted like peacocks through Munich and Nuremburg? Throw in the towel, Herr Hitler. Surely even a man of your asininity can see that against such spirit defeat is inevitable." '

Anne squirmed as Miller tossed the papers back on her desk. 'I swear to God, Hugh, everyone I spoke to insisted there was no such person as Jonas Caudale.'

'Then perhaps they can explain this.' Miller showed her a photograph of a craggy-faced man in an athlete's singlet.

'I got that from the *Picture Post* circa 1938. They ran a profile on Caudale after he set up a new world best.'

Her cheeks flushed. 'What, in God's name, are those people hiding up there?'

'I don't know what they're hiding,' Miller said in a steely voice, 'but if you don't find out, I am going to start seriously re-thinking your future on this newspaper. You're supposed to investigate, not accept every damn thing at face value. Now get yourself back to the Lake District and don't let me see you in London again until you've got this story in the bag.'

Sunlight lit the surrounding peaks as Suzanne walked down the mountain highway. It was a glorious day and the rolling pastures were scattered with spring blossoms. She felt her senses quickening as she saw Greg in the hollow ahead. He was mending a bicycle puncture, his lean face creased in concentration.

She'd missed him, she realized. More than missed. She'd felt a hollow emptiness inside as if some essential part of her had been summarily amputated. Emotions she'd thought long dead had re-emerged, throwing her into a quandary she scarcely knew how to handle. He was hardly the type to inspire affection, she thought. He was taciturn, surly and unresponsive. He built up constant barriers between himself and other people. But when she came right down to it, wasn't it that very quality which attracted her most? She liked him for being human, for being vulnerable like herself.

For weeks, she had hung around the high meadows of the Cirque de Gavarnie while Bruno von Hautle moulded his men into top physical condition. Nothing seemed to matter to Bruno except the thought of outwitting the Englander. He was like a man possessed, bristling with eagerness and anticipation.

She had to admit that her feelings toward the young SS officer had mellowed considerably since their initial meeting. Then, she'd regarded him as a typical example of the worst the enemy had to offer, arrogant, swaggering, pompous and conceited. Now she realized he was also a kind man and though he could be ruthless at times, he was honourable and compassionate too. She liked his humour, his devil-may-care attitude. She even liked his haughtiness. This element, which she despised in other men, seemed in Bruno somehow endearing. In different circumstances she might have fallen in love with him, but no matter how hard she tried, she couldn't get the memory of the lonely young American out of her mind.

She felt a wave of tenderness as she watched him fixing a patch to his inner tube. He made no attempt to look up as she approached.

'You're late,' he said. 'I've been waiting almost an hour.'

The coolness in his tone surprised her and she felt her elation waver. 'I can't wander off as I please. I have to wait until Bruno's occupied, otherwise he might get suspicious.'

'Bruno, is it?'

'Of course, Bruno. What did you expect? I'm here, aren't I?'

He rose to his feet, wiping his fingers on an oily rag. There were ugly scorch marks on his cheeks and a look in his eyes she found difficult to identify. 'You're looking well, I must say. Depravity must agree with you.'

'Depravity? What are you talking about, depravity?'

'Well, you haven't exactly taken holy orders, have you?'

She said angrily, 'Is that why you asked me here? So you could moralize about my behaviour?'

'Hell, no. This is business. I have to find out what your lover boy's up to.'

'Don't call him my lover boy.'

His eyes were cold as he pushed the rag

into his raincoat pocket. 'Look, I don't give a damn about that preening gigolo—your relationship is your own affair—but right now we're only a matter of miles from Gavarnie and if he's planning something we need to be prepared.'

Suzanne held onto her temper with an effort. She knew the possessive nature of men but she knew too that histrionics would get them nowhere.

She kept her voice calm as she said, 'He's gambling on the fact that Jonas will stick to the lower altitudes. He's got a detachment of top mountain runners standing by and he intends to work out Caudale's route through a process of systematic elimination.'

'Can you keep him occupied for the next twenty-four hours?'

'Not a chance. He knows the Englishman's somewhere in the area and he's like a cat on hot bricks. Nothing short of an Allied invasion would distract him at this moment.'

'I was afraid of that.' He knelt down and began to pump up the bicycle tyre, his movements jerky and erratic.

'What are you going to do?'

'None of your damned business.'

'Don't you think I have a right to know? I'm in this as much as you are.'

'By Christ you are. You're in it up

to your neck. You should get a medal from General de Gaulle for your diligence and enthusiasm. You probably sing the Marseillaise as you're climbing into bed.'

'You're such an innocent, *chérie*,' she said tiredly. 'You think you know all the answers but really you know nothing at all. I'm doing this because there's no other way.'

'Maybe I could believe that if you didn't enjoy it so much.'

Suzanne's breasts rose and fell angrily. She said, 'Don't preach at me, Major Anderson. My country has endured four years of tyranny and what I do, I do in the name of freedom. Bruno von Hautle may be arrogant and conceited but he's also noble and decent and kind. So keep your bourgeois middle-class American values to yourself because those are qualities you couldn't even spell.'

Sixty yards above, hidden among the scrub, Bruno watched through his field glasses as Suzanne stormed furiously away. He recognized the man she had been talking to as Auguste Odru, her brother from Viatte. But what was Ordru doing in the Pyrenees? Under the rules of the occupation no Frenchman was allowed to travel more than fifteen miles from his place of residence without an official permit.

A terrible suspicion formed in Bruno's mind as he slipped the binoculars into their leather case and, frowning worriedly, rejoined Willi Fredier on the road above.

Chapter Nine

The secretary of the little Lakeland newspaper looked startled as Anne Huntley stormed angrily into the office. After the long, tedious journey from London, she was bristling with indignation. The editor blinked as she threw the photograph on the desktop in front of him. 'So there's no such person as Jonas Caudale? Then who is this, tell me? General Mongomery?'

The man glanced down at the picture. There was no expression on his face. 'My story still stands.'

'What story? You haven't got a story. You can't tell me Jonas Caudale doesn't exist, because this is Jonas Caudale.'

'I've never seen that man in my life.'

Her eyes narrowed. 'You still insist on sticking to your fairy-tale?'

The man said calmly, 'I tell you I have never heard of Jonas Caudale.'

She snatched up the photograph and tucked it into her handbag. 'I don't know what game you're playing but I intend to find out,' she said, 'and when I do I'll spread your name across every front page in Fleet Street.'

Storming through the door, she met the secretary in the outer office. 'Where can I borrow a car?'

'A car, miss?'

'That's right—a car. It's one of those things with four wheels and an accelerator.'

'But miss, there's a war on.'

'I'm sure it's possible to override the regulations if you've got enough money, even here in the Lake District.'

'Well ...' The girl hesitated. 'There's Barry Jackson. He has a little Austin he sometimes rents out for a bob or two. Working at the hospital, he gets a special petrol allowance.'

'He sounds just the man I'm looking for. Where can I find him?'

'At this time of the afternoon he'll be drinking in the Labour Club. It's at the bottom of the street, directly opposite the bus shelter. You can't miss it.'

'Thank you. I'm glad somebody in this Godforsaken hole knows how to be helpful.'

She flounced haughtily out of the room.

The farm stood slightly back from the road, perched on a tiny rise. Anne turned up the entrance drive, guiding the battered Austin gingerly along the cart-track. As she passed the barn a rough-looking man came out, carrying a sack of animal feed over one shoulder. Dressed in soiled workclothes, he watched her draw to a halt on the cindered forecourt.

She knocked lightly on the farmhouse door and it was opened a moment later by a small, dark-haired woman in her middle twenties.

'Mrs Hendricks?' Anne said.

The woman nodded, watching her nervously.

'I'm Anne Huntley from the *Daily Express*. I found your address in the local records office. I understand your maiden name was Caudale before you married?'

'That's right.'

'Mrs Hendricks, I'm clutching at straws and at this moment you are the only lead I've got. I'm trying to trace a local fellrunner by the name of Jonas Caudale.'

'Jonas?'

Was it Anne's imagination or did the woman's eyes flicker? 'He apparently lived somewhere in the Buttermere area. According to our information, he was a champion athlete before the war yet oddly enough I can find no trace of his achievements anywhere. I wondered if there might be a family link in view of the fact that you both have the same surname.'

A glimmer of fear entered the woman's eyes and Anne sensed a presence hovering at her shoulder. She turned, startled, to find the rough-looking man grinning at her crookedly. His eyes were slightly out of focus, and beard stubble coated his sweaty cheeks. 'What's this then?' he said, wiping his mouth with the back of one hand.

'You are Mr Hendricks?' she said, struggling to hide her confusion.

'Aye, that's right.'

'I'm Anne Huntley from the *Daily Express*.'

'The *Express*, is it?' His lips twisted into an unpleasant sneer. 'What have we done to deserve a visit from such an important celebrity?'

Her cheeks coloured. 'I'm looking for information on a shepherd named Jonas Caudale.'

'Caudale?'

'I understand Caudale was your wife's maiden name.'

'You've been doing your homework, I see. I've heard about you newspaper people, how you're always digging into things you got no business to.'

'Hardly that,' she protested.

'What's he done, this Caudale?'

'It's not what he's done, it's what he's

214

doing. He's running home to Buttermere across German-occupied Europe.'

Chuckling, the man leaned against the side of the door. 'What is he, some kind of mental case?'

'That's what I'm trying to find out.'

'Well, you won't do it here. There's no Jonas Caudale in the Buttermere Valley. Never was. You can take my word on that.'

'Are you sure?' She felt her frustration deepening. 'Perhaps there's someone in your wife's family who might remember this man? A distant cousin, or a relative by marriage.'

'And perhaps you should wash your ears out,' the man said. 'I tell you there's no such person as Jonas Caudale. If there was, I'd know about it.'

Anne looked at the woman. 'Please think. Has there ever been a get-together—a wedding, a funeral, or a Christmas gathering—where you've heard the name Jonas mentioned?'

The woman glanced nervously at her husband, then shook her head. 'Never,' she said in a firm voice.

Anne sighed. It was clear she would get no information from this quarter. 'Well, if you should remember anything, anything at all, please don't hesitate to give me a call. I'm staying at the Glanton Hotel.'

She thanked the woman and drove back to Buttermere through the gathering darkness, feeling bitter and defeated. At the hotel, ignoring the 5″ bath rule for once, she filled the tub full and lay soaking herself for nearly an hour, trying to make sense of the situation confronting her. If Jonas Caudale really did exist—and she had to accept that he must—what strange conspiracy was taking place here?

She was on the point of dressing for dinner when someone tapped lightly on the bedroom door and she found Mrs Hendricks standing on the threshold. The woman looked more frightened than ever and her eyes flickered nervously as she toyed with the belt at her waist. 'Is it true?' she whispered. 'Is it true that Jonas is coming home?'

Anne took a deep breath and gently squeezed the woman's arm. 'Come in, Mrs Hendricks. I think it's time we had a little talk.'

Jonas trotted painfully through the afternoon rain. His body felt listless, as if the endless weeks of running had drained it of energy. Sometimes he marvelled that he managed to move at all for his feet were numb from the ankles down and an aching weariness had settled in his limbs.

His companion, a young Frenchman

named André, gestured toward a winding goat track and they turned along it without a word, their muscles straining to take the grade. I'm getting too old for this, he thought. His limbs, the good strong limbs which had borne him so admirably through his long years on the Lakeland slopes were beginning to wilt at last, worn to a frazzle by the rigours of the last few weeks. Who would have believed it, that so much activity could surround one man? He'd have laughed if he'd had the strength for it, but laughing, like everything else, drained his precious energy reserves.

He'd put on a good show though, nobody could argue with that. Hadn't faltered, hadn't slackened. He couldn't recall how long he'd lasted but it seemed a lifetime. They thought he was crazy of course, the *résistants*. He saw in their faces, he saw it in the way they looked at him each time he arrived at some isolated and secluded rest stop. Well, in their position he'd have figured the same thing. But he did have a reason for this, he did have a purpose, which surely proved, if anything could, that he wasn't completely around the bend.

It was funny though the way things turned out. He hadn't expected so much attention. He was grateful to the *résistants* and grateful too to the American major

217

for his encouragement and support. He was a strange one, Major Anderson, a difficult man to fathom, hard as teak on the outside, sad and lonely underneath. He had an obsessive streak which Jonas recognized and identified with, but only a fool could fail to see that he was out of step with the whole human race. Jonas liked him, liked him better than almost anyone he'd ever met. He owed him his life and when this was over he intended to repay that debt. But first he had to get to the coast, then he had to get across the Bay of Biscay and then he had to get to the mountains of Cumberland. It would not be an easy task and it was not proving easy now.

'How far have we come?' he asked his running companion.

'Five miles.' The Frenchman spoke almost perfect English. 'We can rest a little, if you like.'

'No, I'm OK.'

André was tall and sinewy with tangled hair that curled upwards at the neck. His cheeks were pale, his eyes gentle. Jonas realized that despite the hours they had spent together, he knew almost nothing about the man. That was the craziest part of this whole crazy business. He ran each day with total strangers, sharing risks, sharing physical discomfort, and when nightfall came they were strangers still. There was something reprehensible about that. He ought at least to know the people who were helping him. He studied André curiously, noting the sensitive features, the pale asthetic skin. 'Live around here, do you?' he asked in a conversational tone.

'*Oui*, in the village of Dossola. We graze sheep on the pasturelands there.'

'How many head?'

'About eight hundred.'

'I used to tend Herdwicks myself. Herdwicks and Swaledales and a few Rough Fell Crosses.'

'Really?'

'Swaledales produce more lambs but Herdwicks are tougher. Trouble is, they crop close and put nowt out in the way of manure, so they ruin the land. But they're good survivors, built for the mountain weather. I've known ewes last two months buried under winter snow, feeding on their own wool.'

'You're a shepherd then?'

'Aye. Most of my life.'

'Me too,' André said. 'I tried the city once, Paris. I have a brother who lives in the 12th arrondissement and he got me a job in a clothing store, but I couldn't stand it in the end. I had to come back.'

'Are you married?' Jonas asked.

'No, but there's a girl in the village

219

who works at the local hotel and we've been going out together for almost a year now. I'd like to marry her but I need her father's permission and without money he's unlikely to agree. His daughter brings home a good wage and he'll be sorry to see that go.'

Jonas paused as something caught his eye in the valley below. He wiped the sweat from his face. 'Look,' he said.

A column of trucks wound its way slowly along the mountain road, the roar of the engines strangely muted on the high altitude air.

'*Boche,*' André said contemptuously. 'Looking for us?'

'*Naturellement.*' He spat on the ground. 'Damn fools. By the time they get anywhere near this ridge we'll be miles away.'

Standing up in the scout car, Bruno trained his fieldglasses on the ridge above. His eyes caught a flicker of movement and he held his breath, swivelling the lens into focus. Two men were picking their way toward the mountains' summit. Caught in the cross-hairs of his vision-sight, they looked strangely elongated, as if the glass had distorted them in some obscure way. His senses raced. 'It's Caudale.'

'You're sure?' Willi Fredier shielded his eyes, following Bruno's gaze.

'Who else would be running at such an altitude?'

Swiftly, he scanned the surrounding terrain. He could see the ridge meandering into a series of jagged outcrops; at one point it looped back on itself, forming an irregular 'U', and here a tributary flake of limestone ran from the road to the 'U's' opposite tip. It looked a strenuous ascent route but Bruno felt sure his men could take the grade.

'We'll use that tier to reach the ridge crest,' he said. 'They'll have to swing directly above us.'

Fredier eyed it dubiously. 'It'll be heavy going. More than a thousand feet.'

'What do you think we've been training for?'

He tore the binocular case from his neck. '*Unterfeldwebel*, split the runners into two groups. The four fittest will follow me and cut off the fugitives on the ridge top. The rest will carry rifles and harry our quarry from the rear. Let's see if we can run them into a trap.'

'*Jawhol, Oberleutnant*,' the sergeant snapped.

Willi Fredier chuckled as he watched Bruno pulling on his running shoes. 'You really think you're up to this?'

Bruno said, 'There's nothing the Englander can do that I can't do better.'

'I wouldn't be too sure. Don't forget he's already run half-way across France.'

Bruno grinned as he leaned forward to fasten his laces. 'That's what I'm counting on,' he said.

'Here they come,' André said.

Jonas saw miniscule figures mounting the slope behind them, their slender bodies darting awkwardly among the rocks. There was nothing awkward about their progress however; they were tackling the gradient with astonishing speed. He felt a tremor of uneasiness. 'Those are no ordinary soldiers.'

'Athletes?'

'That's my guess.'

André looked scornful. 'They're carrying rifles. We'll run them to a standstill.'

'They've got one major advantage,' Jonas said, his uncertainty deepening. 'They're fresh and we're tired.'

Bruno picked his way up the tilting flake, sweat stinging his skin. His rib cage ached as he sucked hard at the mountain air but he felt better than he'd felt for months now. The training had paid off, the long hours of pounding relentlessly over the mountain slopes. He was into his second wind at last, filled with a wonderful containment that told him his body was totally under control. He could run all day now without a murmur.

Cliffs rose on both sides, closing in toward the mountain peak, and he felt his senses quickening as he saw the fugitives crossing a shale slope above, their feet clattering on the chill damp air. In another few minutes his men would reach the summit and then they would be pinned neatly at both ends of the ridge.

A stitch lanced Jonas's side. After six weeks of running he was relying on willpower and little else. He massaged his skin ruefully. Maybe André was right, maybe their pursuers, weighed down by weapons, had little chance of overtaking them, but something about the situation worried him and he felt the hairs on the back of his head beginning to prickle.

He saw figures outlined on the ridge above and for a moment could scarcely believe his senses. They were spread across the hilltop, panting heavily as they gazed down at the fugitives' approach. Where, in God's name, had they come from?

'We're trapped,' André gasped.

It was true. With Germans behind and Germans in front, they had been neatly outmanoeuvred. Jonas struggled to control his panic. His tiredness had vanished, lost in the urgent need for survival.

On one side of the ridge, a blanket of cloud slid across the valley, blocking off the lower pastures; on the other, jagged cliffs fell into a fractured gully where they could see a river winding. 'Maybe we can get down there,' Jonas said.

'It's almost perpendicular,' André protested.

'But if we zigzag and keep our speed up—'

'I'd rather take my chances with the *Boche*. You go, I'll try and draw them off.'

'We go together or we die together,' Jonas told him calmly.

André's cheeks turned an unhealthy yellow. He stared at the perilous descent route. 'We'll never make it.'

'We can if we move fast enough. Just a question of balance.'

'If we fall, we're dead.'

'Down there or up here, what's the difference? I don't know about you, but I'd rather take my chances on the precipice.'

André glanced at the Germans above, his eyes blank with fear. 'OK,' he agreed at last.

'Good man.'

Jonas hoped to God he knew what he was doing. It seemed a crazy idea and one he wouldn't have entertained in ordinary circumstances but the incline, steep as it was, offered the only conceivable way out of here.

They started down the precipitous embankment, perspiration streaming from their faces, conscious of the yawning emptiness beneath them. The wind hammered their cheeks as they detoured from side to side in a desperate effort to steady their momentum. There was little pattern to their movements, only a tenacious attempt to remain in place by sheer force of velocity.

Four hundred feet above, Bruno watched in astonishment as the tiny figures weaved and twisted. It wasn't possible, he told himself. The fugitives were defying gravity, running on gradients which staggered the imagination.

He turned to the soldier behind him. 'Give me your rifle.'

Snapping a round into the chamber, he cradled the stock against his cheek and gently squeezed the trigger. Jonas, careering downward, heard the shot, muffled and indistinct, and saw André soar from the slope and hang suspended on the dancing air currents. For a moment he seemed to hover like a bird of prey, then before Jonas's horrified gaze he cartwheeled forward into the terrible void. Jonas watched his body turning as it plummeted past the spires and pinnacles and vanished from sight into the depths below.

He skidded, stricken, to a halt and peered back the way he had come. He saw a man standing on the ridge summit, clutching a smoking rifle. Even at that distance, his features were hauntingly familiar. Jonas recognized the SS officer who had almost run over Yvette several weeks earlier. Twice, the same officer had tried to apprehend him. Now he had murdered André with as much emotion as he might have displayed in dispatching a mad dog. Jonas glared at the man, seething with hatred and fury. Then he sucked in his breath and continued his madcap flight.

Bruno knew he couldn't miss as he lined up the fugitive in his target-sight. One shot was all it would take. A gentle squeeze of the trigger and the Englander would be gone for ever.

He focused the cross-hairs of his eye-piece on the centre of the retreating figure. Easy, easy, he thought, slipping his finger inside the metal guard. Then for no reason he could clearly explain, a paralysing numbness spread through his body and something inside him seemed to falter. He stood frozen to the spot, unable to fire as Jonas vanished behind a rocky pinnacle. Soon nothing moved on the empty hillslope.

Bruno breathed deeply, filling his lungs with air. As he lowered the rifle, he was filled with the strangest feeling of relief.

Anne Huntley stopped her car at the whitewashed cottage where a woman in the garden was planting saplings in the soft moist earth. She wore wellington boots, and her hair looked untidy in the wind.

'Good-morning.' Anne opened the garden gate. 'You must be Mrs McGuire.'

The woman looked up, blinking through her spectacles. She had a small button nose and merry brown eyes. 'That's me,' she said brightly. 'Can I help you?'

'I'm Anne Huntley from the *Daily Express*. I've been talking to Mrs Hendricks down the valley. She tells me she's Jonas Caudale's sister.'

'Does she indeed?' Mrs McGuire smiled. 'It's a long time since I heard that name spoken so boldly.'

'Mrs McGuire, I understand you used to be the schoolmistress here?'

'That's right. Thirty-six years, until I retired last June. They've closed the schoolhouse down now. I told them I was too old to be transferred to Keswick.' She rose to her feet, wiping her hands on a piece of cloth. 'Would you like some tea? It isn't often I get visitors here. Even my pupils have stopped calling since the

227

war put an end to the public transport. And I do love to talk. It's one of the few pleasures I have left.'

'Talking's exactly what I had in mind. And I'd dearly love some tea, thank you.'

The cottage was small and delightfully old-fashioned. The ancient stone fireplace was adorned with horse-brasses, and oak beams straddled the sagging ceiling. Photographs of Mrs McGuire's pupils covered the walls.

Anne munched gratefully on her host's home-made scones. 'These are delicious. They take me back to my childhood. You can't get decent pastry in London any more.'

'It's the eggs.' Mrs McGuire smiled. 'I keep my own chickens in the yard at the back. We're rarely troubled by rationing here.'

'Sometimes I wonder if I'm doing the right thing, living in the city.'

'No question about it, my dear. At your age, you need people and excitement. The mountains are beautiful—I wouldn't leave them for the world—but it can get awfully lonely at times.'

Anne laid her teaspoon gently on the saucer. 'Mrs McGuire, I hope I'm not intruding, but I'd like you to tell me anything you can remember—anything at all—about Jonas Caudale.'

'Jonas?' Mrs McGuire's eyes looked strangely wistful as she poured a drop of milk into her teacup. 'He was a lovely boy, one of my most promising pupils. He had such an inquisitive mind, it used to sadden me to think he would spend his entire life in this forgotten backwater. But the valley was all that Jonas ever wanted. He loved it here, more than anyone I ever knew. He used to wander for hours over the hills. It's hardly surprising that he was the finest fellrunner Lakeland's ever seen. Do you know he set up six new records, including the Armboth Scar, which he won in 1938?'

'Quite an athlete,' Anne said.

'The best. It isn't just physical, you see. It's in here.' She tapped her temple with her fingertip, 'When Jonas sets his mind on something, nothing in the world can dissuade him. He decided he'd become the greatest fellrunner in Cumberland history, and by the time he was twenty-four he'd achieved just that. Unfortunately ...' Mrs McGuire sighed. 'That stubbornness, that total unwillingness to compromise has its blacker side too. Sometimes he can't recognize the truth when it's staring him in the face. That's what happened with the Sanders girl.'

Anne looked at her sharply. 'Did you say Sanders?'

'That's right. The Sanders are one of the oldest families in the valley. They live at the bottom end of Crummock Water.'

'Are you talking about the landowner, Naunton Sanders?'

'You've met him?'

'A few weeks ago. He denied that he'd ever heard of Jonas Caudale.'

Mrs McGuire chuckled as she sipped her tea. 'Naunton would. He'd be trying to protect Jonas, you see. And also, he wouldn't want to go against the feelings of the people. But Jonas and Naunton Sanders' daughter Elizabeth were practically inseparable in the months before the war. I never saw two people so totally devoted to each other. It was a remarkable match. Elizabeth was raised against a background of privilege, enjoying all the luxuries money could buy. Jonas was a shepherd working on one of her father's farms. But you had to know Jonas to understand the electricity between those two. He was sensitive and intelligent, and he had a warm heart and a nimble brain. He loved the hills and the quiet places, but he was well read and well informed. He knew there was a world beyond Buttermere and he knew what was happening in that world. With a little ambition, he could have really made something of himself. As it was ...' She shrugged. 'Being a shepherd was all

230

Jonas cared about. And once he got an idea into his head, it would take an earthquake to shake it.'

'How did old man Sanders feel?'

'Naunton wasn't the problem. Naunton liked Jonas, admired him. He was proud of Jonas's achievements in the local fell races. The problem lay with Naunton's wife, Judith.' Mrs McGuire shook her head. 'I have to confess that Judith is a terrible snob. She's a lovely woman in her own way, but she does like to emphasize the importance of the social order, to put it mildly. She was appalled at the thought of her daughter—on whom she'd lavished such care and attention—falling in love with a common shepherd. She did her darndest to sabotage the relationship but the harder she tried, the closer Jonas and Elizabeth became. It was funny really, to watch Judith's antics. She used every opportunity to belittle Jonas, to humiliate him in public, but Jonas has a natural dignity that can't be shaken. He never responded to Judith's baiting, but he could put her in her place with a lift of his eyebrow.' Mrs McGuire paused, putting down her teacup. 'I'm surprised Sally Hendricks didn't tell you all this.'

Anne said, 'If you want the truth, Mrs Hendricks didn't tell me a damn thing, apart from confirming that there is a

231

Jonas Caudale. She seemed ... I don't know, maybe it's my imagination, but I could swear she seemed frightened.'

Mrs McGuire's face sobered. 'Sally Hendricks *is* frightened. Her husband Larry is quite a tearaway and he hates Jonas more than any man alive. If he discovered that she'd been talking to you, there's no telling how he might react. He has a reputation for violence and he's been in trouble several times with the law.'

'But it isn't only Larry Hendricks. Everyone here pretends they've never heard of Jonas. He's like a non-person, some kind of strange anomaly.'

The humour drained from Mrs McGuire's eyes. Her face grew grave, almost —Anne thought—defensive. 'You have to understand the people here. They're Cumbrians. They belong to a small, tightly-knit community. They never forgive and they never forget. Jonas did a very bad thing.'

'What thing?' Anne asked.

'I'm not at liberty to tell you that.'

Anne looked at her helplessly. 'But surely if a man is guilty of a crime, he has a right to be heard?'

'I didn't say anything about crime,' Mrs McGuire answered tersely. 'I said he did something bad, that's all.'

'Mrs McGuire, until now, you're the

232

only person I've met who's willing to even talk about Jonas Caudale. Please don't stop at the most important point.'

'I have to. It's a question of trust, you see. I've already gone much further than I should. I get so few visitors these days, and ...' She smiled weakly. 'As I said earlier, I do like to chat.'

'But if you won't help me, who will?'

'There's only one person capable of that. Naunton Sanders himself.'

'I've already tried Naunton Sanders.'

'Then I'm afraid, my dear, Jonas Caudale will have to carry his secret to the grave.'

Mrs McGuire reached down and felt the teapot with her hand. Suddenly, she was her old self again. 'Brew's gone cold,' she said in a cheerful voice. 'I'd better put the kettle on for a refill.'

Anne drove back over the mountain pass, her brain in a turmoil. Mrs McGuire's reluctance to finish her story was driving her wild. There were too many questions left unanswered, too many secrets, too many mysteries. Why was the valley so entrenched in its solemn determination to disclaim Jonas Caudale? What terrible act could the man have performed that had led even his closest friends and members of his own family to deny all knowledge of his existence? There was no longer any doubt in her mind that a major story lay hidden here, but how was she to uncover it? She had to find a way to breach the conspiracy of silence.

The road dipped over the hill and she saw the ground sloping away to her right before plunging into a deep ravine. The car picked up speed as she began the long descent, its rusty bodywork clattering on the narrow bends. Gently, she eased her foot on the brake, trying not to look into the yawning chasm. A tremor of uneasiness stirred inside her as she realized her speed was steadily increasing. She pressed the brake pedal flat. There was no response. Her stomach contracted violently. The hillside was flitting by dizzily now, and she could feel the car shuddering as its archaic suspension battled to take the strain.

Below, the lake shimmered in her vision, creating dazzling divisions of light and shade. She slammed the vehicle into reverse and for a fractional second her momentum seemed to ease, then with a metallic ping the lever went slack in her hand and the car rocketed down the final stretch.

A terrible iciness seeped through her limbs as she wrestled feverishly with the wheel. The car was leaping about all over the place, its hull quivering, its wheels shrieking. She bounced across the empty highway and crashed through a field gate in a dizzy fountain of churned-up mud. Skidding across the pasture, she saw the lake hurtling up to meet her, then water sprayed across her windshield and she came to a rest bobbing wildly on the swirling waves.

She was shaking all over, her muscles quivering with tension and fear. She tugged desperately at the door, but the pressure of the water held it stubbornly in place. Winding down the window, she knelt on the driving seat and wriggled through the narrow gap, dragging herself onto the roof. A rock rose directly to her left and gathering her skirts around her thighs, she leapt onto it and waded breathlessly through the shallows to the grassy bank.

Sobbing, she flopped to the ground and looked back at the car still held aloft by some precarious buoyancy. For a moment, it continued floating, its battered roof gleaming with moisture, then in a flurry of swirling bubbles, it vanished abruptly beneath the lake.

Anne was shivering helplessly when she reached the tiny pub. Her stockings were wet, her shoes soggy, and the hem of her skirt clung like papier mâché to her calves and knees.

The bar was half empty as she moved

to the counter. A handful of locals sat in a group around the log fire but they showed little surprise at her bedraggled appearance.

The barman strolled along the counter toward her, a big man with a florid face.

'I'd like a whisky please,' she said in a shaky voice.

'Wouldn't we all, miss. Don't you know there's a war on? Beer's all I've got. Take it or leave it. Pub's get rationed, same as everyone else.'

She felt a ripple of disappointment. She needed something fiery to bolster her shattered nerves, but she supposed beer would have to do. The barman filled a glass and set it on the counter in front of her. 'That'll be ninepence, miss.'

Absent-mindedly, she counted out the money, and turned to face the tiny huddle of customers. She gave a start as she recognized Larry Hendricks and his wife Sally sitting in front of the fireplace. Sally Hendricks' face was bruised and one eye looked almost completely closed. There was a padded dressing taped to her chin and she was hugging herself with both arms as if nursing some hidden pain in her rib cage.

Anne picked up her glass and moved toward her. 'What on earth happened?' she exclaimed. 'Have you had an accident?'

Sally Hendricks glanced at her husband, her eyes suddenly filled with fear. 'I fell down in the barn.'

'It must have been quite a fall. Your face is swollen like a football.'

Sally touched her cheek where the log fire cast ripples across the heavy bruising. 'It was in the loft. The ladder gave way.'

'Have you seen a doctor?'

'She doesn't need a doctor,' Larry Hendricks said, his eyes surly and hostile. 'The swelling will go down in a day or two.'

'How do you know the bone isn't fractured? She should at least have it examined by a qualified physician.'

'I said she doesn't need a doctor. We look after our own ailments here. We've been doing it long enough.'

'Aren't you concerned about your wife's injuries?'

'Who asked you to stick your nose in anyway? You're a total stranger. You come asking questions that are none of your business.'

'You mean questions about Jonas Caudale?'

'That's right.'

'Yesterday, you said you'd never heard of the man.'

'What if I did? Just because you work on one of those swanky London papers,

237

you think you're God Almighty.'

'I'm trying to get at the truth. Why should you care about that, unless you've got something to hide?'

'The truth, is it?' The man's eyes blazed as he rose to his feet and seized her wrist. 'I'll show you the truth, if that's what you want. Let's see how you feel about your precious war hero then.'

He led her to a paddock at the back where an old motorcycle stood propped against the woodshed. He kicked the starter pedal and jerked his head at the passenger pillion. 'Climb on board if it's the truth you're after.'

Wonderingly, she settled herself in the saddle, clasping her arms around his waist. He roared out of the cobbled yard and along a road which traced the rim of the adjoining lake. They passed through a tiny hamlet, then swung left among a baffling labyrinth of side roads which filtered between the sprawling fields. The wind battered her cheeks, making her shiver as it moulded the sodden hem of her dress around the contours of her body. It was impossible to speak with the engine roaring, but she could feel the fury in Hendricks' muscular frame.

He drew to a halt at a country church and switching off the engine, propped the bike against the dry-stone wall. 'This way,' he said, jerking his head.

She followed him into the cemetery at the rear, picking her way among the moss-covered gravestones. Hendricks came to a halt at a row of neat little crosses. Each bore a solitary inscription, the name and identity of the grave's occupant. Anne counted eight in all.

She stared at Hendricks in puzzlement. 'I don't understand. Who are these people?'

He spat on the ground and wiped his mouth with the back of one hand. His face looked wolfish in the sunlight. 'These are the men Jonas Caudale murdered.'

Chapter Ten

Churchill stood at the cabinet room window, staring out over the darkened city. He could see searchlights scouring the skies above, and barrage balloons hovering in the gloom. He pulled down the heavy blind, switched on the desk lamp and leaned forward to select a cigar from the humidor. He lit it carefully, breathing out smoke over the green-embroidered lampshade. He had just settled behind his desk when the telephone rang. It was his personal aide, Anthony

Campbell-Neill. 'General Eisenhower is here, Prime Minister,' Campbell-Neill said.

Eisenhower looked surprisingly spruce as he came through the door. Nothing troubled the general, Churchill thought enviously. Even during the most virulent policy rows, he managed to hold onto his composure.

'I thought you'd be gone,' the general said, his creased face strangely greenish in the filtered lamplight.

'Couldn't sleep. I need to unwind a little.'

Eisenhower was pensive as he seated himself at the other side of the desk. 'How did it go tonight?'

Churchill shrugged. 'Lane doesn't like the idea of the Frome redistribution.'

'Did you explain its purpose?'

'Have you ever tried reasoning with that man?'

'We've got to get him to agree. It's vital to the success of D-Day. Bradley's troops will take two beaches in Normandy, Sir Miles Dempsey's three. Dempsey will also take Caen.'

'What about Patton. I understand he's desperately unhappy.'

'Patton's my insurance policy. I need him to subdue Britanny. If Dempsey can open up the Falaise Plain for Crerar's First

Canadians, Bradley can seize Cherbourg and push through to Avranches. Montgomery will assume the role of Supreme Allied Commander until I can relieve him personally,' Eisenhower asked.

'See the German news reports tonight?'

'Indeed. Our man Caudale made quite a show for himself in the Pyrenees.'

'It's astonishing that he's still at large.'

'Clearly he's beginning to get the Nazis worried. It's the first time they've acknowledged his existence. Officially, that is.' Churchill shifted in his chair. 'I sometimes wonder if we're making the most of this situation.'

'Publicity-wise, you mean?'

'I was thinking in terms of national morale. In the beginning, Caudale was nothing more than a decoy. Now he's turning into a *cause célèbre.*'

'I was thinking the same thing myself. He's thumbing his nose at the German Reich. It would be wonderful to see him actually make it.'

'He *has* to make it,' Churchill said slowly. 'We've started something we've got to finish. Jonas Caudale may seem infinitesimal alongside the Overlord campaign, but our men could do with some kind of encouragement before they attack those beaches and a successful outcome to Caudale's run could inspire the troops at just the right psychological moment.'

Eisenhower looked at him. 'You really believe he can do it?'

'If you'd asked my opinion in the beginning, I'd have said he'd never have got out of the Alps, yet already he's within seventy miles of the French coast.'

'But the Germans aren't playing any longer. Those press reports prove they're beginning to take him seriously.'

'That's why we've got to take him seriously too. Caudale isn't simply one man any more. He's an emblem, a figurehead, a microcosm of what this war's all about. If he succeeds in getting back to Buttermere, he could set the pattern for the final stages.'

'And if he fails?' Eisenhower asked dryly.

Churchill took the cigar from his mouth, breathing out smoke through his lips and nostrils. In the glow of the lamplight, his face looked faintly demoniacal. 'It's up to us to see that he doesn't fail.'

'Mind if I join you?' Theodore Gallagher said, carrying his breakfast tray to Applethwaite's table.

Hastily, Applethwaite cleared a place for Gallagher, moving aside his empty plates. Gallagher flopped into the chair and poured himself a mug of tea. 'Sorry I'm late this morning, Cyril. I've been to

242

a meeting at Winston's office.'

'So early?' Applethwaite glanced at his watch. It was barely half-past eight. 'Must be something pretty momentous.'

'Hardly that, though the P.M. thinks it could have a useful bolstering effect if things work out the way he hopes.' Gallagher picked up a strip of toast and dipped it into his tea, flicking the drops against the side of his mug. 'It's this Caudale fellow again. Apparently he's reached the Pyrenees. In fact, according to our latest reports, he's well on his way to the French coast.'

'That's incredible. What are the Germans playing at?'

'It's beginning to look as though the fellow might actually make it after all. Churchill's determined to get him back to England. He's pulling out all the stops to see that Jonas Caudale finishes the course.'

'It'll be quite a story if he gets to Buttermere.'

'Damn right. Winston will make it his personal business to ensure that his name is blazoned on every front page from Washington to Sydney. It's too good for the Americans, Cyril. We've got to find a way of interceding. When Caudale hits the headlines I don't want this department left out in the cold.'

Applethwaite looked dubious. 'It's a little difficult to know what to do at this late stage.'

Gallagher patted his wrist and reached for another piece of toast. 'Leave it to me, Cyril. I know what it'll take to get Caudale through.'

Vincent La Chaize got off the bus on the Avenue Degas and walked up the narrow alleyway which led to the city square. He was a big man with crinkly black hair, the son of a French father and an Algerian mother. Leader of the FTP, the French Communist resistance movement, La Chaize had devoted himself not merely to overthrowing the German invaders but to the establishment of a Marxist government in Paris. A dedicated Socialist, he now controlled the largest guerrilla movement in France.

When he reached the market square he saw his two subordinates, Conde and Broussel, waiting patiently on a café terrace. La Chaize joined them and snapped his fingers, calling for an *ersatz,* the tasteless substitute which passed for coffee in the Occupied Territories. 'You got my message?' He stared impassively across the square where a group of German infantrymen were flirting with the local girls.

244

'What's up?' Broussel asked. 'Louis made it sound urgent.'

'Have you been listening to the BBC?'

'Of course. What do you take us for, amateurs?'

'Then who is this man Caudale?'

Broussel shrugged. 'Some crazy lunatic who thinks he can run home to England. Who cares?'

'That crazy lunatic has already reached Gavarnie in the Pyrenees. In a few more days, he could be at the coast. The *Boche* have done their damndest to stop him, while the British have been taunting them every step of the way. I want to know why?'

'As a race, the British are notoriously eccentric. Caudale's escapade will appeal to their sense of the absurd. It's something to brighten up the war news, that's all.'

'You fool,' La Chaize said mildly. 'If that's all it amounted to, would the BBC jeopardize the man's chances by broadcasting his position to the enemy? There has to be a military reason, it's the only explanation.'

Broussel and Conde glanced at each other. 'What do you want us to do, Vincent?' Broussel asked.

La Chaize paused as the waiter brought his *ersatz* and laid it carefully on the table. He waited until the man had withdrawn before he spoke again. 'Find Jonas Caudale,' he said.

Josef Goebbels felt nervous as he entered Hitler's office. The Chancellory caretaker had warned him the Führer was in an atrocious mood this morning. Hitler's outbursts of temper, already a legend among the German High Command, were becoming more frequent as their forces awaited the Allied invasion. Goebbels understood the strain his leader was going through but he was also beginning to suspect that the man on whom he had pinned his hopes and aspirations was dangerously unstable.

To Goebbels' relief, Hitler seemed relatively calm as he stepped into the spacious, though, sparsely-furnished office. Seated in front of a huge flag, the Führer seemed to dominate the entire room. This had been the brainchild of Goebbels himself who had designed the office to achieve the maximum effect on anyone entering the Fuhrer's presence for the first time. He reflected absently on how sound his instincts had proved, for despite his unimpressive stature Hitler looked mesmeric with the giant swastika towering behind him.

'Do you realize this man Caudale is still on the run?' Hitler said, without inviting

Goebbels to sit down.

'Caudale?' Goebbels echoed, his mind racing.

'The English POW. The fellrunner.'

'Ah.' Now Goebbels remembered. Having put the initial search into operation, he had forgotten the Caudale affair, concentrating on more urgent issues. Unhappily, the Führer still had his mind set on its original course.

Hitler waved the newspaper he had just been reading. 'He's managed to reach the Pyrenees. Incredible as it seems, he's made a mockery of the troops you sent out to intercept him.'

'My Führer, finding one man in the middle of the mountains is like looking for a needle in a haystack. Also, Caudale appears to have the French terrorist network supporting him. However ...' Goebbels made an expansive gesture. 'Does it really matter if he lives or dies?'

Hitler slapped the desktop with his palm and Goebbels jumped impulsively. He could see the dark eyes smouldering with hysteria.

'He's turning our fighting men into a national joke in the eyes of the world,' Hitler screamed. 'Do you think the British are broadcasting his movements in innocent stupidity? They want us to know where Caudale is. It's a deliberate taunt. Every time he evades our search cordons, he's helping the Allies ridicule the efficiency of the German war machine.'

'I understand, my Führer,' Goebbels said hastily. 'I shall double the number of search units immediately.'

'No.' Hitler's eyes blazed. 'The more men you pour into this pursuit, the more ludicrous the situation becomes.' He patted the newspaper in front of him. 'There is an article here by a journalist named Willi Fredier. He accompanied the only officer who's managed to get within touching distance of Caudale. His name is *Oberleutnant* von Hautle of the *Leibstandarte*. He is himself a trained mountain runner. If the Allies are intent on turning this into an athletic contest, then for the honour of Germany the Englishman must be brought down, not by an entire regiment, but by one man. Judging from his pedigree, von Hautle sounds a perfect candidate.'

'I will see to it at once, my Führer,' Goebbels said, taking the newspaper from Hitler's hand.

'And Josef?' Something in Hitler's voice sent a chill up Goebbel's spine.

'Yes?'

'This Englander has done a great deal of harm to our national reputation. When von Hautle catches up with him, I want Jonas Caudale killed.'

'You've made quite an impression in Berlin,' the colonel said. 'Your old friend Willi Fredier has been singing your praises in the *Nuremburg Gazette.*'

'A man of discernment, Willi,' Bruno answered modestly.

'Please understand, *Oberleutnant,* that I am not, and never have been impressed by your family's title. As far as I am concerned, you are an officer of the *Leibstandarte,* nothing more.'

'I do understand, *Standartenfuhrer.*'

'However ...' The colonel hesitated. 'The Führer wants you personally to take over the Caudale hunt.'

'The Führer?' Bruno shifted in his chair, a faint uneasiness starting inside him. 'Why me, *Standartenfuhrer?*'

'Clearly he has been impressed by Fredier's article.'

'But what can I hope to achieve alone?'

'The Englishman's death naturally. The Führer considers it a matter of supreme importance. Whatever happens, he is not to reach his destination alive.'

'In that case, wouldn't it be more sensible to let the division smoke him out?'

'The Führer wants an end to the practice of entire divisions combing the countryside for one man. He insists the victory should be yours alone. In other words, he's

249

turning this into a personal duel. The finest mountain runner of Bavaria against an undernourished English shepherd. You are not to fail.'

A feeling of dismay filled Bruno. He watched miserably as the colonel laid an envelope on the desktop. 'Here is a letter signed by the Führer. It gives you complete power to requisition any vehicle, piece of equipment or squadron of men as you see fit. Simply show this document to the officer in command and he will place himself at your immediate disposal.'

'*Standartenfuhrer*, I don't know what to say.'

'*Jawhol* will do admirably.'

'But I can't look into a crystal ball and pinpoint where Caudale is.'

'You've almost done it twice. And you know the old saying—third time lucky. The Führer is unfailingly superstitious.'

The colonel was enjoying the situation. Bruno von Hautle's arrogance had irritated him for months. He thought the man was a conceited ass who deserved a good kick in the pants and he was delighted to be giving him one at last. 'Let me explain something else my precocious friend. Hitler considers this prisoner's liberty an affront to the honour of German manhood. He wants him killed, and he wants him killed not by overwhelming force of arms but by an

250

athlete similar to his own standing. Should you fail in your task, it is impossible to imagine how he will react in his present emotional state.'

He lit a cigarette, taking his time, savouring the moment. His eyes were gleaming as he added softly, 'I have a feeling the von Hautle family will find their pedigree very shaky indeed. I might even go so far as to say that in dynastic terms, they could actually cease to exist. Do I make myself clear?'

Bruno felt his stomach tighten. He knew perfectly well what the colonel was getting at. 'Quite clear, *Standartenfuhrer*,' he answered coldly.

'In that case, I wish you luck. Kill this bumptious little Englander, and do it quickly so that we can all get back to the business we were trained for.'

The colonel's aide, Major Stolz, was sunning himself in the cobbled courtyard as Bruno emerged through the doorway. 'How did the meeting go?' he asked in a friendly tone.

Bruno scowled. 'Suddenly, I'm a one-man band.'

'Well, look at the bright side. If you succeed you'll be a national hero. With Hitler's blessing, who knows how far you might go?'

'Speaking personally, the sooner I get

back to the Bavarian ski-slopes, the better I'll like it.'

He paused, frowning, as a deafening roar filled the air. A strange vessel came zooming over the rooftops and Bruno narrowed his eyes, shading his face from the sunlight. Its fuselage was cigar-shaped, its undercarriage supported by thick rubber wheels suspended on metal stems. There was no wingspan and the only propeller Bruno could see was a gyro of rotor blades whirring above the aircraft's roof. He watched in wonderment as it drew to a halt in midair and hovered motionless above the tiny courtyard. Then, with infinite grace, the pilot eased it into a perpendicular descent.

The major laughed at Bruno's expression. 'What do you think of our new flying machine? It's a *Focke-Achgelis Drache,* built on the auto-gyro system—known in some quarters as a helicopter. It can go forwards, backwards, up or down. It can even, as you've just seen, hover motionless in midair. A formidable creation, is it not? It gives a whole new concept to flying. The Drache can land in an area the size of a loading bay.'

Bruno whistled softly as an idea began to form in his mind.

Anne Huntley stood on the lakeshore,

watching the recovery team cranking her automobile out of the water. The crane lifted and the battered vehicle rose dripping into the air.

Sergeant Quinlan, the local police officer, stamped his feet in the morning chill. 'Barry Jackson won't get any more mileage out of that beat-up old wreck. It was falling to bits anyway and two days at the bottom of the lake can't have improved its performance much.'

'Sergeant, I want you to check the brake cables,' she said. 'I have a feeling they may have been tampered with.'

He looked at her sharply. 'That's a serious allegation, young lady. Who on earth would want to interfere with the workings of your car?'

'I really don't know. But ever since I started asking questions about Jonas Caudale people around here have been getting progressively nervous. Particularly Larry Hendricks.'

'That's hardly surprising. Larry blames Jonas for killing his brother, among others.'

'So I gather. He took me to the cemetery to look at the graves. But he refused point blank to tell me anything more. Said it was none of my damned business.'

'Has it occurred to you that Hendricks might be right? You're a stranger here. You belong to a national newspaper. Some things are best kept under wraps. Especially shameful ones.'

'Sergeant Quinlan, can you tell me why Jonas Caudale is such an outcast in this valley?'

'Not my place,' Quinlan said.

'Well, how did he kill those men in the churchyard and why does everyone pretend that he never existed?'

'Only Mr Sanders can tell you that. Nobody else has the right.'

'Naunton Sanders is part of the same latticework of deceit.'

'In that case, I hardly think it would be proper for me to go against the feelings of the people.'

'At least tell me this. If Jonas Caudale is so universally unpopular, why is he risking his life to come back here?'

'What are you talking about?' Quinlan frowned. 'Jonas Caudale is coming to Buttermere?'

'Didn't you know? The BBC French Service has been broadcasting the story for weeks.'

'But he can't. If he does, something terrible will happen.'

'What do you mean, sergeant? Please stop talking in riddles.'

A veil came over the policeman's eyes and his features moulded into an inscrutable mask. 'Anything else, you'll have to get from Mr Sanders,' he said, and strolled back to the dripping crane.

Jonas paused, the rain hammering his cratered cheeks. The sound reached him again, harsh and discordant, like a maddening insect that wouldn't go away. He saw the machine moving slowly up the valley and sweat bathed his narrow face. Tubular and elongated, it was coasting backwards and forwards, pausing birdlike to examine a patch of rock or undergrowth, hovering motionless in midair. Without wings it looked strangely unreal, its grotesque body held aloft by whirring rotors spinning above its fuselage.

Banking, it came soaring up toward him and Jonas dove into a cluster of firs, burrowing low as the underbelly glided by above his head. The downdraught from its blades ripped the foliage from the branches and he felt the solid whoomph-whoomph-whoomph of the air currents as they thrashed at the frozen earth. Zigzagging up the ridge, the machine looked like a grotesque dragonfly. Twice, it landed, settling onto the unstable ground with a delicacy he would scarcely have believed possible. Then it fluttered off to the north, framed against the swirling sky.

Eyes red, face beard-stubbled, Jonas

watched it slowly vanish from sight. Now the Germans could come at him from the sky as well as the ground, he thought.

He began to run, heading erratically across the mountain shoulder. The summit was blanketed in mist but he steered his way toward a narrow saddle, using his wrist compass as a guide. For two whole days he had been scrambling alone around these Godforsaken peaks, lost and disorientated. Food was what he needed now—something to fuel his flagging energy. He'd gobbled some watercress from a stream in an adjoining valley and at first light had uncovered a nest of pheasant eggs which he'd forced himself to devour raw, but with his strength depleted and his muscles numb with fatigue, lack of nourishment was beginning to warp his senses.

The memory of André hung hauntingly in his mind. He hadn't known the young Frenchman well but he was filled with a consuming hatred for the man who had murdered him so pitilessly. The hatred rankled in his breast and the air grew colder as he gained altitude. Soon he had risen above the cloud base and was able to see snowcapped mountains reaching away in every direction. Several times he sank up to his thighs in snow, and once, slipping on an ice-glazed boulder, he almost tumbled over a cliff edge which would have sent him crashing into pine forest a thousand feet below.

The rest of the morning he blundered his way across chill streams and serrated ice slopes, grateful at last when just after noon the ground began to tilt downwards and he left the high country behind, entering a series of small, tightly-knit valleys which formed a baffling labyrinth to the west. Here, he was forced to run against the grain of the land, dropping into each individual gully in turn. It was a bad system and one which strained his endurance to the utmost, for the terrain mocked him, defying him to test his judgement, even his sanity.

But sanity had gone, he reflected, sanity was drifting somewhere above the mountain tips, and in its place he was conscious of a new sensation, a feeling startling in its virulence. Fury. Fury at himself and at the people chasing him. Fury at the war and all the things which stood in the way of what he was trying to do. The fury gave him strength, it was the one thing in the world he could rely on.

The fury was like life itself.

Crouched in the helicopter cockpit, Bruno gazed down at the confusion of valleys below. For more than seven hours they had scoured the countryside, spotting few signs of life. Four times, they'd been forced to return to base while the pilot refuelled, and now, as the afternoon lengthened, he felt his spirits beginning to flounder. Viewed from the air, the land looked a chaotic hotchpotch of sharktooth ridges, bottomless crevasses and savage buttresses. How could they hope to find a solitary figure in such bewildering terrain?

He had left Suzanne at Garrison head-quarters where Colonel Schneider (not out of the goodness of his heart, Bruno knew, but simply for expediency's sake) had assigned them living quarters on the chateau's upper level, a small, self-contained apartment with kitchen and bathroom attached. Bruno had been grateful for that—at least it offered a base to work from—but now, gazing down at the awesome expanse he had to cover, he was filled with a sense of hopelessness and defeat.

Beside him, clutching the roofrack for support, the sergeant Bruno had commandeered—Richner was his name, a short thickset man with brutish, peasant-like features—sat with his Schmeisser cradled across his knees. Since no safety harnesses were available, both he and Bruno had to cling doggedly to the wall pipes to keep from sliding out through the open hatch.

Staring down at the mountains, Bruno

reflected that he could quite happily murder Willi Fredier for landing him in such a mess. To call it an inconvenience was putting it mildly. If Willi hadn't written that stupid article, he, Bruno, would still be an anonymous SS officer. No name for Hitler to quote, no mission to be lumbered with. His chances of running Caudale to earth seemed ludicrously remote but he knew that displeasing the Führer in such unsettled times could be a hazardous exercise. He had heard rumours from the Russian front of officers executed wholesale on trumped-up incompetence charges. His whole family could be at risk, according to Colonel Schneider.

And he had other things to worry about apart from Jonas Caudale. His feelings for Suzanne Le Gras were getting dangerously out of hand. What had started as an amiable flirtation, a pleasant interlude to while away the time, had developed into something he could no longer control. He knew his duty as a *Leibstandarte* officer was to report her to the Gestapo—he had suspected her for some time of being a member of the Resistance—but he simply couldn't bear the thought of losing her. She was a formidable lady without a doubt, and Bruno realized he was completely infatuated.

The pilot interrupted his reverie by

tapping him on the shoulder. 'We have to refuel,' the man bellowed, mouthing his words above the thunder of the rotor blades.

'Again?'

'The tank is almost empty, *Oberleutnant.*'

'But we've been back four times already.'

The pilot raised his eyebrows expressively.

'All right.' Bruno sighed. 'Let's get it over with. I want to try another sortie before nightfall.'

The ruined farmhouse stood at the roadside, framed by a line of trees. Greg propped his bicycle against the wall and stepped through its derelict doorway. He could see a hollow where the fireplace had been, the line of its chimney blackened with soot.

Fumbling in his pocket, he lit himself a cigarette and settled back to wait. The memory of his last meeting with Suzanne still filled him with embarrassment and discomfort. It had been unforgivable, the way he'd behaved, but he hadn't been able to help himself. He was in love with the woman and the thought of she and Bruno von Hautle had driven him almost to distraction.

Greg had never experienced jealousy before. He'd read about it often enough but he'd never been able to understand the foolishness of people governed by their own emotions. He had always believed that the measure of a man lay in the level and effectiveness of his restraint. His father had taught him that, impressing upon him from the earliest age the virtues of self-control. But his father had been a fool, he realized now. His father had never experienced the fire in the senses, the emptiness of impending loss. His father had never been alive.

No wonder he'd felt so isolated all these years. Suzanne Le Gras had helped him to identify his folly but accepting the truth could be even more painful than keeping up the pretence and as far as she was concerned, he had the most terrible feeling he could already be too late.

He spotted a movement in the trees ahead and saw Suzanne herself crossing the empty roadway. Even on the most miserable day she carried her own special radiance, he thought. He watched her approach the farmhouse and hesitate in the shattered doorway.

'It's OK,' he told her.

She stepped over the threshold, the wind ruffling her hair. He could tell by her eyes that she too remembered their last encounter.

'I thought you'd be gone,' she said awkwardly. 'The Germans have set up a checkpoint at the edge of the village.'

'Where's von Hautle?' He kept his voice calm and businesslike.

'He's taken off in some new kind of flying machine. He's hoping to pick up Jonas from the air.'

'So he hasn't found him yet?' Greg breathed a sigh of relief. 'Thank God.'

She studied him shrewdly, noting the tension in his face. 'What's wrong?'

'Jonas has disappeared.'

'I thought you had people accompanying him everywhere?'

'We did. His companion's gone too. I've put out an alert through the French underground. Can you contact me if anything happens?'

'That won't be easy. Bruno's becoming suspicious.' She hesitated. 'I think he's in love with me.'

Despite himself, he felt a flash of anger. He'd resolved to keep their dealings on a professional level—no more outbursts, everything cool and orderly—but her directness startled him.

He snapped, 'You little fool, you're supposed to infatuate him, that's all. You don't have to put your body and soul into it.'

'I like him. Is that a crime?'

'Yes, it's a crime. He happens to be the enemy.'

She felt her own temper rising. It was several weeks since they'd last quarrelled but his accusations had wounded her deeply. 'He happens to be a very nice man—a gentleman, in case you've ever heard of the word.'

'In times like these, gentlemen are dropping like flies.'

She said, 'Why don't you admit the truth? You don't give a damn about Bruno's nationality.'

'OK, I'm jealous, I admit it.'

'You've got no hold on me. I promised you nothing.'

'I know, I know. But I'm not a bloody machine, for Christ's sake.'

She stared at him in wonder. His eyes looked feverish and tiny muscles had begun to tremble under his skin. Never in her life had she seen such pain in the face of a human being. She knew he wanted her, she'd be a fool not to have recognized that, but she could scarcely believe the torment in his features.

Greg's lips twisted into a stricken grimace. For weeks he had tried to purge the spectres from his mind but it was more than ordinary flesh and blood could stand. He felt a sudden contraction in his throat and unable to help himself, seized her in his arms and kissed her savagely on the mouth. She sagged against him, taken completely by surprise. It was the last thing in the world she had expected. 'This is madness,' she whispered. 'Remember the war.'

'To hell with the war,' he snapped. 'For the first time in my life, I feel like a human being.'

Then he kissed her again and she gave herself up to the tyranny of love.

Chapter Eleven

Greg cycled back along the country road, his mind in a turmoil. He could scarcely believe what had taken place. It seemed blurred in his memory as if he had dreamed it somehow, an erotic illusion created by his own fevered imaginings. He wasn't as a rule an impulsive man. He planned things out, examined consequences, but with Suzanne his most primitive desires had taken control and far from assuaging his hunger the amatory interlude seemed merely to have intensified it. Now he wanted her more than ever and to his astonishment she wanted him too.

Could she really care for him in a meaningful way? he wondered. She'd certainly acted like it; she'd been like a wild animal as they'd struggled breathlessly in a tangle of discarded clothing. He knew women were experts at pretending but pretence wasn't in Suzanne's nature. He believed she'd meant it when she'd whispered to him in the dust, her mouth hot and moist against his ear. He believed in the frenzied urgency of her body. He wasn't such a hopeless case after all. He wasn't a deadbeat or a write-off. It was an intoxicating realization and he was humming happily to himself as he pedalled through the surrounding woodland.

He saw the cottage emerging through the trees and gently applied his brakes. The long, low-roofed building had belonged initially to a local woodsman but the Resistance had taken it over as a temporary refuge.

Two men approached him from the cottage door and Greg recognized Rene and Yves, *maquisards* from the Pamiers country, sent by Marcel to accompany Jonas to the coast.

'Where have you been?' Rene asked, balancing his rifle across his shoulder. 'You're more than an hour late.'

'I got held up. Any news of Caudale?'

'Nothing yet. But we've got company. An Englishman. He parachuted in this morning.'

Greg was surprised. He had received no word of any newcomer. 'What's he doing here?'

'Says he's come to take over.'

Frowning, Greg propped his bicycle against the porch and stepped inside. The cottage was small and smelled unpleasantly of cooking fat, an odour he particularly disliked; his nostrils wrinkled as he stared at the thickset man who sat at the battered table, checking the contents of a leather-bound suitcase. The newcomer was fleshy and barrel-chested with a face that displayed the indulgences of easy living; his hair was thick, and there were tiny blue veins crisscrossing the skin above his cheeks. He was examining bottles of pills and lotions, and he half turned in his chair as Greg entered.

'Who are you?' Greg demanded.

The man's features twisted into a grin. 'Name's Herrington,' he drawled in a lazy English accent. 'You must be Major Anderson? London thought you might need a helping hand to keep Caudale mobile.'

'London?'

'Section D-14.'

'Gallagher's department?'

'Ah, you know Gallagher?'

'We've met,' Greg said.

He tossed his raincoat onto a chair and

266

leaned over the fire, warming his hands. 'London must have agents to burn.'

Herrington's face looked boyish beneath the ravages wrought by time. 'Caudale's hitting the headlines on both sides in this war, theirs and ours. That makes him a very important figure indeed.'

'Important to whom?'

'Everyone, though for different reasons. The Germans want him stopped, we want to keep him moving.'

'Gallagher's idea?'

'Churchill's.' Herrington crossed his legs languidly. 'He's looking for something to inspire the troops on D-Day and he's chosen Caudale. Our job is to make sure he gets through to Buttermere.'

Greg glanced at the suitcase filled with drugs. 'What are those?'

'Caudale's spent two years on POW rations. He musn't be allowed to flag.'

'You're some kind of doctor?'

'A very good doctor, as it happens. Sportsmen were my speciality before the war.'

'An athletics medic?'

'Let's say I helped them achieve their full potential.'

Greg's lips twisted humourlessly. 'Helped them to cheat, you mean.'

'That's a little near the knuckle, old chum, though I have to admit you are uncannily intuitive.' There was no malice in Herrington's features, no sign of resentment or reproach. He smiled as if the matter was of little consequence. 'True, I was struck off the register for unprofessional conduct but happily the War Office has discovered a whole new use for my talents.'

'So it isn't enough to feed Caudale's neurosis any more. Now we've got to drug him as well.'

'They told me you might be difficult. I'm sorry if you think it a little inhuman but war itself is inhuman. Caudale isn't an individual any longer, he's a declaration of intent.'

'Your thesis, or Gallagher's.'

'Statement of fact, old chum.'

'I think I'm beginning to dislike you, Herrington.'

'I have that affect on people,' the Englishman admitted blithely. 'However, our own feelings are scarcely important here. Only Caudale matters now.'

Greg stood with his back to the fire, warming his thighs and calves. He felt a malicious satisfaction as he said coolly, 'There's one little thing you haven't accounted for. I haven't the faintest idea of where Jonas Caudale is.'

Bruno leaned through the helicopter hatch,

studying the mountain peaks below. 'You're sure this is the same valley?' he shouted at the pilot.

'It's where we looked earlier, *Oberleutnant*. But spotting a man in such a landscape ...' The pilot shrugged.

'He has to be here. There's a limit to how much ground a man can cover on foot.'

'He could hide in the scrub where an army wouldn't find him.'

'He's got to eat, hasn't he? He's got to move. Sooner or later he's bound to make a mistake.'

'Then what, *Oberleutnant?*'

Bruno hesitated. The colonel had outlined with chilling emphasis what was expected of him and the awful consequences if he failed to carry it out. He glanced at Sergeant Richner who was gently fingering his Schmeisser. Something about the man reminded him of a battering ram. Which was just as well, Bruno thought, since somebody had to do the necessary.

'We'll leave that to the sergeant.'

Jonas heard the helicopter as he mounted a narrow couloir. He saw the machine etched against the sky, its ugly fuselage suspended beneath whirring rotor blades. Frost coated the windshield, giving it the appearance of a sleepily-lidded reptile.

269

He surveyed the landscape ahead. His only route lay across the open plateau; there was no visible cover but he knew he had to chance it. If he stayed where he was he would stick out like a sore thumb.

He began to run, picking his way through the scattered boulders, ignoring the aching lassitude in his limbs. He was operating by reflex almost, his knees buckling with each crippling step. A sharp pain lanced his side and he groaned as he clapped his hand to it; a stitch was the last thing in the world he needed now.

The plateau spread before him, honeycombed with gullies of dry, frozen peat. No matter how hard he tried, he seemed unable to quicken his pace. A rocky spur reared among the mist and he headed toward it, making for the foliage beyond.

He had scarcely mounted the rise when he heard the thunder of rotors and saw the helicopter sweeping up behind him.

'There he is,' Bruno shouted, waving at the incline below.

The pilot seemed unimpressed by his enthusiasm. 'That could be anyone, *Oberleutnant.*'

'At this altitude? Get this aircraft around, damn you.'

The pilot swung the craft to starboard,

270

and Bruno felt his stomach tense as the running figure grew rapidly larger. At his side, Sergeant Richner eased the Schmeisser across his knees.

'Think you can hit him?'

'I can try, *Oberleutnant.*'

'Do it quick. No misses.'

'*Jawohl.*'

The fugitive was zigzagging in a desperate attempt at evasion and Bruno's lips tightened as the sergeant flicked off his safety catch. 'Take her in as steady as you can,' he bellowed at the pilot.

Jonas, weaving and dipping down the slope below, tried desperately to run faster, but his body seemed to be moving in slow motion. Never in his life had he felt so vulnerable.

The stutter of a machine gun made his stomach cringe. Bullets ricocheted off the fractured rock as the aircraft, hovering above him like a gigantic bird of prey, struggled for purchase on the mercurial air currents and Jonas felt the downdraught from its rotors pounding the back of his skull.

The incline levelled and with a gasp of relief he spotted the scrub directly in front. He dove full length into its spiky foliage and fifty feet above, Bruno cursed under his breath as he watched their quarry vanish from sight.

'Forgive me, *Oberleutnant*,' Sergeant Richner said.

'It wasn't your fault.'

He ordered the pilot to circle the scrub while the sergeant changed magazines and sprayed the bushes with bursts of machine gun fire. For several minutes, they poured repeated salvos into the leafy eiderdown.

'Think you got him?' Bruno said at length.

The sergeant shook his head. 'Can't be sure, not from this height.'

'Take her down and land on the plateau,' he told the pilot.

The man looked unhappy. 'It'll be tricky, *Oberleutnant*. There's a hell of a crosswind here.'

'Don't argue. Just do it, damn you.'

The helicopter settled on a level outcrop and Bruno and the sergeant leapt down and began circling the thicket. Flies gathered around Bruno's face and he swatted them irritably, his body tingling with tension. He disliked hunting another human being, particularly a man whose only crime—if it could be called a crime—was a simple desire to return to his homeland, and if Caudale was wounded he couldn't bear the idea of administering the *coup de grace*.

There was no sign of movement, however, as he waved Richner to a halt and stood listening intently. Any crackling among the scrub was being obliterated by the roar of the helicopter but the damned pilot had refused to switch off his engine, arguing—rightly, Bruno realized—that it would take twenty minutes to get the machine airborne again.

'Any luck?' he shouted at the sergeant.

Richner shook his head. 'The man has vanished, *Oberleutnant.*'

'Well, he can't have left the scrub. You try that corner and I'll try this. If you see anything, yell out.'

Bruno moved the bushes aside and a marmot darted from his path, vanishing into the underbrush. His nostrils caught the odour of stagnant water and he saw a slime-covered pool flanked by heavy foliage. The scrub gathered around him, its razor-sharp boughs tearing at his clothing.

Suddenly, he heard the sergeant shout and saw a dishevelled figure burst from the underbrush and sprint toward a line of granite cliffs. The man mounted the shale and began climbing desperately, picking his way up the semi-vertical rock-face. A colony of birds, nesting on neighbouring ledges, squawked in protest as he wormed his way into their midst.

'Back to the aircraft,' Bruno bellowed.

Together, they charged across the plateau and hurled themselves through the entrance hatch as the pilot swung into the air, banking toward the escaping fugitive. Bruno saw the cliff approaching, saw the solitary climber clinging to the precipitous wall. Richner fired two quick bursts, his bullets ricocheting wildly, then with a deftness which surprised them all the fugitive slipped into a narrow cavity.

Their pilot struggled to bring his machine to a hover but the thermal currents swirling around the cliff-base danced them dangerously close to the rock and swearing under his breath, he banked to starboard, soaring over the adjoining crest.

Huddled inside his refuge, Jonas watched the aircraft turning rapidly. It had almost crashed back there—would have, if the pilot hadn't, by a master stroke of judgement, drawn back at the last crucial moment—but now he was bringing the machine around and Jonas watched dazedly as the aircraft came streaking in toward him. Surprisingly, he felt no panic. Fear seemed diminished by the inevitability of death. He'd always believed it would come to this, he thought. He'd never expected to complete his run alive. It had been too much to expect, there'd been too many forces ranged against him, but he didn't regret it for a moment.

The squawking of the birds rose above the helicopter's roar. He could see them clearly, nesting on the ledges below. They were large and black with yellow beaks and fiercely-tapered tail feathers. He did not recognize the species. The colony formed a living blanket covering the entire cliff and his heart began to thump as a wild idea occurred to him.

He picked up a pebble and hurled it at the shelves below. A few fledglings rose into the air, flapping their wings in a half-hearted protest. He wiped the sweat from his eyes, feeling the downdraught from the helicopter as the pilot homed in for the kill. All he had were a few meagre seconds. If he timed this wrongly there would be no second chance.

Balanced against the cliff-face, he peppered the birds with rocks, directing his missiles into the very heart of the colony. At first, the salvo had little effect. The bulk of the flock remained defiantly in place, then just as he was about to abandon the idea there was an ear-splitting clamour and with a thunder of flapping wings, the entire multitude rose into the air, blotting out the sun.

He watched dry-mouthed as they engulfed the helicopter in a fluttering shroud. Caught in their flight path, the great machine struggled desperately for altitude. Like an eagle engulfed by a locust swarm it bucked and lunged in a frantic effort to remain aloft. He heard the rotor blades splintering, saw the windshield shattering and unable to believe his senses, waited in silence, holding his breath.

Thirty feet above, Bruno struggled for balance on the tilting deck. The crippled aircraft was dancing about all over the place. He saw the pilot's eyes blazing with panic. 'Can't you hold her?' he shouted.

'The pitch-rod's fractured, *Oberleutnant*. We're out of control.'

'Then settle down somewhere, you fool.'

'I'm trying,' the man choked. 'God help me, I'm trying.'

Bruno heard the sergeant mouthing obscenities as, like a needle drawn by some strange magnetic pull, the great machine began to spin.

'We're going to hit the cliff,' the pilot screamed.

Bruno sensed the rampart towering behind them and tossed his pistol through the open hatch.

'Jump,' he yelled and without hesitation, hurled himself desperately into space.

Jonas saw two figures leap from the stricken machine and mouth dry, watched it swaying closer and closer to the cliff wall. The fuselage swung to one side, hitting the buttress with a thunderous crack. The shattered rotors whirled through the air like a pair of scything wheels and the roar

276

of the explosion deadened his senses. He huddled back in his refuge as the metal flanks burst outwards in a shimmering pumpkin of flame. For a long, interminable moment the shower of debris bombarded the precipice and when at last he eased himself to the chimney mouth, he saw wreckage blazing on the rocks below.

Two Germans lay among the shale, their bodies coated with a thin layer of dust. One, the nearest, was drenched in blood and even at that distance Jonas could tell that the man was dead. The other began to stir and he sucked in his breath as he recognized the man's features. It was the SS officer who had murdered André. A surge of fury rose inside him. He could scarcely believe his fortune. By some incredible miracle, he was being given a chance to redress the balance. He spotted a pistol lying on the lower slope, tossed from the aircraft at the moment of impact. He scrambled toward it, trembling with rage.

Below, Bruno felt slivers of pain running through his limbs as he rolled onto his stomach and eased himself to his knees. He saw the wreckage of the flying machine, bits of it still blazing, and what was left of the pilot still perched among the flames, his body a charred, unrecognizable mass. Sergeant Richner lay fifteen feet away on the shale. Something about the grotesque alignment of his limbs told Bruno the sergeant was dead. Two men gone and the flying machine ruined. It would take some explaining when he got back to base.

A bullet pinged from a rock close by and he felt his stomach tense. He saw the Englander slithering down the slope toward him, clutching his discarded pistol. A spasm of fear knotted in his chest. Sergeant Richner's Schmeisser lay at the gully bottom but he knew he had no hope of reaching it. He watched Jonas rapidly approaching and something in the craggy features filled him with terror. The Englander looked insane, as if he'd been driven beyond the boundaries of rational behaviour.

Bruno dragged himself to his feet and began to run, picking an uneven route up a ragged incline. He had never been so frightened in his life. He heard a bullet thud into the rocks as he worked his way higher, his muscles straining to take the grade. There was a gritty taste in his mouth and blood was trickling into his eyes but the worst thing of all was the sickening hysteria which came sweeping over him in waves, destabilizing his senses. His slobber was everywhere, on his cheeks, on his throat, on his chest.

He reached the top of the hill and a

feeling of dismay filled him as he found his route blocked by a perpendicular cliff. The drop was not entirely vertical but it was steep enough to defy any kind of rational descent. It fell almost a thousand feet to a carpet of pines in the valley below.

A sob issued from his lips. He had no choice but to turn and make a fight of it. He spun wildly, his stomach dissolving, and scooped up a handful of dust. He saw the Englander mounting the rise and without hesitation, hurled the grit directly into his face. Caudale skidded to a halt and Bruno drove headlong into his stomach, feeling the wiry resilience of his opponent's body as they rolled, thrashing and kicking, along the precipice rim.

Bruno was conscious of the cliff at his rear but even worse was the realization that the man he was fighting carried the strength of a cornered tiger. Jonas wrestled him against the ground, straddling his chest, digging his fingers into the German's windpipe. Bruno pushed the heel of his palm against his assailant's chin and thrust upwards with all his might but the Englander was like a terrier, sinewy and unyielding. With a surge of panic, he realized he was beginning to lose con-sciousness.

He reached out with his free hand, groping through the dust. His fingers closed on a jagged rock and he swung the missile in a vicious arc. The rock thudded against Caudale's left temple and Bruno snatched a mouthful of air as the pressure on his windpipe slackened. He swung again and saw the Englander's eyes flicker. He kicked upwards and sent Caudale sprawling. Caudale rolled over the precipice rim, his flailing limbs sending up clouds of spiralling grey dust, and Bruno, coughing painfully, watched him tumble down the sloping cliff-wall and vanish into the trees below.

The postman smiled at Anne Huntley as he drew to a halt at Naunton Sander's drive. 'Strictly speaking, we're not supposed to carry passengers but with the war putting an end to the local bus service, the authorities tend to turn a blind eye when we pick up hitchhikers.'

'You've been very kind,' she said, climbing from the van. 'I appreciate the ride.'

He waved cheerfully, and swinging her handbag over her shoulder, she walked through the gate and rang the front bell. The door was opened by an attractive young woman in the uniform of a WAAF pilot officer. She was slim and dark-haired, and she carried an air of innate confidence which surrounded her like an electric force. 'Can I help you?'

Anne felt her heartbeat quickening. 'Are you, by any chance, Naunton Sanders' daughter, Elizabeth?'

'Yes, I am. May I ask who you might be?'

'My name's Anne Huntley. I work for the *Daily Express*. I called several weeks ago. Perhaps your father mentioned it?'

'I don't think so. Daddy has such a notoriously bad memory. He'd forget his own head if it wasn't screwed on properly. However, he's upstairs in his study at the moment. Would you like me to call him?'

'No. Miss Sanders, it isn't really your father I want to see at all. It's you.'

'Me?' The young woman laughed. 'Your editor must be hard up for stories if he's sent you all this way to interview Elizabeth Huntley. I'm about as interesting as last week's laundry.'

'I'd like to talk, if I may, about Jonas Caudale.'

Elizabeth Sanders' eyes flickered. 'Whom did you say?'

'Please don't play games with me, Miss Sanders. Everyone else is doing that and it's making my job enormously difficult. I know all about your relationship with Jonas. I just wondered, is it possible that you're the reason he's running home?'

The young woman frowned. She glanced over her shoulder then stepped outside, closing the door behind her. 'Jonas is coming here?'

'Didn't you know?'

'Of course not. How could I?' She shook her head desperately. 'He can't. It's impossible. Doesn't he realize what will happen?'

'That's what I wanted to ask you, Miss Sanders. What exactly *will* happen if Jonas Caudale returns to Buttermere?'

Elizabeth steered her across the cindered forecourt. 'We can't talk at the house. If my mother finds out that Jonas is coming back ...' She shuddered. 'You don't know what she's like. She was always against him, from the beginning, and she's never forgiven the terrible thing he did.'

'Nor has anyone else as far as I can gather. I wonder if that includes you, Miss Sanders?'

'Please call me Elizabeth. I can't stand formality. I get enough of that in the RAF.'

She stopped at a blue staff car parked alongside the rhododendrons and smiled faintly as she opened the door. 'It's really the Wing Commander's, but he took pity on me when I told him how isolated Buttermere had become. He even threw in a week's petrol coupons to make sure

I didn't get stranded.'

Anne didn't say anything. She had a feeling Elizabeth Sander's stunning looks may have had something to do with the Wing Commander's generosity.

They drove through the gate, heading south along the lakeshore and Elizabeth fumbled in her tunic for her cigarettes. 'Do you use these things?'

Anne shook her head and Elizabeth lit one for herself, breathing out smoke as she swung to the left along a narrow car-track. Anne noticed that her fingers were trembling.

'Please tell me about Jonas,' she said.

'What's to tell?'

'Everything. As far as this valley is concerned, he doesn't even exist.'

Elizabeth Sanders laughed dryly. 'They'll have to acknowledge him sooner or later.'

'Including Larry Hendricks?'

'Larry's a slob. He likes to think he's the neanderthal type, but that Tarzan routine is nothing but an act.'

Anne hesitated at Elizabeth's words, feeling embarrassed, then she said, 'I'm beginning to realize that. I thought for a while he'd been tampering with my car brakes, but the mechanics put the failure down to natural causes.'

'Oh Larry wouldn't go that far. But he's a nasty piece of work just the same.

'Once, when he'd been beating up Jonas's sister, Sally, Jonas whipped him within an inch of his life. He put the fear of God into the man and Larry never laid a finger on Sally again. At least ... not until after Jonas had gone.'

Anne felt a small twinge of envy as she examined Elizabeth's sensual mouth, her dark lustrous eyes. 'Have you known Jonas all your life?'

'I suppose so, but he didn't register much in the early days. We came from different worlds, you see. Also, when I was eleven, my parents sent me to school in Devon. That rather shut me off a bit from the people in the valley. I came back during the holidays but most of the friends I knew—friends of my own age—were ones chosen by my mother, children of similar backgrounds and position. Jonas lived only a mile or two away but in terms of human contact it might have been the other side of the moon.'

'So how did you meet?'

Her lips twisted into a fleeting smile. 'It was during my last year at school. I'd come home for the summer break and the local sports committee asked me to present the prizes at the Buttermere Fell Race. Jonas won, naturally. He always did. I recognized him as soon as he stepped onto the platform. I'd seen him often over the years, wandering about, except that he looked different now—older, shrewder, a little less callow and gawkish.' She chuckled. 'He didn't make a very good impression on me that afternoon.'

'Why's that?'

'After the prize-giving the shepherds held a singsong. It's sort of a local tradition in Lakeland. Whenever Cumbrians get together, sooner or later somebody starts singing.'

'Like the Welsh.'

'Not quite. Here, they sing songs which have been passed down over the generations—songs about the mountains and the valleys, about the fell packs and the fox hunts and all the other things which make up a sheep farmer's life. Things haven't changed much, despite the advent of the Twentieth Century.'

She wound down the window, tapping ash from her cigarette. 'Jonas sang along with the others. There was a lot of beer drinking—that's part of the custom—and I suppose he got pie-eyed, most people did. Anyhow, he threw up over the refreshments table.' She laughed. 'He completely disgraced himself. They had to chuck the whole lot out, sandwiches, scones, everything. If the barman hadn't found a few packets of potato crisps, the event would have been a disaster.'

'Not exactly a romantic first meeting.'

'Definitely not. And if you'd asked me what drew me to Jonas, I wouldn't have been able to answer in those early days because I didn't fully understand it myself. But he was different to anyone I'd ever met. He was so calm, so sure, so graceful. I realize that's a strange word to describe a hill shepherd but when Jonas moves you can feel the power in him, the absolute certainty in everything he does. I'd never encountered that before. Most of the boys I came into contact with were hand-chosen by my mother—not effete exactly, but compared with Jonas they seemed like schoolkids. When Jonas spoke, everyone stopped to listen. He had that effect on people.'

The track came to an end and Elizabeth stopped the car where they could see the craggy ramparts of Brackenthwaite Fell and the tumbling waterfall of Sourmilk Gill. 'Let's walk,' she said, switching off the engine.

They strolled across a grassy hummock, the dappled sunlight warming their faces in the bright May morning.

'How did you meet again, after the prize-giving ceremony?' Anne asked.

'The next time was only a few days later. I'd borrowed Daddy's car to drive over to Grasmere and on the way back, the engine stalled on the top of Honister Pass. Jonas came along on one of his training runs and got the thing going again. I gave him a lift into the valley. We came here.'

'Here?' Anne was surprised.

'It was one of those lazy summer afternoons, the kind you dream about when we're in the middle of winter. Jonas wanted to cool off after his run. He said he knew a place, a secret place. This was it.'

Anne drew to a halt as the ground opened suddenly in front of her and she saw a narrow brook running into a deep rocky pool. The water was so clear she could see the bottom twelve or fifteen feet below. It shimmered invitingly in the sunlight.

'We swam,' Elizabeth said. 'Just the two of us. I was a little embarrassed at first. After all, I hardly knew Jonas. I took care to keep my bra and pants on but Jonas never worried about things like that. He stripped off and dived in fully naked, which was a bit of a shock for me, since I'd never seen a nude man in the flesh before. However, he was so guileless and unaffected it seemed the most natural thing in the world. Afterwards, we lay in the sun and listened to the birds singing.'

She paused, looking intently at her cigarette. 'Then we made love.' Her eyes met Anne's, challenging and defiant. 'I didn't feel bad about it. It seemed a perfectly normal progression. And Jonas wasn't like some men, who paw you about like a piece of meat. He was thoughtful and considerate and he always seemed to appreciate my feelings. He taught me to enjoy physical relationships. Why should I be ashamed of that?'

'No reason at all,' Anne said.

Elizabeth dropped her cigarette into the water. It sizzled briefly before sinking to the shale-covered bottom. 'After that, we were practically inseparable. We went everywhere together. He started coming up to the house. My mother was appalled.'

She pushed her hands into her tunic pockets. 'It was difficult at the time but I think now I understand her feelings. She'd had such hopes for me. She'd groomed me and pampered me, and God knows, she wouldn't have been human if she hadn't set her heart on a prestigious marriage. The realization that I'd become besotted with a local shepherd was anathema to her. She did everything in her power to break us up but it didn't work. I was in love with Jonas, he was all I cared about.

'When I went back to school we wrote to each other every day. He sent me lists of books to read. It was ironic, in a way. I was enjoying the finest education that

288

money could buy but it was Jonas Caudale who taught me about art and literature. He was like that. He threw himself into life with all the vigour of a spitfire and I suppose that's what Mummy found most repellent of all. In her world, people knew their place. They knew how to behave, how to sublimate their emotions. Jonas terrified her with his obsessive commitment to living.'

'How did your father feel about all this?'

'Daddy was wonderful. He admired Jonas, you see. The way Jonas dominated the fell-racing scene was something my father could appreciate. He did his best to smooth things over, but my mother was adamant. She didn't want Jonas as a son-in-law at any price. We had some terrible rows.'

Elizabeth picked up a pebble, toyed with it absently for a moment, then lobbed it gently into the water. 'When war broke out, Daddy came up with what seemed a perfect solution. He persuaded Jonas to enlist in the Northumberland Fusiliers then used his influence to get him a position at officer's school. The idea was to change his social status. Daddy felt that if Jonas could distinguish himself as a British officer, Mother'd be forced to accept him as an equal. It would be the first step in breaking down the barriers in her mind.'

'And did the strategy work?'

Elizabeth's eyes clouded. 'It might have, if it hadn't been for Jonas.'

'Jonas?'

'He did something ... unforgivable. After that, nothing could ever be the same again.'

Anne looked at her expectantly but she made no attempt to elaborate. She stood staring into the rocky pool, her eyes dark and fathomless. Then she shivered, folding her arms and rubbing her shoulders.

'It's turning cold,' she said. 'Let's get back to the car.'

Chapter Twelve

Cyril Applethwaite whistled happily as he tucked his bicycle clips into his pocket and trotted up the oak-panelled stairway of Government Offices in London's Great George Street.

His boss, Theodore Gallagher, watched sourly as the young intelligence officer tossed his cap at the wall peg, nodded a pleasant 'good-morning' and made himself comfortable behind his desk. There were times, Gallagher had to admit, when Applethwaite's good humour drove him to distraction.

'Why is it, Cyril, that nothing in the world ever seems to bother you? Ration books, food queues, enemy bombers—they're all like water off a duck's back.'

'It's my nature,' Applethwaite admitted.

'I know it's your nature. But have you any idea of how irritating it can be?'

'I keep telling myself that I ought to be a little more restrained—in view of the war and all—but I just can't seem to help myself.' Applethwaite paused. He had worked with Gallagher long enough to recognize when the man was in a filthy temper. 'What's wrong, Theo?'

Gallagher shook his head, nipping the bridge of his nose with his fingertips. 'We've made a fool of ourselves with this Caudale fellow. We shouldn't have touched him with a bargepole.'

'What's he done now?'

'Well, for starters, he's fallen over a cliff. It's a miracle the idiot's still alive. He's in a pretty bad way, I gather. Unconscious most of the time, though no bones broken physically.'

'How do you know all this?'

'We've had a radio message from the FTP.'

Applethwaite was surprised.

'How on earth did the FTP become involved?'

'They saw a plane crash in the Pyrenees and went to investigate. They found Caudale at the foot of a hundred-foot drop, pretty beat up. He looked as though he'd tumbled from the top. They've got him hidden in some old water mill.'

'This come through on radio traffic?'

Gallagher nodded. 'The message said, quote: "Tell the world that Jonas Caudale is under the protection of the People's Communist Liberation Front," unquote. They're trying to turn him into a political crusade. They're using him to legitimize the French Communist cause and de Gaulle is hopping mad.'

'Does it really matter about de Gaulle?'

'Of course it matters. When our boys go in, the *Maquis* will rise in their support. There'll be a power struggle behind the lines, *résistants* against *résistants*. Supposing the Communists gain control? Can you imagine what life will be like if France follows the Soviet Union after the war? They're only twenty miles across the Channel, for God's sake.'

'But surely the French people will decide that.'

'Exactly. Which is why we have to persuade them, Cyril. We have to discredit those FTP bastards in the eyes of the world.'

'They're outside our jurisdiction, Theo.'

'Not quite. They're using Caudale to bolster their credibility. Ergo—Caudale has to be stopped. It's time to put an end to this pantomime once and for all. You still have contacts among the German agents in Biarritz?'

Applethwaite looked startled. 'You're not suggesting we turn Caudale in?'

'Not directly. But you do have ways of getting your messages through. Check where Caudale's hiding at the moment, then persuade one of your people to surreptitiously divulge the information.'

'But Caudale could be killed,' Applethwaite protested.

'How many people have died already in this war? How many more are likely to die when our troops hit those beaches on D-Day? Make up your mind, Cyril. We've fought long and hard against the Fascist threat. Do you want to achieve victory only to find Communism sitting right on our doorstep?'

Silently, Applethwaite shook his head.

'I thought not. See that message is leaked, and let the Germans think it came from the FTP. When Caudale's picked up, I want no doubt in anyone's mind about where the treachery lies.'

'If Churchill finds out, or General Eisenhower—my God, there'll be hell to pay.'

'Then keep it close to your chest. Everything on a need-to-know basis. It'll be our little secret—how we saved France from Communist tyranny.'

As Applethwaite left the room Gallagher reflected that it was the first time in his life he had seen the young man lose his insufferable cheerfulness. The realization pleased him and he was humming softly as he picked up his fountain pen.

Greg stopped the *gazogene* and removed the blinkers from his headlamps. He flashed them twice before settling back behind the driving wheel to wait.

'You're sure this is the right place?' Herrington said.

'Where else could it be?'

After a moment, a light flickered in the thicket. 'There's the signal.'

A group of men moved out of the trees, circling warily to flank the vehicle on two sides. Greg recognized the cloth caps and bedraggled raincoats of mountain partisans. He opened the door and stepped into the starlight.

'Death is a fearful thing,' a man said.

'And shamed life a hateful,' Greg answered.

The man motioned him to place his palms on the car roof and rough hands searched him from head to foot. Herrington was forced to open his suitcase while the *résistants* sifted through the bottles inside. When they were satisfied, the first man jerked his head. 'This way.'

In silent procession, they set off along a barely discernible footpath meandering through the trees. Greg heard a river gurgling, then the thicket parted and he saw the outline of a water mill ahead. Two men guarded its entrance.

The windows had been sealed with heavy drapes and the only light came from hurricane lamps as they followed the *résistant* leader up a creaking stairway, the redolence of damp straw and human sweat lingering in their nostrils.

They found Jonas lying on a battered mattress, his eyes closed, his face swathed in surgical dressings. His sweat suit, what was left of it, had been ripped to shreds, and Greg saw a series of lacerations crisscrossing his wiry body. Beneath the lint and gauze pads, Jonas looked like a living corpse. His breathing was shallow and faint tremors ran along his bony limbs.

A man rose to his feet as Greg and Herrington entered. 'Major Anderson?'

'That's right.'

'I'm La Chaize.'

Greg shook the man's hand. Vincent La Chaize, head of the Communist FTP, was already a legend in Occupied France. A shrewd strategist and a brilliant guerrilla leader, he had plagued the Germans for three long years.

Greg said, 'Thanks for your message. We came as soon as we could. This is Dr Herrington.'

La Chaize nodded at Herrington as the doctor placed his suitcase on the ground and knelt at Jonas's side. In the lamplight, the Frenchman's eyes were the colour of dark Burgundy. 'We came across him by accident,' he said. 'My men were investigating an air crash. They found Caudale instead.'

'How long has he been in this state?'

'Off and on, since we brought him here. Sometimes he's logical, sometimes not. He passes out at the drop of a hat. I think he's lucky to be alive.'

Greg watched Herrington carrying out his examination, running his fingers across the back of the Englishman's neck then sliding them down the slender body, checking the rib cage and limbs. Jonas gave no indication that he was aware of the doctor's presence. His body was shivering like a rabid dog's.

La Chaize drew Greg gently aside.

'What's this is all about, Major.'

'It's very simple. Caudale's running home to England and London's planning to use him as a publicity stunt.'

La Chaize frowned, rubbing his cheek. 'Running home?'

'That's right.'

'Why?'

'He won't say.'

'But it doesn't make sense.'

'Jonas isn't a sensible person.'

The light from the hurricane lamps cast shadows across the Frenchman's bushy hair as he watched Herrington lifting Jonas's eyelids with his fingertips. At length, he said, 'We're prepared to give you our support on one condition.'

'What's that?'

'When the story breaks, I want the FTP publicly credited.'

Greg considered for a moment. 'I'm sure that'll be OK. The only problem is, our fellrunner may have reached the end of his road.'

Herrington looked up at them, his raddled face unusually sombre. 'I need to be left alone. I can't work in a bloody railway station.'

'What are you fixing to do?'

'Examine him properly, of course.'

A terrible suspicion formed in Greg's mind. He said, 'No drugs, Herrington.'

'Let me be the judge of that.'

'No drugs goddammit.'

Herrington stared at him for a moment, then wiped his hands on a cloth and rose to his feet. 'Will you excuse us for a moment, M'sieur La Chaize?'

The Frenchman looked at them shrewdly before withdrawing to the outside landing. Herrington glared at Greg, his fleshy face purple in the lamplight. 'Who's side are you on anyhow?'

'I'm on Caudale's side. He's a human being.'

'What does that mean, for God's sake?'

'It means he's somebody I happen to like.'

'That's great. Bosom pals, that's terrific. If you liked Adolf Hitler, would you be fighting for Das Reich?'

'Don't be a damn fool.'

'It's not me who's the fool. Look at this man. Have you ever seen such a mess in your life?'

Greg glanced down at Jonas sprawled on the battered palliasse. He had to admit that Herrington was right. Jonas looked almost at death's door. The surface of his face was drawn tight against the bones, and there were deep craters where the eyes should be. The skin itself carried the texture of burnt porridge.

'He's a wreck,' Herrington said. 'He's

suffering from concussion and after only a cursory examination, I'd say he's probably bleeding internally as well.'

'In other words, he's a hospital case.'

'Damn right he's a hospital case. Except that I can't allow him to be a hospital case because I'm the miserable sod who has to stuff all the bits together and make sure that he gets to Buttermere. So why don't you keep your bleeding heart, Joan of Arc sentiments to yourself, and let me get on with my bloody job?'

Greg felt his lips tightening. He knew that what Herrington said made sense but something in his nature rebelled at the man's callousness. 'I was right about you the first time, Herrington. You may be a brilliant doctor but as a human being, you're a grade-A asshole.'

Sunlight streamed through the open window, casting dappled patterns across the gloomy apartment. Bruno sat at the table and poured himself a whisky from the bottle at his wrist. Spread out in front of him was the cardboard file which had been forwarded from Gestapo Headquarters on the Avenue Foch in Paris. The file contained Jonas Caudale's POW medical reports, translations of the BBC broadcasts on the progress of his run and even a British magazine article on his sporting achievements before the war. They offered a comprehensive picture of the man he had been trying so desperately to capture.

He rolled the whisky around his mouth before swallowing, grunting as the fiery liquid sent a pleasant glow through his empty stomach. He wondered why he was getting so upset. After all, he had seen the Englander go over the cliff and it was hard to believe that any man could have survived such a fall, but to Bruno's concern the patrols he had sent to investigate had found no sign of any body.

Until now he had been ambivalent in his attitude toward the Englander—he had even, to some extent, admired the man—but the episode on the clifftop had changed all that. Throughout his life Bruno had regarded himself as a superior being, a creature who by the very nature of his genes was a cut above the common herd. Now he couldn't dismiss the terror he'd felt as he'd fled in panic up the ragged hillslope. The memory filled him with shame. He wanted revenge. Retribution. His hunt for Caudale had become a sacred crusade. Nothing would satisfy him but the ultimate consummation—the Englander's death, pure and simple.

He closed the file as Suzanne came into the room, carrying two loaves of French bread which she deposited in the kitchen.

He watched as she hung her coat on the door peg. 'Been far?'

'Just into the village. Where else would I go?'

He rose to his feet and kissed her lightly on the side of the neck.

'Don't smudge my make-up,' she said, pulling away and glancing down at his file. 'What are you reading?'

'Some stuff on Jonas Caudale. I picked it up from the Gestapo.'

'I thought you said Caudale was dead?'

'I said he *might* be dead. The fellow has an irritating habit of springing back to life again. These papers will help me to understand him better. It's the first rule of combat, know thine enemy.'

'So you do think he's still alive? You're talking about him in the present tense.'

'*Touché.*' Bruno smiled.

He was silent for a moment as he watched her take a marrow from the cupboard and begin to slice it on the kitchen bench. Something in her movements told him she was unnaturally nervous. Curious, he thought. His worries about Suzanne were growing stronger by the hour. He suspected he loved her, a situation he didn't dare to contemplate, but even worse was the conviction—etched deep into his psyche—that she was consciously and deliberately betraying him.

'What did you think of the bunting in the village?' he asked casually.

'Bunting?'

'The streamers and decorations. You must have seen them?'

'Oh yes, of course.'

'The local soldiers put it there. It's to celebrate a German festival—the feast of Lammerding. I thought it a bit provocative though, sticking an effigy of General de Gaulle on the bonfire. How do the locals feel?'

She shrugged. 'They realize it's only a bit of fun. You Germans don't have a monopoly on humour, after all.'

He picked up a piece of marrow and rolled it thoughtfully between his fingers. His face was casual but his eyes carried a sharpness she had never seen before. 'I've been meaning to ask you something. You wouldn't have any old friends around here, would you?'

'What kind of friends?'

'People you might remember from the old days. A relative perhaps—like your brother, say.'

She looked at him, frowning. 'What is this, some kind of interrogation?'

'If you like.' He squeezed the vegetable with his fingers and threw it back on the bench-top. 'Some days ago, you were seen talking to a cyclist who has since been

302

identified as Auguste Odru.'

'So you've been having me watched?'

'It's my duty to have you watched. I'm a German officer. I have the security of my men to consider.' He studied her keenly. 'What was Odru doing here? You know he isn't supposed to leave Viatte without official permission.'

She sighed. 'It wasn't Auguste. The man may have looked like Auguste but he was simply a local peasant mending a bicycle puncture. In this country we often stop to help people in trouble. That's probably difficult for your Teutonic brain to comprehend.'

'He must have been pleased then. At an offer of help from a total stranger.'

'I expect so.'

'Odd, he looked anything but pleased to me. I could have sworn—I was watching from a distance, mind you—but I could have sworn the man was extremely angry.' His voice hardened. 'You may also be curious to know that as far as I am aware there is no bunting in the local village, no dummy of General de Gaulle and I have never heard of a German celebration called Lammerding.'

Her mouth opened and closed but there was no sign of submission in her gaze. She stared back at him, her eyes challenging and defiant, and he thought sadly: she's a woman in a million.

He ran his finger down the curve of her cheek. 'You have brought me great pleasure, my dear. I'd forgotten what it is like to care for another human being. However, a friendly word of warning. Until now, I have given you the benefit of the doubt but you would be wise to remember that I will not allow emotion to sway my judgement a second time.'

He paused as someone tapped on the door. A sentry stood on the threshold, clad in the uniform of an SS stormtrooper. Suzanne struggled desperately to compose herself as she heard the man speaking to Bruno in a low, urgent whisper. The realization that her masquerade was over, that somehow or other he had penetrated her cover made her muscles chill, but something rose above her terror, a feeling of puzzlement. If Bruno knew she was working for the Resistance, why was he being so reasonable? There could be only one explanation. He was using her as bait to ensnare her friends. She would have to keep her wits about her. She would have to ensure she didn't make the slightest mistake.

When he returned his eyes were shining with excitement. 'Change your things and meet me downstairs,' he said. 'We've just had a tip-off from one of your FTP people.

Caudale's hiding in a derelict water mill above the Pol Valley.'

'You want me to come along?' She looked surprised.

He chuckled as he plucked his cap from the bedroom door. *'Chérie,* until Jonas Caudale is dead, I haven't the slightest intention of allowing you out of my sight.'

Anne Huntley heard the door open behind her and turned to see Naunton Sanders entering the room. Sanders had lost some of his poise in her presence. Now he looked guilty and faintly subdued. 'My daughter Elizabeth sends her apologies. She hopes you'll forgive her but she has a blinding headache and she's had to lie down for a while. She's asked me to drive you back to your hotel.'

'That won't be necessary. I can easily walk from here.'

Her voice was cool and his cheeks coloured under her gaze. She stared at him steadily, relishing his discomfort. He'd made a fool of her with his avuncular charm. It would do him good to stew a bit.

'I know what you're thinking,' he said after a moment. 'I lied to you about Jonas.'

'You said he didn't exist.'

305

'What did you expect? You came here from a national newspaper. You wanted to rake everything into the open, spread my daughter's name across your pages for the whole world to read. I wouldn't have been doing my duty as a father if I hadn't made some attempt to protect her.'

She considered the point for a moment. The man was right of course. He owed her nothing, neither loyalty nor explanations. But she had a job to do and only Sanders could help her get to the truth of things. She said, 'Mr Sanders, if Jonas Caudale does reach Buttermere, he's going to be international news. This valley will be so flooded with media people, there'll be no question of keeping the story secret any longer. At least give me the courtesy of an interview. I do think you owe me that.'

'What can I tell you that you don't already know?'

'The most important thing of all. What did Jonas Caudale do that made him a pariah among his own people? And why is he running home across enemy-occupied territory?'

Sanders stared moodily into the fireplace. 'It isn't easy to explain after all this time.'

'You might try.'

'Very well. On the understanding that whatever you print, you keep my daughter's name out of it.'

'I can't make such a promise, Mr Sanders. Your daughter's involved whether she likes it or not. But I can give you my word that her part in the affair will be handled as sympathetically as possible.'

Sanders looked unhappy and she didn't blame him. There was an air of defeat in his slumped, bony shoulders but after a moment he nodded. 'That's good enough for me. As long as Elizabeth isn't hurt. It's high time the truth came out anyway.'

He stood with his back to the fireplace, resting his heels on the metal fender; she settled herself on the sofa. In the wintry light, his cheeks were unnaturally pale. 'I hardly know where to begin.'

'You can skip the background stuff. Most of it I already know.'

'What did Elizabeth tell you?'

'She told me how you sent Jonas off to officer's school.'

He shook his head in surprise but his eyes had no life in them at all. 'It seemed a good idea at the time,' he said, 'helping Jonas to make something of himself. And I have to admit that it certainly eased the tension here.'

'Meaning things were quieter without Jonas around?'

'More placid anyhow. At least as far as my wife was concerned. Elizabeth probably found life a good deal duller. But there

307

were compensations. In those early days of the war, they used to train commando units on the Buttermere fells.'

'Army?'

'Marines mostly, but some infantry troops as well. The old Dobson house was converted into a makeshift barracks and men were ferried in each month to go through a mountain warfare course. They were taught by a major named Gavin Cheever. He was a New Zealander—an expert in outdoor survival—a personable young man from a good family with a brilliant future in front of him.' A faint smile etched the corners of Sanders' mouth. 'Gavin fell for my daughter almost at first glance, which was hardly surprising considering Elizabeth's looks.'

'How did she feel?'

'Flattered, I suppose. Intrigued in a mild sort of way. But to tell the truth it was my wife who arranged things. She invited Major Cheever to the house for tea. "To break the ice," she said—a friendly gesture to a foreign soldier serving in a distant country—but she made damned sure Elizabeth was present when he arrived.' Sanders chuckled. 'You must understand, Miss Huntley, my wife—bless her soul—has very entrenched views on things. She likes to maintain the social order. I realize it's terribly old-fashioned in this day and age but Judith can't help herself. She was brought up that way, and sees an inalienable division between her own status and what she regards as the lower orders. To Judith, Gavin Cheever was a far worthier prospect for Elizabeth's hand than Jonas Caudale could ever be.'

'Where was Jonas at this time?'

'Still at officer's school. Gavin took advantage of his absence to call at the house every day. He was besotted with Elizabeth and Judith was delighted of course. She thought that with Jonas out of the way, it could be only a matter of time before things began to develop between those two.'

'And did they?'

'They might have. But one day, by extraordinary coincidence, Jonas himself turned up at the school. He'd been sent, together with a number of other cadets, to take part in a mountain warfare course. You can imagine how embarrassing it was. The two men kept coming up to the house at the most difficult moments. Strictly speaking, Gavin was Jonas's commanding officer but if you'd ever met Jonas, you'd know that subservience is not in his nature. It took all my powers of diplomacy to prevent Gavin slapping him on a fizzer.'

'How did Elizabeth handle all this?'

'With her usual poise. It'd take an

earthquake to shake that girl. Besides, she wasn't really interested in Gavin Cheever. In fact, the rivalry between the two men might have sizzled out if things hadn't come to a head in February 1942. 1 don't know if you remember but it was one of the worst winters Britain's seen in almost fifty years. Most of the mountain passes were blocked with snow and the lakes were frozen solid. Judith had arranged a dinner for some of the officers serving in the valley and Jonas, without warning, turned up uninvited. He could be an exasperating devil when he put his mind to it.'

'How did Mrs Sanders react?'

'What could she do? Elizabeth was in love with the man. She had to swallow her annoyance and put a brave face on things. But Gavin—jealous, I suppose—did his damndest to make Jonas feel inferior. He kept bringing up his schooling, his lack of etiquette. It was all a nonsense really because Jonas, despite his humble beginnings, was very well informed. Then finally Gavin went too far. He started belittling Jonas's sporting achievements and that's when I felt my own hackles rising.'

Sanders shook his head indignantly. Now that he was into his stride, he had lost his hangdog look. She had the feeling that he welcomed the opportunity to talk as

310

if in some strange way he was exorcizing himself.

'Cheevers claimed anyone could run in such low-lying terrain, especially when the weather was good. He claimed that in New Zealand, they had a race called the Balfour Footstool which they held in the middle of winter.'

'And Jonas challenged him?'

'Not Jonas.' A shadow crossed his face. 'Me.'

'You?' Anne was surprised.

'I was irritated, I suppose, by the man's arrogance. I suggested we hold our own Balfour Footstool.'

'In England?'

'Why not? Conditions couldn't have been more suitable if they'd tried. I suggested Gavin pit his commando team against Jonas and a few of the locals. It seemed, at the time, a perfectly sound idea and I thought it might give Jonas an opportunity to put Gavin in his place.'

'But surely most of your men would be away doing military service?'

'Well, we still had a few veterans around—exempted from the army because of the farm labour shortage—and there were any number of youngsters just itching to show their paces. Cheever jumped at the chance. He'd been a mountain runner himself and felt he could whip Jonas to a standstill in wintry conditions.'

The firelight cast ripples across Sanders' cheeks. There was a look of pain in his eyes as if something inside had begun to hurt. 'Because the race was unofficial, we decided to dispense with stewards and registrations stops. We drew up two teams, the top eight athletes from Gavin's commando unit and seven locals headed by Jonas. Then we mapped out a route across the Catbells to Keswick-on-Derwentwater, a straightforward run all the way. The competitors were given directions and left to their own resources.'

He rested his hand on the mantelpiece and Anne saw the knuckles gleaming white through the skin. 'The day started bright as crystal, one of those winter mornings you only dream about. We saw the runners off, then used an army truck to take us around to the finishing line. We had to drive via Cockermouth because the passes over Newlands and Honister were blocked with snow. We set up base on the Keswick side of the lake and settled down to wait.'

Sanders looked down at his hand, clenching his fist angrily as if he wanted to smash the mirror on the wall behind. 'The weather deteriorated toward midday,' he said. 'It's the sort of thing that happens in these mountains. Conditions can change in the twinkling of an eye. By noon, a raging blizzard had blotted out everything in sight and it was impossible to see the lake even, only a blinding veil of snow. We lit stoves and brewed hot coffee to warm the runners when they reached the finishing line. We'd worked out exactly how long the race should take but after an hour passed with no sign of life I knew something had gone seriously wrong.'

'Why didn't you alert the rescue team?'

'In those days, there were no rescue teams and since the race was a private affair we hadn't made any safety provisions either.'

'How long did you wait?'

'An hour-and-fifty minutes. Then Jonas emerged out of the storm, running like a drunken man. He was followed at various intervals by a handful of survivors—eight participants out of the original sixteen.'

'What happened to the others?'

'Dead, all of them.'

'Including Gavin Cheever?'

'Him too.' He rubbed his face with his fingertips. 'The story came out bit by bit. Apparently, they'd dropped off Catbells with Jonas in the lead. As he'd reached the Keswick road, instead of turning left, he'd headed across the frozen lake. The others saw his footprints and followed blindly, disorientated by the storm. God knows how they moved at all on such a slippery surface but the snow was so thick they didn't realize they were running on ice until the first warning cracks echoed beneath them. Maybe one man might have made it, but not the entire team. When the stuff gave way, eight of the competitors plunged into the freezing water.'

He paused, gazing down at the mantel-piece as if somewhere on its marbled surface he could see the terrible scene unfolding. 'Try to imagine the horror of that moment. The others tried desperately to help but every time they approached the hole, the ice splintered under their feet. They were forced to watch as their companions vanished beneath the surface. The accident happened on the 18th of February. It was late March before we got the bodies out.'

Anne was silent for a moment, picturing the terrible tragedy. She swallowed hard to moisten her throat. 'A story like that should have made the national papers. Why have I never heard of it?'

'Oh, it was in the papers all right. But the war news tended to dominate the headlines at the time. The victims were listed as trainee commandos who'd died whilst taking part in an endurance exercise. In reality, only three of the dead were soldiers. The others were local teenagers from the Buttermere Valley.'

'But Jonas Caudale could hardly be blamed for an act of God.'

'You don't understand. In such atrocious conditions the others might be forgiven for getting disorientated, but not Jonas. He knew those mountains blindfolded.'

'Meaning?'

'Meaning there can be only one explanation for his behaviour. Jonas was cheating.'

'Cheating?'

'He was trying to slice a couple of miles off the final stretch, not realizing the others would follow instinctively in his footprints.'

Sanders wiped his palms against the front of his shirt. 'Can you imagine what it means to a tiny community like this, losing five young men in a single tragedy? There wasn't a family in the valley which didn't have a relative to mourn.'

'What did Jonas say?'

'He protested his innocence, of course, but nobody believed him. He was too wrapped up in Elizabeth to even think straight.'

'So you think he deliberately tried to destroy Gavin Cheever?'

'Not destroy. Defeat. I'm sure he didn't want to see the man killed, but you have to admit that things worked out very neatly from Jonas's point of view.'

He rose to his feet. 'Come with me.'

She followed him up the stairway to a tiny attic on the topmost landing. The room was cluttered with assorted pieces of junk. He switched on the electric light and pulled out a battered chest. Opening it, he waved at a collection of sporting trophies inside. 'All these belonged to Jonas. He won them over a period of years. Some list details of records which have never been broken but you'll find no reference to them on the official files. After the coroner's misadventure verdict, Jonas's awards were confiscated and placed here for safekeeping. The race-books were reprinted to eliminate all mention of his name. He was ordered out of the valley and warned never to return. If he does, at least one man—Larry Hendricks, who lost a brother in the tragedy—has sworn to kill him.'

'It's like something out of the Old Testament, sending a man into exile.'

'It may be hard for a city girl to understand but these are mountain people. They have their own rules, their own way of doing things.'

'How about Jonas?'

'Well, he went to pieces after that. Scarcely a day went by without our hearing about some new spot of trouble he'd got himself into. Eventually, they reduced him to the ranks and transferred him to North Africa. Soon afterwards, we heard he'd been taken prisoner. Elizabeth tried writing via the Swiss Red Cross, but we have no way of knowing if the letters ever arrived.'

Anne was silent as she considered Sanders' story. 'If everything you say is true, why would Jonas risk his neck running the German gauntlet to reach a place where the inhabitants have disowned him?'

Sanders sat back on the floor, one strand of his immaculate grey hair dangling untidily over his forehead. 'I've been asking myself that question for days. The only thing I know is that Jonas loved this valley more than any place in the world. The mountains were in his blood. Try to imagine what happens to a man when he's locked up like a caged animal, especially a man like Jonas. Perhaps, by his own reasoning, he sees this run as an act of contrition. Perhaps he's demonstrating to the people of Buttermere how badly he needs to be here, and hoping in some curious and perverse way that he can somehow buy forgiveness.'

'That's too glib,' Anne said flatly. 'A man who can take on the German war machine single-handed is hardly going to do it because of some deluded fantasy. I think he has another object in mind.'

'What's that?' Sanders asked.

'I don't know,' she admitted softly. 'But one way or another, I intend to find out.'

Chapter Thirteen

Greg watched worriedly as Jonas emerged from the water mill, supported on each side by *résistants*. He moved in disjointed bursts like a man who had lost control of his limbs. A surgical dressing formed an incongruous bulge on the side of his skull and there were purple bruises under his cheekbones.

'How're you feeling, champ?' Greg asked.

Jonas didn't answer. His features were locked into a trance-like mask, his eyes strangely out of focus.

'What have you done to this man?' Greg's voice was cold as Herrington checked Jonas's pulse rate.

'Stop worrying, old chum. He's on his feet, isn't he?' The doctor's movements were deft and sure, like a trainer handling a thoroughbred.

'He's a zombie, for Christ's sake. You can't expect him to run in this state?'

'He has to run. He's only a stone's throw

318

from the French coast. If we can get him to Bayonne, we'll be home and dry.'

He took out a hypodermic needle, examining it briefly in the morning light.

'What's that stuff?'

'Nothing for you to worry about.'

'I want to know what you're pumping into him, dammit.'

'Just a little depressant cocktail, something to dull the inhibitory sensors, plus a touch of cocaine as a pick-me-up.'

'You fool, he can't take any more of your crazy concoctions. What are you trying to do, kill him?'

'No, Major Anderson, I am not trying to kill him. I am trying to keep him on his feet until he finishes what he has to. Then he isn't my concern any more.'

'Terrific, that's terrific. Whose concern is he, may I ask?'

Herrington sighed as he rolled up Jonas's sleeve. 'Major, I'm doing what's necessary to get the job done and considering the consequences of this run, so—if I may say so—should you.'

'Herrington, by the time you've finished with Jonas, the only thing he'll be good for will be a funny farm.'

Herrington's face remained unmoved. 'In which case, he'll be a damn sight luckier than a lot of the men who'll hit those beaches on D-Day.'

Seated in the staff car, Bruno saw the sergeant hurrying toward him.

'They are at the mill, *Oberleutnant*. About seventeen in all—terrorists without a doubt.'

'Are the men in position?'

'*Ja.*'

Bruno glanced at Suzanne in the vehicle rear. Her cheeks were pale but her eyes looked surprisingly calm. 'So our information was correct. Not all your countrymen, it seems, oppose German rule.'

She watched him owlishly over her woollen neckscarf. Even in the semi-darkness she looked devastating, he thought. He said, 'You'd better remain in the car. There could be shooting.'

'I want to come with you.'

'Try not to worry, *chérie*. You know I lead a charmed life.'

The dawn air chilled his skin as he climbed from the car, buttoning his overcoat. A faint mist rose among the hedgerows, and he could see his troops crouching in the underbrush. 'Detail two men to guard Madame Le Gras,' he ordered the sergeant. 'Under no circumstances is she to leave the vehicle.'

'What if she insists, *Oberleutnant?*'

'Then shoot her.'

He took out his pistol and checked its load, then he waved at his men who spread into the thicket. There was little to see, despite the pale streak in the eastern sky. Ground mist obscured the furrows of a ploughed field immediately to Bruno's left, and somewhere nearby he heard a river gurgling. It was hard going, for the overhead branches shut off the lifting sun and he heard his troops panting as they wormed their way through the heavy foliage.

The woods parted and he saw the outline of a water mill in the clearing ahead. A group of figures stood around its base, clad in bedraggled clothing. They looked, at first glance, like ordinary farmhands, except for the weapons they were carrying. Twigs crackled at Bruno's rear as the sergeant came wriggling toward him, his face sweaty with strain. 'Shall I give the order to fire, *Oberleutnant*?'

'No. We'll try to take them alive.'

It was crazy, he knew; men caught in such circumstances would hardly give up without a fight, but he hated unnecessary slaughter. He rose to his feet in the semi-darkness. 'Attention,' he shouted in French. 'Throw down your arms and place your hands in the air. You are under arrest.'

The terrorists froze and for one elongated

moment he thought they were going to obey. Then with a suddenness which took him by surprise, they scattered wildly in every direction.

Bruno's men did not wait for the command to fire. The entire world seemed to explode—he could think of no other way to describe it—and his insides shuddered as the roar of their carbines numbed his senses and night dissolved into violent day.

Dimly, to his left, he saw figures scampering into the nearby trees. One of them dropped his sten gun as he ran. 'Come with me,' Bruno bellowed at the sergeant.

He tore through the shrubbery, his body filled with a savage elation. Branches swept into his face and he brushed them aside, his pistol slippery in his fingers. A man turned, bringing his rifle to his shoulder, and still in motion, Bruno twisted to the left as the bullet whistled past his ear. Without pausing, he swung his Luger in a vicious arc, laying the *résistant's* skull open to the bone. As the man pitched sideways, he leapt across his motionless body.

He saw the terrorists crashing through the trees and fired blindly. A figure dropped, thrashing in the grass, and his companion seized him around the middle, dragging him toward the scrub.

322

For a fractional moment, the rescuer's face was caught in the reflected glare of the gunfire and Bruno blinked in astonishment. It was Suzanne's brother, Auguste Odru. And he had cursed loudly in an American accent.

The *gazogene* roared down the mountain road, skidding as it took the bends. Greg felt sick, as if his entire body was disintegrating from the inside out. A fiasco, it had been back there, a complete and utter fiasco. Where had the Germans come from? There'd been no warning, no hint of anything at all until it had been too late. Christ knew how many men had died. Worse still, he had lost Jonas and that was unforgivable. Greg had seen Jonas being spirited into the trees by a group of escaping *résistants* but he had no way of knowing whether the Englishman had managed to survive.

In the *gazogene's* rear, Herrington gritted his teeth, moaning softly under his breath. Struggling to staunch the flow of blood from his rib cage, Greg glared at the two *résistants* in front. 'Can't you slow down a bit? You're killing him, for Chrissake.'

'If the *Boche* catch us, we'll all be dead, Major,' one of the men answered in a surly voice.

Greg used his scarf to pad the blue-rimmed wound. 'Try to keep still, Herrington. I've got to stem the bleeding.'

Herrington's veins bulged along his corded throat. 'Christ, the pain, it's tearing me apart.'

'Let me get this dressing fixed.'

Greg knew it was a flimsy application at best and the way the vehicle was lurching it would be a miracle if the damned thing stayed in place but somehow he managed to secure the bunched-up neckscarf over the ugly puncture.

Sweat coated Herrington's skin and his cheeks looked sallow in the early light. He reached out, clutching Greg's wrist. 'Anderson, you've got to give me something for the pain.'

'I've nothing to give. You'll have to stick it out, at least for the moment.'

'Look in the box.'

Greg hesitated. He glanced at Herrington's drug case lying unopened on the seat by his side. 'I'm not too familiar with that stuff,' he said uncertainly.

'You'll find a bottle with a blue label.'

Greg flipped open the suitcase lid, fumbling among the phials. He took one out and held it in front of Herrington's nose.

'That's it,' Herrington croaked. 'Use the syringe. Hurry.'

Struggling for balance, Greg fitted a needle to the hypodermic, and Herrington's face relaxed as he felt the drug flooding his bloodstream.

Ahead, the gradient slackened and Greg realized the ground was beginning to level. He peered through the window but all he could see was a line of pines flanking the hedgerows on their right. 'Where are we?'

'Just south of Bayonne,' the driver said. 'If we can reach the city, we'll be able to lose ourselves in the suburbs. It's only ten miles, maybe less.'

Suddenly, the driver cursed, jamming his foot on the brake and Greg felt a quiver of alarm as he saw a line of vehicles parked across their path.

Roadblock.

Figures moved in the gathering light. '*Boche?*' Greg asked.

'*Milice.*'

The driver swung the vehicle into reverse and roared back the way they had come. Greg glanced through the rear window and saw the *miliciens* galloping frantically to their trucks. At his side, Herrington moaned through fiercely-clenched teeth.

'For God's sake, are you trying to kill him?' Greg barked. 'Slow down, damn you.'

The Frenchman ignored the command as the *miliciens* started in furious pursuit, their internal-combustion engines quickly gaining on the charcoal-burning *gazogene*. Greg saw their headlamps slicing through the semi-darkness. 'They're narrowing the gap.'

The driver topped a rise and brought the vehicle to a screeching halt. 'We'll have to escape on foot.'

'You're nuts. Herrington's bleeding like a pig.'

'We'll help him the best way we can. Get him out of the car.'

Greg knew the Frenchman was right. Inside the *gazogene*, they didn't stand a chance. Somehow, panting and straining, they wrestled Herrington from his seat and supporting him clumsily between them, manoeuvred him into the surrounding pines.

Greg never forgot the next few hours, propelling Herrington through the prickly underbrush, trapped in an endless jungle of smothering scrub. At length the woods gave way to open pastures but here the going proved even tougher still, for they had to pause continually to check for enemy observation posts. He saw the city lying across the horizon in a grey, metallic sprawl, smoke from its chimneys forming a hazy blur which merged with the shimmer of the rising sun.

It was broad daylight by the time they reached a small-holding on the outskirts of the suburbs where the farmer was a Resistance sympathizer. He led them to a draughty barn and they eased Herrington into the straw where he lay for over an hour, coughing blood and wheezing painfully. It was clear to Greg that the Englishman was in a very bad way. 'How do you feel?' he asked, gently mopping his forehead.

Herrington's cheeks looked yellow as he struggled for breath. 'Like I've got an elephant sitting on my chest.'

'I think the lung is punctured. We've got to find you a doctor.'

The farmer, a corpulent man with a weather-beaten face, said, 'Help is already on its way, m'sieur. Your companion looks bad but I have seen such wounds before. With careful handling, he may still survive.'

Greg groped for his pistol as the sound of a vehicle reached them from the compound outside but the farmer gently patted his wrist. 'Do not worry, it is a friend.'

Feet crunched on the gravel forecourt then a man entered, ducking his head beneath the roof-beams. He was thickset and ruddy-cheeked, and he carried a leather bag which he placed in the straw at Herrington's feet.

'This is M'sieur Jadot,' the farmer said. 'He will take care of your wounded comrade.'

'You're a doctor?' Greg asked.

'No, m'sieur, I am a vet, but in such unsettled times, I am the only comfort your friend can hope for.'

Herrington's breathing wheezed as Jadot removed the dressing from his rib cage and examined the blue-rimmed hole intently. Greg could see his skull gleaming in the filtered sunlight.

'You must be Major Anderson?' the man said without looking up.

'That's right,' Greg answered in surprise.

'I have a message for you. Your friend Caudale, he is safe. Some of our people managed to smuggle him into the city.'

Greg felt his pulses quicken. 'Where is he now?'

'Resting at my home.'

'Thank God.'

Jadot took out a hypodermic and injected Herrington's forearm, then with delicate care began cleaning blood and bone fragments from the Englishman's chest. He said, 'Caudale's ill and appears to be hallucinating. There is some evidence of internal damage. Strictly speaking, he shouldn't be moved but we have to get him out tonight.'

'Why tonight?'

'Because there's an Irish merchant ship sitting in the harbour. If we can smuggle him on board we might get him as far as Dublin at least.'

'That's great.'

'We'll do everything we can to keep your friend alive,' the farmer promised, 'but you must go now with M'sieur Jadot. Caudale is the important one here. He's what this is all about.'

Greg knew the farmer was right. He nodded at Jadot who was working delicately with a metal probe. 'You're the doctor,' he said.

The corporal was a slightly-built man who looked more like an insurance clerk than a soldier of the Wehrmacht. Bruno noticed that his fingers were trembling as he put down the coffee tray and quickly left the room.

'It's your uniform,' the garrison commander explained. 'Us common soldiers always feel uneasy in the presence of the SS.'

Bruno sipped his coffee, grunting in satisfaction as the steaming liquid sent a glow of warmth through his chilled stomach. All things considered, it had been a successful day. They had failed to pick up Jonas Caudale but they had killed seven *maquisards* and brought four in handcuffs to Bayonne. He felt certain the Englander would now attempt to cross the Bay of Biscay on one of the vessels in the city harbour.

'I need your support,' he told the commander.

The man smiled graciously. 'Naturally, for an officer of the *Leibstandarte*, my garrison is at your disposal.'

'It is not for me, but for the Führer.'

He took out the letter of authority Colonel Scheider had given him and slid it across the desk. The commander read it in silence. He seemed impressed. 'What do you require of me?' he asked, handing the letter back.

'I am looking for an Englishman, an escaping POW heading for the coast. I suspect he'll attempt to leave France by jumping one of the ships moored in the river and I want the waterfront placed under heavy guard.'

'I can set up roadblocks on the city approaches if you like.'

'No, the man's too elusive in the open countryside. If I can corner him on the wharf, it'll make his arrest much easier.' He glanced at his watch. 'How many vessels do you have at anchor?'

'Seven. Four French fishing boats, two German freighters and an Irish merchantman.'

'Irish?' Bruno felt his senses sharpen. 'When is she due to sail?'

'Just after dawn, I believe.'

Bruno thought for a moment. The Irish ship would be the most obvious choice of all. It could carry Caudale across the Bay of Biscay and deposit him safely in Dublin. Suddenly, he knew—knew beyond any shadow of doubt that the freighter would be Caudale's target.

His hands were trembling as he placed his coffee mug on the desk. 'Commander, I want you to quarantine the Irishman and post sentries on its decks and bridge.'

'But *Oberleutnant,* the vessel belongs to a neutral country. The diplomatic consequences could be disastrous.'

'Not nearly as disastrous as allowing Caudale to slip through our fingers. Forget protocol, Commander. Under the authority granted me by the Führer, I order you to place that ship under arrest.'

Cathyl Tuohy, master of the SS *Tara,* swore under his breath as he saw German soldiers running across his deck and hatch-covers. He had been sailing to Bayonne for almost a year now and until this moment had suffered little interference from the occupying forces. Tuohy was a big man with an irascible temper and he felt his cheeks reddening as he glared at the local garrison commander. 'What the hell's going on here? Who gave you permission to board my ship?'

'My apologies, captain,' the commander said. 'I'm afraid there may be a slight delay to your departure.'

'You'd better have a bloody good reason. I've got a schedule to meet.'

'The reason is not your concern, captain,' a voice said behind him and he turned to see a good-looking young officer in SS uniform strolling casually up the gangplank. Something in the man's manner shook Tuohy's confidence for a moment. 'Who the hell are you?'

The officer touched his cap. 'Lieutenant von Hautle of the 5th *Leibstandarte* SS Adolf Hitler. Forgive me, but your vessel is under temporary German protection. We believe a certain fugitive will attempt to board her sometime this evening and I am asking for your co-operation in the interests of German-Irish relations.'

'Supposing I refuse?'

'Then you leave me no alternative but to place you under arrest.'

'You bloody fool, when Berlin discovers what you're doing, they'll have your guts for garters.'

'Possibly. But in time of war, the usual niceties do not apply.'

Tuohy was about to speak again when a

young woman emerged out of the darkness and his voice seemed to lodge in his throat. Her cheeks were exquisitely formed and her eyes carried an expression he couldn't quite decipher. He thought he had never seen anyone quite so beautiful.

The SS officer smiled as he took her arm. 'Perhaps you will escort us to your cabin, captain. We have a long night ahead so we might as well make ourselves comfortable.'

Winston Churchill sat on the Members' Terrace at the House of Commons, thumbing through a pile of report sheets. The other MPs left him wisely alone as he paused from time to time to scribble lengthy comments in the margin columns. Churchill's demeanour was becoming progressively less cordial with D-Day approaching.

Several MPs glanced up as General Eisenhower strode on to the terrace, led by a House of Commons usher. The man escorted the general to the Prime Minister's table, and taking off his glasses, Churchill waved Eisenhower into a vacant chair. 'I'm just going through the Balister reports.'

'And rewriting them to your own specifications, I see.' Eisenhower glanced at the margin scribblings.

'I thought Balister might appreciate a pointer or two.'

'The trouble with your pointers is they always sound like pronouncements from God.'

'You think I'm too overbearing?'

'You, Winston?' The general's expression was archly innocent. 'I would never dream of suggesting such a thing.'

Churchill placed the papers on the table at his side and reached for the coffee pot. 'Would you care for a little refreshment? It's an American brand. I had it ordered from one of your KP stores.'

'No, thanks. I've been drinking coffee till my insides feel awash.'

Churchill carefully refilled his own cup. 'What brings you to the House?'

Despite the balminess of the day, Eisenhower looked desperately tired. Churchill knew he'd been working flat out to get the invasion details finalized.

'You remember that man Caudale?'

'The fellrunner?'

'It seems he's reached the French coast.'

The Prime Minister was surprised. 'You came all this way to tell me that?'

'Not quite. The situation has taken a turn we didn't foresee. Caudale has surrounded himself with a group of unsavoury bedfellows. The FTP.'

'Communists?'

'They're claiming Caudale as one of their own, using him as a political pawn.'

'I see.' In the sunlight, Churchill's domed forehead looked unusually pronounced. 'Does it really matter? We're already supporting Tito's people in Yugoslavia.'

'In the short term, probably not. But consider what will happen if we have to announce that Caudale has completed his run thanks to the courtesy of the French Communist party. De Gaulle will go beserk.'

'It does seem an awful lot of fuss for just one man.'

'Caudale isn't one man, Winston. Caudale's a symbol. God knows, I'd love to see the fellow make it but not under these terms.'

'What are you going to do?'

'The submarine we detailed to pick him up off the French coast—I'm issuing an order to cancel it.'

'But what about the man you put in—what was his name again—Major Anderson?'

Eisenhower looked miserable as he glanced across the Thames to where a patrol boat chugged beneath the arches of Westminster Bridge. 'I'm afraid Major Anderson will just have to find his own way home,' he said.

Suzanne stood at the porthole window, staring down at the darkened quayside. Voices rose in the cabin behind her as Bruno and the captain engaged in a game of chess. From time to time Bruno's laughter echoed in Suzanne's ears but Captain Tuohy made his moves with the air of a man who was struggling hard to control his temper. Suzanne knew he deeply resented the takeover of his ship. She knew too that Bruno's strategy was chillingly accurate. If Jonas Caudale had survived the ambush, the SS *Tara* would be his most logical objective.

She turned as a crewman appeared and asked the captain to accompany him to the bridge. Excusing herself, she followed them along the companionway. The captain glanced angrily over his shoulder, his wind-baked face redder than ever. 'No one's allowed on this bridge without my permission. You don't have the run of the entire ship.'

Suzanne spoke quickly in English. 'Captain, have you a gun on board?'

He eyed her suspiciously. 'Who wants to know?'

'Please don't play games with me. We're running short of time. The man the Germans are looking for will almost certainly try to board this vessel tonight. We

336

have to stop the *Boche* from killing him.'

Tuohy hesitated, and jerked his head at the crewman. He waited until the man had withdrawn, then examined Suzanne again, a faint smile twisting the corners of his mouth. 'So,' he said, 'you're a member of the Resistance.'

'Please answer me, captain. Have you a gun on board?'

'Supposing I do?'

'If you want your ship back, give it to me.'

'My God, you've got a nerve. You come in here as calm as you please, and expect me to accept your cock-and-bull story without a single shred of evidence.'

'There are seven Germans on this vessel. If I take von Hautle prisoner, do you think your men could handle the others?'

'You're out of your mind. Those Jerries are armed, for Pete's sake.'

'But they're watching the waterfront. They'll hardly expect an attack from the crew itself.'

He looked at her with disbelief 'Even if we pulled it off, we'd never get out of the harbour. They've got artillery emplacements all over the rivermouth.'

'Trust me,' she told him firmly.

She waited in silence, willing him to co-operate. She was counting on the man's stubbornness, on his rebellious nature, and when she saw his eyes begin to gleam she knew she hadn't been mistaken. He laughed as he came to a decision. Opening a panel in the base of the azimuth, he took out an object wrapped in a ragged tea towel. When he drew back the material, she saw a Blackhawk Rueger revolver.

'You know how to handle one of these things?'

Suzanne nodded, and the captain pushed it into her hand. 'I'll need thirty minutes to organize the crew. Can you keep von Hautle occupied?'

'I'll make sure you are not disturbed,' she promised.

Greg awoke to find Jadot gently shaking his shoulder. Behind the Frenchman stood two youths carrying rifles and short-barrelled revolvers. He sat up, running his fingers through his hair. All day long, he'd slept like a baby, hidden with Jonas in the tiny apartment. Now he rose to his feet and opened the bedroom door. In the semi-darkness, they saw Jonas shivering miserably on the narrow bunk. His eyes were stricken, his cheeks wax-like.

'He's suffering withdrawal symptoms from the drugs,' Jadot said. 'Let's hope to God he can make it.'

'He'll make it. Jonas is the one thing in this war you can count on.'

'It will not be easy getting through the streets with the curfew in force.'

'Won't the harbour gates be guarded?'

'We'll create a diversion. A few bursts of rifle fire should give you enough time to sneak Caudale over the wall.'

Greg looked at him in wonder. It always astonished him that men like Jadot—ordinary, respectable men—could risk their lives on madcap escapades only an idiot would contemplate. The two *résistants* accompanying him looked scarcely more than boys, spotty-cheeked and sallow-featured.

'You'll be running a hell of a risk,' he said.

'Don't worry about us, Major. We aren't planning to take up permanent residence out there. Once we get the Germans occupied, we'll pull out fast.'

'How about the ship itself?'

'Hard to tell. The Irish like to remain neutral. You'll have to play that as it comes.'

It seemed a shaky plan at best, but it was the only one they had. Greg hooked Jonas's arm around his shoulder and pulled him into a sitting position. 'Give me a hand as far as the door.'

They moved outside, pausing on the threshold as one of Jadot's companions checked that the street was clear, then with Greg manhandling Jonas along they picked their way through a line of empty gardens. The city was silent in the pre-dawn darkness. Jonas moved like a man in a trance, his body shuddering as he responded to Greg's touch. It was impossible to tell if he was rational or not.

They crossed the deserted sidewalks taking full advantage of the available cover, pausing in doorways to check the route ahead. Twice, they had to hide as enemy patrols rattled by.

After a while, the harbour wall emerged out of the gloom. Greg saw the barbed wire fence bordering its gateway as Jadot brought his companions to a halt and examined Jonas critically. 'Just make sure he gets back to England. If I'm putting my neck on the line, I'd like to know it's been worth it.'

'I'll get him back,' Greg promised.

Jadot shook his hand, his breath steaming on the cool night air. 'Take him down the alley and as soon as you hear the shooting, head for the wall. We'll withdraw after thirty seconds.' His lips twitched as he added dryly, 'That should be just about long enough for the *Boche* to do something unpleasant in their trousers.'

'You never cease to amaze me,' Bruno

smiled as he moved a queen to block Suzanne's knave. 'I didn't know you could play chess.'

'You never asked.'

'Pity. It might have helped to while away the time.'

'I wasn't conscious you had any problems in that direction.'

Bruno whistled in approval as Suzanne brought up a pawn from the rear. 'Bravo, you're a natural.'

Outside, they heard the rattle of a truck. Their hull creaked as the vessel stirred in the swell.

Bruno's face was bland as he said nonchalantly, 'Is the captain amenable?'

She looked at him. 'What are you talking about?'

'I mean has he promised to help you take over the ship?'

His eyes were mild, his manner casual. 'You did suggest it, didn't you? That he use his crew to dispose of my guards?'

She felt her senses quickening. 'If you believe that, why are we still sitting here?'

'My dear *chérie*, I'm assuming the captain isn't a fool. Not only are there two Wehrmacht companies on the waterfront but nothing can leave this harbour without passing under our artillery emplacements.'

Fingers trembling, Suzanne lit a cigarette while Bruno studied her with amusement.

'A wise general watches his enemy,' he said. 'I've always known you were a member of the Resistance. Why do you think I insisted that you accompany me everywhere?'

'If that's true, shouldn't you have turned me over to the Gestapo?'

'It's one of the anomalies in my nature that I never do what is expected of me. Besides, I have to admit that I find your beauty irresistible. A crying shame we have to be on opposites sides in this war but then, if I weren't the foe, would you I wonder have been drawn to me in the first place?'

Suzanne said nothing. She could feel her nerve beginning to snap.

'The American posing as your brother, I suppose he's your contact?' He chuckled as her cheeks paled. 'You imagined I was both blind and stupid? *Chérie*, there is nothing you can do that will still surprise me.'

Struggling to keep her face impassive, she said, 'What happens now?'

'To tell the truth, I really don't know. In the strict military sense, I ought to have you shot but that would be such a tragic waste. Besides ...' He smiled again. 'I've grown rather used to having you around.'

'What about your duty as a German officer? You'd abandon that to save me?'

'I'd abandon anything.'

'Including Jonas Caudale?'

'Caudale?' Bruno was surprised.

'Why don't you let him go?' she urged.

'Out of the question.'

'He's nothing to you, nothing to the Reich. All the poor man cares about is getting home.'

'You're wrong. There's a personal thing between Caudale and me. I can't explain it, but that's the way it is.'

He was about to speak again when the sound of gunfire reached them from the quay outside. 'What the hell's that?'

He pushed back his chair, rising swiftly to his feet and without a word she drew the pistol from her handbag and aimed it at his chest. He froze in his tracks as he watched her finger tightening on the trigger. 'I was wrong about you, *chérie,*' he said. 'You *can* still surprise me.'

Cathyl Tuohy heard the rattle of gunfire as he crept along the darkened companionway. He paused, glancing back at his mate, Daniel O'Donnel who was staring at him in alarm. 'We're under attack,' O'Donnel said.

'Not us. It's over by the harbour gate. Must be that bloody Englishman trying to get into the docks.'

'What if they kill him?'

'That's his lookout. Just keep your mind

343

on your job. Everything as we discussed it and no mistakes, OK?'

Tuohy had spread his men throughout the ship, two crew members to a sentry. His orders had been terse and explicit—hit hard, disarm quickly.

Boots clattered on the deck as the German guard, drawn by the commotion, ran toward the ship's rail. Tuohy cursed under his breath. There was no longer any hope of approaching the man undetected. They would have to act boldly.

'Come on,' he whispered.

Thrusting his hands in his pockets, he strolled into the moonlight, making no attempt to conceal his approach. His mate followed, blinking in confusion. Tuohy wandered to the sentry's side and stared across the waterfront at the staccato flashes lighting the darkened sky. 'What's going on out there?'

The sentry muttered something in German, his pale eyes filled with alarm.

'Looks like our friend here doesn't understand English,' Tuohy told his mate. 'Get down behind him, and tuck in your head.'

O'Donnel dropped to his knees, crouching behind the German's thighs. Tuohy hesitated a moment, judging his timing. His eyes swept the deserted quayside but most of the soldiers had headed toward the gate as soon as the shooting had started. There was no one in sight.

Moving so fast his arm was a blur, he hit the sentry across the thorax, seizing his rifle as the man tumbled over. The German collapsed in a heap, his helmet rattling across the empty deck. Tuohy motioned to O'Donnel and the two men dragged the unconscious figure into the cover of the nearest cargo hatch.

Panting hard, Greg manoeuvred Jonas over the harbour wall. The rim had been topped by several strands of barbed wire but he used his raincoat to smother the ugly spikes. Jadot had been as good as his word, the diversion had worked like a dream.

Greg's limbs shivered as he manhandled Jonas into the cobbled yard and stood listening to voices drifting from the entrance gate. The shooting had stopped now but men were running in all directions and despite the blackout, he could see searchlights probing the streets beyond. A fine old panic the Frenchies had started.

Moonlight glimmered on the rigging of ships moored at the river's edge as he steered Jonas across the gleaming cobbles. Somehow, weaving and stumbling, he picked an uneven route along the silent waterfront, checking each of the vessels in turn. The SS *Tara* was fourth from the end. Its gangplank looked deserted.

A figure appeared on the deck and stood grinning down at them as they started up the narrow ramp. 'Jonas Caudale?' The voice was Irish and faintly lyrical.

'Who are you?' Greg frowned.

The man chuckled, helping Jonas up the shuddering catwalk. He was large and husky and his bulbous nose clung to his beefy face as if it had been stuck on as an afterthought. 'Cathyl Tuohy's the name, master of the SS *Tara*. You made it just in time. We're getting ready to cast off.'

'In the middle of the night?'

Tuohy laughed. 'Damned Germans tried to stop us leaving port, but I have a touch of obstinacy in my nature. Bloody-mindedness, my wife calls it.'

Greg had expected arguments, protests, refusals, but Tuohy's welcome took him completely by surprise. The captain helped him steer Jonas down to the lower deck and his muscles froze as he saw a German officer in full SS uniform being guarded by a crewman with a heavy revolver. Then someone else moved into the lamplight and his tension dissolved into joyous relief as he recognized Suzanne. He leapt forward and seized her in his arms, kissing her wildly on the mouth.

The German officer watched them with

a mocking expression, a faint smile creasing his lips. 'I'd advise you to make the most of your freedom,' he said. 'You'll never get past the guns at the river mouth.'

The garrison commander felt the slipstream bathing his cheeks as his staff car roared along the harbour wall. His life was a peaceful one as a rule—an occasional air raid, a visit by the local *oberkommandant* —but nothing to get alarmed about. Now he was beginning to feel as if the war had exploded in his own back yard.

His driver screeched to a halt and he clattered briskly up the steps of the sandbagged artillery emplacement. The platoon sergeant saluted as he entered. 'The vessel is nearing the harbour mouth and heading for the open sea, *Sturmbannfuhrer*. We are awaiting the order to fire.'

The commander stared across the dancing wave crests. He could see the freighter clearly in the gathering dawn. It was the SS *Tara* without a doubt. Too bad, he reflected. He'd have taken a chance with one of the Frenchmen but attacking a foreign vessel, especially a ship belonging to a neutral country, filled him with the gravest misgivings. If he got it wrong there'd be hell to pay.

He glanced at the gun-crews in their *Waffenrock* scorch smocks. 'Switch on the searchlamps.'

A cluster of beams lanced across the salt-grey swell, illuminating the *Tara* in a pool of dazzling light. Raising his field glasses, the commander swivelled the lens into focus. He knew if he fired now he could blow the vessel out of the water with one well-timed broadside, but he had to be sure that what he was doing was right.

'Have you tried contacting them by radio?'

'They do not answer, *Sturmbannfuhrer*. Either they are using a different frequency, or ...' The man left the sentence unfinished.

The commander swept the decks with his binoculars, grunting as he spotted a group of figures standing on the bridge. One, he recognized instantly. It was *Oberleutnant* von Hautle, standing with his arm around the woman, Madame Le Gras. As the commander watched, von Hautle waved at him in a friendly manner.

'Shall I order the men to fire, *Sturm-bannfuhrer*?' the sergeant asked.

The commander lowered the field glasses. It seemed strange that von Hautle should depart in such an unorthodox fashion, but the commander was a cautious man who disliked taking risks and he had no intention of doing so now. 'No,' he said, pushing the binoculars into their leather case. 'Allow the vessel to proceed.'

Chapter Fourteen

Bruno sighed as he watched the artillery post receding into the darkness. 'What simpletons we put in command.'

He felt the pressure of Suzanne's pistol. 'Step back inside,' she ordered, disengaging herself from his arm. There was no hint of gentleness in her eyes and if he had any doubts about her ability to squeeze the trigger, he dispelled them now. Suzanne Le Gras would shoot him at the drop of a hat. 'You're a remarkable woman,' he said, moving down the companionway. 'You let nothing stand in the way of your duty. I admire that.'

Suzanne didn't answer. Her face was a frozen mask.

'I'll admit you had me fooled in the beginning,' he added. 'But that was because I allowed my heart to rule my head. After I'd thought about it—actually thought about it—I realized how unlikely it was for a lady of such strong convictions to succumb so easily to my masculine charm. The trouble was, you were always so convincing.'

Still no response. What hurt most, he thought, was not the fact that she'd outwitted him but the realization that despite everything, he was still in love with her. He was careful however, to keep his features relaxed as he entered the crowded saloon. The captain was watching him with a crooked little smile and behind the captain stood the American, Major Anderson, his eyes smouldering darkly. Anderson hardly seemed the type a woman would fall for, Bruno thought, but if there was one thing he'd learned in his short and happy life, it was that nothing was as mercurial as human nature.

'Congratulations, Major,' he said cheerfully in English. 'I believe you have a saying "May the best man win?"'

'You can't charm your way out of this one, von Hautle.'

My God, the fool's still angry, Bruno thought. He felt the deck lift beneath his feet as the ship headed into the open sea. 'May I ask what is going to happen to me?'

'You'll be handed over to the British authorities,' Greg told him. 'After that, it's a matter for the War Office. Imprisonment, I imagine.'

'Hey now,' the captain said. 'May I remind you Major, the lieutenant is my prisoner, not yours, and until Eire declares war on Germany, there'll be no question of handing him over to the British or anyone else.'

'What are you talking about? He's an enemy officer.'

'Wrong, Major Anderson. Lieutenant von Hautle is my guest, together with the six troopers presently residing in the forward hold. When we reach port, they'll be delivered to the local Garda and then only on condition that they'll be repatriated to their own country as quickly as possible.'

'For God's sake, whose side are you on?'

'I'm not an Englishman, Major, and I'm not one of your allies either. I'm a neutral remember, and a qualified neutral, at that. I make my living trading with these people and I wouldn't have lifted a finger if the idiots hadn't commandeered my ship.' His eyes twinkled as he examined Greg and Bruno knowingly. 'And since it's clear that you and the good lieutenant here are about to settle the war on a more personal basis, I think it might be better for everyone concerned if I invite Mr von Hautle to join me in my private quarters. Lieutenant, will you come this way please?'

Smiling pleasantly, Bruno followed the captain along the companionway.

'That was quite a speech back there,' Bruno said as the captain poured them each a drink.

'Something in my blood. Can't stand people telling me what to do. A hereditary trait, I suppose. My father fought in the Easter Rising.' Tuohy handed the glass to Bruno. 'Besides, I felt a little guilty about imprisoning you and your men. It's not as if we're enemies, after all. If you hadn't been so bombastic back there, I mightn't have acted so strongly.'

'Diplomacy was never my strong point,' Bruno admitted.

'Mind if I ask you something? How long have you and the major known each other?'

'I never met the man before tonight, but we do have a common bond.'

'The lady?'

'Exactly.'

'I figured that was it. Ah, the vagaries of the human heart.'

'I hate to admit it, but I think I'm in love with her.'

'And naturally the major resents that.'

'The major's jealous—a normal human emotion. I'm going through rather a bad bout myself at the moment.'

The captain laughed, draining his glass. 'Well, you're not the first man to make a fool of himself over a woman and I dare say you won't be the last.'

Bruno listened to the engines throbbing beneath the lower deck. He was beginning to relax after the shock of finding himself a prisoner. Even the pain of seeing Suzanne in the American officer's arms had eased to some extent. His eyes were calm as he rolled his whisky gently in the glass. 'Did you mean that about turning me loose?'

'Why not? If the Garda prove uncooperative, I have friends who'll see you get back to Germany in one piece.'

'Friends?'

'Comrades. Associates. People I trust.'

'What kind of people?'

'Idealists and fellow patriots.'

The wind blew spray against the porthole window and Bruno heard it rattling like the murmur of a distant storm. He leaned forward in the chair, his senses suddenly alert. 'Are you talking about the IRA?'

Tuohy chuckled as he picked up the bottle and refilled his glass. 'Who said anything about the IRA? I told you, I'm not a man who cares to take sides.'

'But your father did. In the Easter Rebellion, he took sides all right. "Ireland One Nation", isn't that the saying? Tell me the truth, are you a member of the IRA?'

Tuohy studied him with amusement. 'What an inquisitive fellow you are and no mistake. The IRA, is it? Now what would a respectable mariner like myself be doing in such irresponsible company?'

Bruno sank back, his eyes dancing. 'You're one of them, I knew it.'

'I do have certain sympathies, I will admit. I've done them favours, from time to time—an arms shipment here, a bit of contraband there. Being a merchantman has its uses.'

'Don't you realize that our intelligence forces maintain links with your Republican friends?'

'I've heard it rumoured,' Tuohy admitted.

'For God's sake man, when you're fighting a war it stands to reason that your enemy's enemy is your natural ally. Can you contact your people in Dublin and get a message through?'

'What kind of message?'

Bruno glanced quickly around. A jotting pad lay on the table, and he began to scribble. 'Give this to your radio operator. Tell him to transmit it letter by letter. It's written in a simple code which we use to communicate with foreign sympathizers. The IRA will understand. They can contact German intelligence for confirmation.'

'You never quit, do you?' Tuohy said

with a crooked smile.

'Not while I still have something to fight with. Will you send it?'

'Why not? I'll do anything for a friend and ally.'

Bruno picked up the whisky bottle and refilled his empty glass. Raising it in the air, he grinned happily. 'Up the Republic,' he said.

The ferry pulled into Dublin harbour and leaping ashore, Donald Rourke secured his rope around the leading capstan. He called to one of his colleagues to toss his jacket from the deckrail, then slinging it over his shoulder, strolled toward the harbour entrance, a thickset man with a skull which merged into the compact musculature of his shoulders with no discernible dividing line. At the age of fifty-two, Donald Rourke had worked on the Dublin ferries for almost a quarter of a century and was only eight years off retirement. He was also, unknown to the Garda or the Irish authorities, supreme commander of the IRA's Dublin Brigade.

When he reached the harbour gate, he saw Alex Stebbings the taxi driver, waiting on the opposite side of the road. He knew Stebbings would never give up the prospect of a fare unless something important was afoot and pulling on his jacket, he crossed the street, dodging nimbly among the traffic. 'What's up?' he asked as Stebbings slid down the taxi window.

'There's an emergency, Donald. They need you at headquarters right away.'

'OK. Give me a lift. I'll pay you back at the end of the week.'

'Headquarters', as Stebbings called it, was nothing more than a simple terraced house, indistinguishable from a thousand others in the same area of the city, but its very innocuousness made it an ideal centre for plotting out Republican campaigns. Since the outbreak of war when the Irish Prime Minister de Valera had made it clear that any threat to Irish neutrality would be ruthlessly crushed, the IRA had moved underground, watching the war raging through Europe and waiting for an opportunity to strike back at its ancient enemy, the British government.

When Rourke arrived at brigade head-quarters, he found seven men sitting in the upstairs room. The uncarpeted floorboards were studded with cigarette butts and the window shades had been drawn to shut out the evening sun. The seven men gathered solemnly around the simple trestle table were, like Rourke himself, nondescript in appearance, but they made up the ruling council of the Dublin IRA.

'We've been waiting for you all day,

Donald,' a man said, opening the proceedings without ceremony. 'We've received an unusual request from the German intelligence forces.'

Rourke listened in silence as the man quickly outlined the details of Bruno's radio message from the SS *Tara*. 'We checked the broadcast's validity with our contacts in Hamburg and it seems authentic, right enough.'

Rourke was thoughtful as he considered the matter. Behind him, the gas fire roared in the evening stillness. 'What's the feeling of the council?' he asked at last.

A second man cleared his throat. 'We've never helped the Germans before, why should we do it now? Who cares what happens to this idiot Brit?'

'The Germans are our allies,' Rourke said.

'Adolf Hitler?' a man exclaimed contemptuously. 'Jesus, Donald, I'd sooner be involved with the devil himself.'

'Anything which embarrasses Westminster is a victory for the movement. We're not talking about ethics here, we're talking about fighting and winning. When your back's against the wall, you can't always choose the perfect soulmates. We'll drop Hitler soon enough when we get the Brits out of Ulster, but at the moment, Germany's all we've got.'

'But what's the percentage in this for us?'

'Goodwill,' Rourke said. 'It'll show the Germans we're dependable. Who knows where it might lead? Arms shipments? Money? If the invasion takes place, Hitler will be desperate to divert the Allies' attention. It's up to us to prove we're just the people to do it.'

He looked quickly around the muggy room. Outside, they heard the roar of a bus heading toward the Liffey. 'Go to the harbour,' Rourke ordered one of his men. 'Find out if Trigg's fishing boat is free. Tell him to get it ready to sail.'

Greg heard a footstep on the threshold and turned to see Suzanne entering the cabin. She glanced at Jonas who was shivering visibly under the blanket. 'How is he?'

'Running a fever. He needs hospital treatment fast.'

'The captain's got a medical chest on the bridge. Shall I fetch it?'

'No. I'm not pumping him full of any more drugs.'

Suzanne looked down at Jonas's ashen features. His eyes were closed and beads of sweat clung to his craggy forehead. Tiny, almost imperceptible tremors ran through his facial muscles as if his countenance was about to collapse at any moment. 'Perhaps we should let him rest. It'll be better if he sleeps.'

'I guess you're right.'

They stepped into the companionway, mounting the ladder to the deck above. Greg switched on the saloon lights and drew the shades across the porthole windows. It seemed hard to believe their escapade was almost over. A few more hours and they would be in Dublin. After that, it would be hospital for Jonas, and for him—the boat-train back to London.

He hesitated. 'Will you come with me to England?'

'I haven't thought about that yet.'

'Well, you can't go home. London's safer.'

'But what about my people?'

'You won't help them by getting yourself arrested.'

'It isn't as simple as that and you know it.'

He turned to face her. 'I'm not going without you, that's how simple it is.'

Suzanne stared up at him for a moment, then ran her fingers along the brass fittings lining the porthole windows. Her eyes were sad. 'Things were different in France. You needed me there.'

'I need you here,' Greg insisted.

'You're wrong. You'll never forget what happened with Bruno. I watched the way you looked at him on deck. I've never seen such hatred in my life.'

'He's the enemy, for God's sake. How did you expect me to look?'

'I'm not talking about the war, I'm talking about us. Living together, little things—unimportant things—get blown out of all proportion. When you're angry at me—and you will be—do you think you'll forget Bruno then?'

'I've forgotten him already.'

She shook her head, sighing. 'How naïve you are sometimes.'

Greg said, 'Listen to me. All my life, I've been out of step with the whole human race. Now, for the first time, I've found someone I can relate to. Do you think I'm going to let that go?'

She was about to answer when they heard the roar of a motor launch outside. He frowned. 'What the hell's that?'

He drew back the window shade and saw a fishing boat pulling alongside the *Tara's* hull. Shadowy figures shinned up a rope ladder tossed from the deck above. A tremor of uneasiness stirred inside him. 'We've got visitors.'

They hurried to the bridge where they found the wheelhouse occupied by four strangers in wellington boots. Across their arms, they carried Thompson submachine guns. With them, to Greg's astonishment, was Bruno. The SS officer smiled at Greg with a casual insolence that made the American's stomach crawl.

'What's going on here?' he asked. 'Who are these people?'

The captain chuckled amiably. 'Major Anderson, I'd like you to meet some friends of mine—fellow patriots, you might say, whose only wish is the unification of their homeland.'

'What the hell are you talking about?'

The newcomers' leader, a heavy-set man in his early fifties, motioned the captain to be quiet. He studied Greg in silence for a moment and Greg was conscious of a curious deadness in the stranger's eyes. 'Major Anderson, in the name of the Irish Republican Army, we are taking you into our custody—you, the lady, and your companion, Mr Jonas Caudale. You will kindly join my associates on the motor launch below.'

Greg gaped. He couldn't believe what he was hearing. These men were Irish, not German, and the captain, despite the iron tenacity he had displayed earlier in the evening, was allowing them to dictate orders on his own bridge.

'I'm an American,' Greg protested.

For a moment, a glimmer of regret showed in the newcomers' eyes. 'I give you my word you will not be harmed,

Major. Neither you, nor the lady.'

'And Caudale?'

'We've arranged a rendezvous with a German gunboat. The Englishman will be handed back as a prisoner of war.'

'You'd do that? Help the enemy?'

'Your enemy, not ours, Major. They're fighting the British, and that's good enough for us.'

Bruno smiled at Greg, settling his cap more jauntily on his forehead. His eyes were mocking and amused. 'Fortunes of war, Major Anderson. What is life but a gamble, and you know the old saying—"lucky in love, unlucky at chance".'

Afterwards, Greg never quite knew how it happened but something in the German's handsome features pushed him beyond the boundaries of reason. Before he realized what he was doing, he had hit Bruno on the side of the jaw. Bruno crashed backwards over the azimuth, his arms and legs whirling, and four machine guns thrust themselves against Greg's chest as he struggled to control his rage. Bruno stared up at him dazedly, blood trickling from the corner of his mouth.

The IRA leader snapped, 'I am not a man noted for his patience, Major. I advise you to board the motor launch immediately before I lose my temper. That is an order.'

The Irishman's eyes were like flakes of obsidian. Greg obeyed without a word.

The rain was strengthening as Anne Huntley cycled into the drive at the home of Sergeant Quinlan, the Buttermere policeman. She propped the bike she had borrowed against a nearby tree and holding her coat above her head, tugged hard at the doorbell.

For several minutes, she fumed and fretted but there was no sound of movement from the building's interior. Muttering under her breath, she followed the garden path to a rainwashed patio at the building's rear. To her surprise, she found the back door open and stepped inside, shaking the moisture from her hair. She rattled the latch loudly but there was no response.

Puzzled, she moved through the tiny kitchen to the corridor beyond. The sound of music drifted from the living room and she recognized the strains of Francis Langford singing 'You'll Never Know'.

She tapped on the door and pushed it open but one glance told her the room was empty. The log fire had died in the grate and a mug of tea, only half drunk, stood on the table beside an open newspaper. She moved toward it and glanced at the top page. She noticed a short report on the ice tragedy at Derwentwater. There was no mention of the fell race. The victims were listed as farm youths and army commandos taking part in an outdoor survival course. The paper was dated February 1942.

A feeling of uneasiness gathered in Anne as she moved further along the corridor. Something about the half drunk tea and the wireless playing unnoticed disturbed her. She felt her premonition strengthening.

When she opened the adjoining door, she froze on the threshold. The room was clearly a study of sorts, probably used by Sergeant Quinlan to fill in his arrest forms and deal with all the other paperwork associated with the job of an English country policeman. The walls were covered with public service posters and detailed maps of the surrounding area.

A solitary desk stood in front of the slate fireplace, its surface scrupulously clean and tidy. Behind the desk sat Sergeant Quinlan. He was leaning back in his chair, staring mutely at some indeterminate point on the ceiling. His mouth was open, and the twin muzzles of a twelve bore shotgun lay propped between his lips. He had used his toe to squeeze the trigger and part of his skull and most of his brains were sprayed across the gilt-edge mirror on the wall behind. A handful of flies had gathered around the ugly wound at the back of Sergeant Quinlan's head.

Steeling herself against the gruesome sight, Anne moved to the desk and examined it briefly. A handwritten note lay on the blotting pad. Picking it up, she held it to the light, her lips silently moulding the words. When she finished reading, her cheeks were ashen. 'Dear God in Heaven,' she whispered.

Her hands trembled as she picked up the telephone and jangled the receiver rest for the operator.

Rourke stood in the wheelhouse of the little fishing launch and watched the waves breaking over the bow in front. Two hours had passed since he had intercepted the SS *Tara* and taken her passengers prisoner and during that time, Rourke—a reflective rather than an emotional man—had begun to have serious second thoughts.

In the beginning, the benefits had seemed obvious—impress the Germans give his men a taste of much-needed action and, hopefully, set up a relationship in which future arms deals might be negotiated—but Rourke had to admit he cared little for the policies of Adolf Hitler. Moreover, it was clear to anyone with half an eye that the Germans were losing badly in this war. Was he really gaining a useful ally or risking everything on a disastrous gamble? The

British fellrunner had affected him more than he cared to admit. Jonas Caudale looked almost at death's door yet there was no sign of 'give' in the man, no hint of surrender or defeat. Rourke admired that. He disliked being the instrument of the Englishman's downfall.

The wheelhouse door opened and Frank Murat entered, carrying a mug of coffee. Murat was a tall man with a permanent beard stubble. He placed the coffee at Rourke's wrist and stared through the spray-battered windshield. 'How far is it now, Donald?'

'Another three hours. We'll be there before dark.'

Murat made no attempt to withdraw. He stood drumming his fingers against the bulkhead.

'What's on your mind, Frank?' Rourke asked, casting him a sideways glance.

'We've been thinking,' Murat said. 'About what we're doing here. It isn't right, Donald. You know it, and we know it. It isn't right at all. Have you taken a look at that little sod down there? He's dying, Donald. He'll be lucky to make it through the night. We shouldn't be handing him over to the bloody Germans. It's crazy, that's what it is. And it has damn all to do with the Republic.'

Rourke took a mouthful of coffee,

grunting as the scalding liquid scorched his throat and stomach. He held the vessel steady as the swell lifted her bows, spraying foam across the glistening deck.

'We want to take him home, Donald,' Murat said softly. 'We've been talking it over and we want to take him home.'

Rourke's blunt face flushed. 'You talked it over? What the hell does that mean, you talked it over? Since when are policy decisions made by soldiers in the field?'

'Nobody's challenging your authority, Donald, but we can't see what we're gaining by this exercise. That man down there, he's one of our own. We can't hand him over like a sacrificial lamb.'

'So now we're running things by bloody committee, are we?'

'Be reasonable, Donald. At least let's reconsider our position.'

'I have considered it,' Rourke snapped.

He paused as a wave crashed across the decks, hurling itself at the salt-flecked windshield. The vessel danced under its impact and cursing, he wrestled with the controls, holding the bow on an even keel. What was he getting so testy about? He couldn't blame a man for speaking his mind, especially when his words made sense. They had nothing against Caudale, nothing in the world. What right had they to interfere, after everything he'd gone through? Rourke felt his resolution wilting. 'Take over for a bit,' he ordered. 'I'm going below.'

The prisoners were seated around the table when Rourke climbed down the ladder into the hold. They glanced up as he entered, the girl cool and resigned, the American crimson with fury. Only the German seemed happy with the situation. Humming softly, he was trimming his fingernails with a pair of metal clippers.

Caudale, the Englishman, lay on a bunk, his eyes fixed dazedly on the deckbeams above. There was sweat on his cheeks and his body was shivering. Rarely had Rourke seen a human being so ravaged and helpless. 'How is he?'

'He's awful sick, Donald,' one of his crewmen said. 'He needs a doctor bad.'

Jonas's face seemed to have lost its shape. His skin looked bloodless, like soggy blotting paper.

Without turning, Rourke said, 'Simon, I want you to lock Lieutenant von Hautle in the forward hold.'

Bruno lowered his nail clippers, frowning. 'What's that?'

'A precautionary measure, lieutenant. Please accompany Mr Lennihan, if you will. I'm placing you in temporary custody.'

'I don't understand.'

It's very simple,' Rourke told him. 'We're taking Jonas Caudale home.'

It was something in the air, nothing Jonas could put a name to, a faint, indefinable odour of bracken and moorgrass, but he knew he could smell the mountains of Cumbria and he felt his senses quickening, his heart beginning to hammer. You never completely lost that, he thought—the good clean scent of rain on the hills, clouds massing, the earth preparing to renew itself—he belonged here as he had never belonged anywhere in his life and he had come back, prodigal-like, to the mountains which bore him to find the only truth he had ever wanted, the only peace he had ever known.

He half rose from the bunk, his pulses throbbing, then a wave of nausea swept his body and he fell back panting against the mattress.

Several feet away, Greg watched him in silence, his brain numbed by the rapid sequence of events. It was hard to believe circumstances had tilted so sharply in their favour. That was the Irish for you, he reflected. Perversity was in their nature.

He glanced up as the hatch opened and Rourke came down the stairway, his cheeks glistening with spray. 'Almost there, Major. This is as close to the shore as I dare get. If we run into a British gunboat, we'll be in serious trouble.'

Two crew members carried Jonas delicately into the open air and Greg followed, shepherding Suzanne in front of him. The two men lowered a rubber boat over the side and laid Jonas, still swathed in blankets, carefully in its bottom. Through the darkness, Greg saw the distant outline of the land ahead.

'That's Whitehaven,' Rourke said, hunching his shoulders against the wind. 'You can't see the town because of the blackout regulations, but keep rowing and you'll hit it spot on. Watch out for sentries. It's the principle port on the Cumbrian coast so it'll be heavily guarded. Don't try to be a hero.'

'Being a hero is the last thing I had in mind,' Greg said. He hesitated. 'You've been very kind, commander.'

'Kindness doesn't come into it. The poor bugger deserves to win. He doesn't belong in this stinking war.'

Rourke shook Greg's hand, then helped Suzanne down the rope ladder. Greg followed, picking up the oars. He fixed them into the dinghy's sockets and began rowing determinedly for shore.

The spray picked up, lashing their cheeks as he focused his strength into his arms and shoulders. He could see the faces of the IRA men vanishing into the darkness.

'Why did they help us?' Suzanne

shivered. 'It doesn't make sense.'

'They don't have to make sense,' he said. 'They're Irish.'

The wind picked up droplets from the dancing waves, hurling them into his face, and he had to work hard to stop the boat twisting in the swell. He went on rowing, conscious of the land growing steadily closer, his hands chilled to the bone. Then he saw the walls of the harbour emerging out of the gloom and suddenly a searchbeam shot across the water, illuminating them in a ball of shimmering light. He raised one of his paddles, waving it in the air.

'Who the hell are you?' a voice bellowed. 'What d'you think you're playing at?'

'Major Anderson, U.S. Special Operations, returning from Occupied France.'

'France, is it? Well, get your backside over here, sunshine, and keep your hands on those bloody paddles.'

He steered the dinghy toward a rusting staircase which led down from the quay above. As he approached, soldiers ran onto the landing bay and pulled his vessel alongside. Greg helped Suzanne onto the platform where a sergeant with a bushy moustache studied them under his flashlight beam. 'Major, you say? You don't look like no bloody major to me.'

The long hours of tension had left Greg

feeling testy and irritable. 'Take us to your commanding officer,' he snapped angrily. 'We have an extremely sick man here.'

Rourke examined the hole in the fishing boat's hull. It was almost three feet in diameter, its edges jagged and serrated. Through the opening, the wind hurled salty droplets against his cheeks.

'Bloody kraut used one of the metal stools to smash the porthole's outer rim,' Frank Murat said. 'He made it just large enough for a man to wriggle through.'

'There must've been a hell of a racket. How come nobody heard him?'

'Paddy had the wireless on. Probably blotted out the noise.'

Rourke grunted, running his fingers over the splintered bulkhead. 'Some mess he's made. Trigg'll be hopping mad.'

'How about the German?'

'Forget the German. He's probably drowned by now. If he hasn't, he'll be somewhere on the English coast. Either way, he isn't our concern any more.'

General Eisenhower was seated in his office when his aide, Major Shellburn walked into the room. 'De Gaulle's arriving tomorrow,' Shellburn said.

Eisenhower sat back in his chair, rubbing the top of his head. It had been Churchill's idea to involve General De Gaulle in the D-Day landings but both the British and Americans had taken considerable care to keep the general safely in Algiers in case he communicated details to members of his personal staff. Now at last it looked as if the final restriction on the Allied offensive was about to be eliminated. 'We're ready to go then?'

'I'm sorry, sir, not quite.' Major Shellburn shuffled among the papers under his arm. 'This is the latest weather report, just in from the Met Office. There's a severe depression moving in from the west. It looks like things are going to get pretty bloody over the next twenty-four hours.'

Eisenhower examined the weather sheet, then rose to his feet and stood at the window. Already, rain was drifting across the soggy lawns outside. He stared at the sky which hung in a welter of swirling black clouds. 'Put out a general communiqué to all units. Tell them that Operation Overlord has been postponed until further notice.'

Forty-eight miles away, Lieutenant General Mark Kitman, deputy commander of the U.S. Fifth Army Group, was looking at the same sky from the cover of his rain-slicker. Behind him, in rows of tents reaching as far as the eye could see, his men waited in combat readiness for the order which would send them into enemy-occupied France. The worsening weather filled General Kitman with foreboding. He knew the dangers of attempting landing manoeuvres in such unstable conditions and as he eyed the rain sweeping ominously in from the west, the scowl on his face grew more and more pronounced.

Captain Jeff Clayman came trotting toward him across the muddy compound, his slim body scarcely distinguishable beneath his dripping poncho. 'Message from SHAEF headquarters, general. D-Day's been cancelled on account of the weather.'

General Kitman kicked angrily at a stone and watched it sail into the swirling rain gusts. 'We've been sitting around this craphole like virgins on a wedding night,' he said. 'Who in Christ's name's going to tell the men?'

On Sunday, June 4th, Winston Churchill, toured army groups waiting in readiness on the Southampton coast. Afterwards, he returned to his special train which was parked on a siding near the outskirts of the city to await General De Gaulle's party from Algiers.

The general arrived by car early on the morning of Monday 5th, accompanied by

Churchill's Foreign Secretary, Anthony Eden. Conscious of the historic significance of such a moment, Churchill walked along the track to greet his old friend and rival.

De Gaulle's face remained stony as Churchill approached and when the Prime Minister tried to embrace him, he drew back in disdain.

'Is something wrong?' Churchill asked.

'You have not been honest with me,' De Gaulle answered in French.

Churchill switched languages with consummate ease. 'It was impossible to get you here any earlier, but at least I've told our American friends that no assault can be attempted on French soil without your explicit approval.'

'That is not what I am talking about,' De Gaulle said frostily.

Churchill glanced at Anthony Eden. 'I'm afraid I don't understand.'

'You are supporting the Communists in my country.'

'Ah.' Churchill's eyes narrowed. He pulled up his collar against the rain and a trickle of moisture ran from his hat brim down his overcoat front. 'You're talking about the Caudale affair, I take it.'

General De Gaulle scowled. 'The FTP is using this Englishman to drum up cheap publicity. Their objective is not simply a German defeat but the establishment of a

Marxist government in France.'

'Yes, yes,' Churchill said, understanding at last. He threw his arm around De Gaulle's shoulders, shepherding him toward the waiting railway carriage. 'Well, we'll just have to do something about it, won't we?'

Chapter Fifteen

Morning came with a coolness which stunned Bruno's senses. He'd expected some semblance of warmth with the rising sun, but the day was cloaked in a wintry aura—which didn't help much when a man was clad in sodden clothing. It had been a gruelling swim from the Irish fishing launch, a constant battle through the twisting foam-flecked waves, the water—icier than anything he'd imagined—numbing his brain and paralysing his flesh.

Half-dead, he'd reached the shoreline only to discover his troubles were just beginning; the rocky crags were studded with mines and it had taken him nearly two hours to pick a delicate path through the ugly soup-plate canisters buried beneath the shifting shale. Now, in the first pale light of day, his clothing wet, his body exhausted, he realized he was in serious trouble. Not only was he alone in enemy territory, he was also in grave danger of perishing from exposure.

He hugged his chest as he studied the terrain ahead. He was in an area of rural farmland, bordered at the rear by the gunmetal glimmer of the Irish Sea. Villages nestled in the meadow folds and directly in front rose the craggy ramparts of the Cumberland mountains, dour and menacing under the storm-laden sky. Somewhere amid that complexity of peaks lay the place Caudale was making for—Buttermere. There was no doubt in Bruno's mind that Caudale would attempt to finish his run. Despite the Englishman's debilitated state, he was still driven by the same incessant fever and this was Bruno's last chance for ridding his mind of the obsession which had so plagued and tormented him.

But first he had to find warmth, dry clothes, food, succour. He moved along the hedgerows, his eyes watchful and wary, studying the landscape as he headed inland. Toward mid-morning, he spotted a scarecrow in a little hollow. The bizarre figure, stuffed with straw, was clad in a tattered boiler suit which had been covered with waterproof sheeting to prevent its insides dissolving in the rain. With a grateful murmur, he stripped off his drenched uniform, pulled on the dummy's outer-garments which were mercifully still dry, then wrapped the slicker around his shoulders and headed for the cover of a nearby wood.

'Major Anderson?' the doctor said.

Greg reached down, taking Suzanne's hand. The doctor removed his spectacles as he entered the hospital waiting room. 'He's in a mess. Worn to a frazzle, I'd say. Exhaustion. Malnutrition. He's also injured internally, though we haven't been able to establish the extent of that yet. For the moment, it's better if he sleeps. We'll carry out exploratory tests later in the day.'

'Will he survive, doctor?'

'He's tough and resilient so he has an excellent chance.' The doctor's face softened. 'Which is more than I can say for you two, if you don't get some rest. You look about dead on your feet.'

'The harbour commander's found us rooms at the local hotel,' Greg told him, 'but I had to check on Jonas first. We've come a long way together. I don't want him flunking out on me now.'

'No fear of that, I should think. I'll call if anything happens. I promise you'll be the first to know.'

'Thanks doctor, I appreciate all you've done.'

Greg and Suzanne strolled wearily out into the morning rain.

Anne Huntley's clothing was drenched as she cycled into the drive at the front of the Sanders' house. She rang the bell and stood squeezing the moisture from her bedraggled hair. After a moment, the door opened and Naunton Sanders stood on the step, staring at her in bewilderment. 'Miss Huntley—my God, I didn't recognize you. You look like a drowned rat.'

'It's raining cats and dogs out here.'

'Please come inside. You must get out of that damp clothing. I'll ask Elizabeth to find you something warm.'

She followed him into the drawing room where Elizabeth sat in front of the fire, nursing a small child. The child was plump and rosy-cheeked with curly hair and laughing blue eyes. It gurgled happily as Anne entered and she stared at it in mild surprise. 'Yours?' she asked Elizabeth Sanders.

Elizabeth's cheeks were pale. 'Jonas's,' she corrected softly.

Anne sucked in her breath, shivering a little as moisture streamed from her sodden clothing. It was the last thing in the world she had expected. She'd thought she had

379

got to the bottom of things, dispelled the mystery, identified the obsession that was driving Jonas Caudale on, but the existence of the child threw an entirely new light on the affair. 'Does he know?' she whispered.

'I wrote to him through the Swiss Red Cross but we have no idea if he received the letter.'

'But supposing he did,' Anne said. 'It would probably explain a lot.'

'Can you get Miss Huntley a robe or something?' Sanders asked.

Anne shook her head as Elizabeth placed the child on the seat beside her and rose to her feet. 'Please, this isn't a social call. I came to tell you that Sergeant Quinlan has killed himself.'

Both Sanders and his daughter reacted to the news with stunned astonishment. 'I can't believe it,' Sanders whispered.

'I found him less than an hour ago. He'd used a shotgun to blow out his brains.'

'My God.' He moved to the fireplace and stared dumbly into the flames.

'Have the police been notified?' Elizabeth asked, her cheeks ashen.

'I called them immediately. They're at Quinlan's house now.' She looked at Sanders. 'I think you ought to know that Sergeant Quinlan left a suicide note admitting everything.'

380

On his left cheek, a tiny nerve had begun to throb. 'I always knew the secret would come out sooner or later,' he said. He turned like a condemned man facing a firing squad. 'Perhaps it's time I told you the truth.'

Jonas awoke slowly, coming out of a dreamless sleep. For a moment, he lay perfectly still, trying to identify his surroundings. Then he remembered. The hospital. He heard rain pounding the window-pane and smelled—or imagined he could smell—the redolence of the mountain peaks outside. He was almost home. A few more miles would do it.

Moaning under his breath, he threw back the bedclothes and swung his feet to the floor. Hunched on the edge of the bed, he explored his body mentally. Legs all right. Still some feeling there, thank God. Head swimming, but otherwise intact. The bulk of his distress seemed centred in his stomach. But pain was a relative thing, he reasoned. Like guilt, pain could be exorcized.

He glanced around dully. They had placed him in a private ward, the window curtained to shut out the daylight. Wincing, he eased himself to his feet and tottered toward the door. Three times, he had to pause and hold onto the bed for support.

It didn't look good, he had to admit; his body felt as weak as a kitten's but he was damned if he'd quit with his destination in reach.

He checked the outside corridor. Nurses moved in and out of the adjoining wards. A porter wheeled a trolley toward the distant X-Ray chamber.

Jonas gently closed the door and tugged back the curtains, peering at the rain. A flash of lightning lit the sky. Another. The weather was building into a fearful storm. Beneath the window, a metal fire escape led into the yard below and he saw the street, through a narrow arch.

He eased up the window and stepped out, gritting his teeth as the icy gridwork chilled his naked feet. The rain pounded his head and shoulders, drenching his flimsy pyjamas.

He padded down the stairway and into the road beyond. There was scarcely a soul in sight, and few vehicles either—the petrol rationing had seen to that.

He hesitated, filling his lungs with air. Then hunching his body against the storm, he slipped out of the alley and began to run.

Greg opened his eyes to hear someone hammering on his bedroom door. For a moment, he lay blinking at the unfamiliar hotel room, then seizing a towel from the nearby rail, he wrapped it around his middle and padded across the creaking floor.

In the passageway outside stood the local harbour commander, Captain Jeremy Meadows, an earnest young man with a bushy RAF moustache. With him was Suzanne, wearing a borrowed houserobe.

'What's up?' Greg stepped back to let them in.

'It's Caudale,' Meadows said in a clipped voice. 'He's escaped.'

'Escaped? How can he escape? He's a patient, not a prisoner.'

'All right, he's run off. The orderly found his ward room empty.'

'Dear God.' A terrible premonition gathered in Greg as he looked at the storm raging against the hotel window. Jonas had seemed in no fit shape to even stand on his feet, let alone move. 'He's out in that?'

Captain Meadows nodded.

If Jonas had gone, Greg thought, there was only one place he could be making for. 'You have a car, captain?'

'A car, sir? Yes, sir.'

'I'll join you in the lobby downstairs.'

'Where are we going, Major Anderson?' Meadows asked.

Greg was already scrambling around

383

the room, pulling on articles of clothing. 'Where do you think? To Buttermere, of course.'

The rain lashed Jonas in blinding, freezing veils, moulding the sodden pyjamas against his sinewy body. His dark hair hung lankly over his forehead and water streamed in a relentless flow into his eyes and mouth. He'd seldom seen rain like it, he had to admit; not even during his long years in the Buttermere hills had he known the heavens to open with such relentless fury. The effect was demoralizing to say the least, but his body was moving which was something to be thankful for. He'd thought himself finished back there but somewhere amid the dim recesses of his brain, he had dragged out the last vestiges of willpower he needed to keep him going.

He was home now. Only a few more miles. The idea filled him with determination. If he could make it home, he would see his son. That alone was something worth fighting for.

The pain in his feet had already diminished; it had been bad at first with sharp stones ripping his naked flesh, but as time progressed the biting cold had chilled his skin until his legs felt numb from the ankles down. He had no sense of loneliness now; the loneliness had left him, dissipated by the realization that victory was within his grasp.

He ran easily, not forcing the pace, ignoring the downpour which ripped through his sodden clothing, thinking instead of the objective ahead. Journey's end.

Mewing under his breath, he headed determinedly toward the beckoning mountains.

What a climate, Bruno thought, ambling along the glistening roadway. He was making his way toward the hills but the cloud was so low, the visibility so deceptive, that he was constantly forced to switch direction. He knew his chances of avoiding detection in enemy terrain were fairly remote and he realized too that he should be grateful for the storm which kept the roads relatively free of people, but there was a limit to how far his luck would stretch and if he wanted his mission to succeed, he would have to act quickly.

He had no idea why he was doing this, no clear idea anyway. Maybe Caudale had challenged him in some elusive way. Maybe he felt humiliated after their desperate chase through the Pyrenees. But he knew the real issue wasn't about Jonas Caudale at all. It was about Bruno von Hautle, and he had been fighting it all his life.

The drone of a motorcycle reached him above the pounding wind and he glanced around for somewhere to hide. He saw the white helmet of a military policeman and realized with a sinking heart that the man had already spotted him. His muscles tensed as the rider roared by, showering him with spray, then turned back the way he had come, drawing to a halt at Bruno's shoulder.

'Hell of a day for a walk,' the man said, studying him through visored wind goggles. Bruno could see raindrops bouncing off his helmet top.

'Storm took me by surprise. I've just been down to the village to visit the bank.'

'Oh yes?' The man used his glove to wipe his glistening cheeks. 'Which village is that?'

'The one in the valley.'

'Which valley are you talking about, squire?'

'Swinford,' Bruno replied, plucking a name out of the air.

'Never heard of the place.' Behind the goggles, the MP's eyes flickered. 'Live around here, do you?'

Bruno shivered as his drenched clothing sent driblets of moisture trickling down his chilled skin. 'I work at the farm up the road.'

'You're not an Englishman. Not with an accent like that.'

'Polish,' Bruno answered hurriedly. 'I came from Warsaw to fight with the Free Polish Army, but they invalided me out. Blood pressure. The doctors prescribed manual labour.'

'Where's your gas mask? Don't you know civilians are required to carry gas masks at all times?'

'I ... I left it behind at the farm. Stupid of me, I realize, but I was in such a terrible hurry.'

'Let me see your papers,' the man said.

Bruno's spirits sank. There was no longer any question of brazening things out. Only a fool would venture afield in wartime without proper identity papers. He reached up to his overall pocket, the man watching his every movement. Bruno didn't give him time to speculate. He let the rain-slicker slip from his shoulders and as the man's eyes followed the unexpected flurry, he spun sharply to the right, swinging his arm in a vicious arc. His fist drove into the MP's temple, causing the man to choke and splutter. He rose from his bike, one hand groping at his weapon holster, and Bruno hit him a second blow, this time on the side of the jaw. It was a classic right hook and he felt a crunch as the impact jarred the MP's helmetted skull. The man pitched backwards over the roadway and collapsed unconscious into the ditch.

Seizing the MP's ankles, Bruno dragged him onto the grassy verge and kneeling, removed the man's pistol, tucking it into his waistband. Quickly, he rummaged through the soldier's things, confiscating his field glasses and compass. He discovered a map in a pouch at the motorcyclist's waist and spread it out on the grass, examining the surrounding landscape.

The mountains rose several miles from the coastline, forming a natural cartwheel in the throat of England. Buttermere lay at their centre. He calculated swiftly. Jonas, he estimated, had been dropped at the tiny port of Whitehaven, therefore there were two routes he could take to complete his journey. The first lay to the north, swinging around the mouth of Ennerdale and approaching Buttermere from a westerly direction. The second took a direct line across the topmost peaks, dropping into the valley from the southernmost point.

It was a gamble, he knew, but he was willing to bet Jonas would opt for the shorter distance, despite the arduous terrain. Tucking the map into his boiler-suit pocket, he rose to his feet and picked up the motorcycle. The MP was beginning to stir as he kicked the engine into life, and rattled off along the rain-soaked roadway.

The ground was steepening, Jonas realized. He had left the fields behind and was entering the lower hill-slopes. The light faded as the cloud grew thicker and he moved by instinct, feeling his way by touch and luck. His bare feet slithered in the peat but somehow, doggedly, he kept moving upward. There was nothing to see but the driving rain, nothing to think of but the prospect of home.

He could smell the good rich odour of the Cumbrian earth, feel its vitality coursing through him. There was a communion with the land when you ran upon it, he thought. You couldn't describe that, couldn't explain it in any logical sense, but he felt its power like a magical force. Pain and discomfort seemed incidental by comparison, as if all the suffering his body had endured was dissolving in a wave of rapture. He was running home on a winter's evening with the lights of the cottage blazing across the fell and the good stomach-warming, life-imbibing odour of fresh broth drifting across the open hearth. He had returned to the mountains of his youth and he knew now the mountains would reward him. No more quandries to prick his troubled soul. Only peace, solitude and contentment.

Mist drifted into his face and he saw crags looming through the raindrenched bracken. Something splashed across his lips and when he rubbed his hand against it his knuckles came away wet with blood. God knew what damage he'd done to his insides, but nothing could stop him now, nothing.

The wind whipped in with a terrifying clamour and he gritted his teeth as it drove against him in successive waves, pounding his sodden pyjamas in a chilling spray. Lightning flashed across the sky and his head rang with a deafening explosion as thunder clattered over the forbidding mountains. It was a wild day to mark his returning, he thought, a wild, glorious and unforgettable day. But there was nothing to worry on with his legs pounding and his heart pumping.

Nothing in the world to worry a shepherd, on a hillside, coming home.

A fire roared in the metal grate, casting a glow of warmth across the empty barroom. Greg and Suzanne stood at the window of the little inn, staring out at the raging storm. They could scarcely see the mountains for cloud.

'What possessed him to go out in such appalling weather?' Suzanne said.

'The same madness that's been driving

him on from the very beginning. All he cares about is getting home.'

'Why? Why, for God's sake?'

'I guess only Jonas can answer that.'

She shivered impulsively as she watched the rain streaming down the window pane. 'And this is what he's running to? Buttermere?'

'What you can see of it. On a good day, it's one of the most beautiful places on earth but in weather like this ...' He shrugged.

'Making it back to England should be achievement enough. What's the difference in a few odd miles?'

'To Jonas Caudale, apparently everything.'

Behind the bar, they heard the low drone of Captain Meadows' voice speaking on the telephone. The receiver clicked and he came back into the lounge, his flushed face unusually tense. 'We've had a report from one of our army units near Kinniside. An MP has been attacked by a stranger he was questioning. The man had a foreign accent and claimed to be Polish. When the soldier asked for his papers, the suspect knocked him cold and stole his pistol and motorcycle.'

Greg felt his senses chill. 'What did he look like, this stranger?'

'Tall and personable, the MP says.'

'Bruno,' Suzanne whispered, her cheeks paling. 'It has to be Bruno.'

'Contact your people,' Greg ordered. 'Tell them to put out a full alert. That Pole your MP so unwisely halted was an SS officer named Bruno von Hautle.'

Meadows looked startled. He ran his fingers along his beefy moustache. 'What, in Christ's name, would a German officer be doing here?'

'He's on his way to murder Jonas Caudale,' Greg told him.

Jonas sprawled in the mud, blinking as he saw the grass tufts rising above him. He couldn't remember falling, not clearly anyhow, but he knew it was the fourth time he'd taken a tumble in the last few minutes. Curious that, the way his body kept tilting out of alignment. His strength was fading, he'd be a fool to deny it, but he knew in his heart that no matter how often he floundered, some inner spark would always keep him going. He would move because his survival depended upon movement.

A sheet of lightning lit the sky and thunder jarred his eardrums as he struggled to his knees, focusing his willpower into the simple task of working his way upright. Somehow he managed it, swaying and teetering. He was mobile at least, and that was a victory in itself but there was still a worrying lassitude in his limbs and an aching emptiness in his insides. He felt as if he had been cleaned and gutted, like a rabbit ready for market. Tentatively, he let his body fall forward, wincing as his buckling legs took the strain.

Sodden sheep watched curiously as he staggered through the dripping bracken, his mind lost in a torpor of its own making.

Bruno swung the motorcycle to a halt, revving the engine as he peered over the valley below. The land at this point was heavily cultivated, especially in the fertile bottomlands bordering the river, but above the road the hills rose green and brown, vanishing mysteriously into the cloud-cluttered summits. Directly beneath, he saw troop convoys moving along the network of narrow roads and as he watched, men spilled from the trucks and began setting up a barrier where the highway divided. He wiped his face with his sleeve, grunting softly.

He opened up the throttle, roaring along a winding farmroad which skirted the base of a ragged ridge-crest. The rain ripped into his cheeks, blinding his vision. He spotted the farm ahead, nestling among a thatch of fir trees, and brought his machine to a halt, contemplating the options confronting him. If his guess was correct, Jonas Caudale must be somewhere among the summits above. He had followed the route for more than an hour, checking the hillslopes inch by meticulous inch, but apart from a few occasional sheep, he had seen no sign of movement or human presence. Now, scanning the ridge with his field glasses, he felt the breath catch in his throat as he spotted an ant-like creature of minuscule size, moving with agonizing slowness across the rainsoaked heather.

Caudale, it had to be Caudale. Who else would traverse the hills in such atrocious weather?

He opened the throttle and thundered up the hillslope above.

Something was terribly wrong with Jonas's legs. His muscles were ignoring the signals sent out by his ravaged brain and he knew he was reeling and floundering like a man in a state of progressive dementia. If I fall here, he thought, I'll never get on my feet again.

A spasm in his chest almost made him tumble but he recovered his balance in time and staggered on, one hand clutched to his rib cage as his naked soles slithered across the rainwashed rocks. Though he couldn't say why, the side of his chest seemed swollen; he'd been bumping into things, tripping and stumbling crazily for the past few hours, and at one point a thatch of brambles had caught him full in the face, ripping his skin to shreds.

The hills had lost their texture now, their density dissolving into a featureless expanse where the peat bogs got boggier, the grass clumps clumpier, and he sank to his knees in treacly brown slime. The land seemed drained of colour, its surface bathed in wavering mist spirals from which jagged outcrops reared with terrifying suddenness.

He saw a figure approaching from his rear and startled, wiped the rain from his eyes with his fingers. A man came jogging toward him and his spirits quickened as he recognized the tangled hair and lantern jaw of Bobby Teasdale, the one-armed runner from Pooley Bridge.

Another figure approached from the opposite bank—it was George Fisher from Keswick, his sinewy body glistening with rain. Suddenly, there were runners all over the place, gathering around him in a comforting shroud. He saw Lennie Birkett grinning in that crazy way he had, and he knew that couldn't be right because Lennie Birkett was dead. Lennie had taken a shrapnel blast in the Allied invasion at Salerno, yet here he was running as if his life depended upon it, his long limbs covering the ground with an almost effortless grace.

'Gan on, Jonas,' Lennie bellowed, his teeth flashing wildly. 'Last man in buys t'first round.'

Jonas laughed, felt the pain draining from his body, felt his heart steadying and his muscles strengthening. A flicker of warmth started inside him, spreading outwards through his limbs. Now there was no sense of strain, only a wonderful feeling of vitality. Now he was running hard and true, better than he had ever run in his life. He was like a feather in the wind, knowing he could do it because this was what he had been born to, gliding over the grassclumps with his arms pumping, his legs flailing, his friends gathering in a sustaining cordon at his rear. His lips drew back into a triumphant grin as he sprinted wildly into the fog.

Bruno chose his position well. He could see the point where the ridge narrowed, forming a splintered knife-edge so that anyone approaching would be forced to pick a delicate path along its rocky spine. He lay in the boulders, his pistol extended, waiting for Caudale to appear. It was a sorry ambition for a man to harbour and no mistake, but Bruno couldn't help himself. He wasn't doing it for the Führer.

He wasn't doing it for the Reich. It was ingrained into his soul like a strange, psychotic compulsion. He couldn't explain his reasons, but he couldn't ignore them either.

He heard the wind roaring along the valley, then something rose above its clamour and he recognized the harsh rasp of laboured breathing. He blinked the rain from his eyes, his finger tightening on the trigger. A head appeared above the ridge, a pair of muddy shoulders. He steeled himself, steadying his aim. He could see Jonas clearly now, his pyjama-clad body shapeless, barely recognizable.

Bruno lowered his pistol, dry-mouthed. Jonas looked like a monster from some grotesque vision, his tattered clothing dangling in shreds from his decimated body. His feet were raw and even through their coating of peat, he could see the swollen, blood-crusted flesh. Jonas was reeling and staggering like a drunken man, his face demented as he floundered past Bruno.

Caught in a horrified fascination, Bruno watched the tormented creature blundering blindly up the hillside above.

Breasting Fleetwith Pike, Jonas saw the clouds beginning to part. It was a glorious sight, as if the sky had suddenly peeled itself, the sun coming out to welcome him home. Its rays lit the hills and valleys ahead, and there, directly in front, lay Buttermere with its twin lakes and little alluvial plain. Never in his life had he seen it look so beautiful. Here, in this unbelievable land was the only home he could ever know, the only happiness he could ever wish for.

He started down the track, putting his mind to the final descent, his muscles taking the strain with a smooth and supple ease. He was strong and young and filled with an unquenchable vitality. These were his hills and his valley, and there was the lake shimmering gently at his front.

And now the track dipped toward Gatesgarth and his heart leapt with joy as he saw Elizabeth waiting to greet him, her lithe body framed by the sunlight. She was holding his child, a beautiful thing, more delicate than anything he had ever imagined, with rosy cheeks and laughing eyes and dark curls dancing in the wind. Nothing had changed, that was the extraordinary thing, not even the dress Elizabeth wore, and he was laughing excitedly as he poured everything into one last determined sprint. He could hear the crowd welcoming him home, their voices blending into a single obsessive chorus, 'Jonas,' they roared. 'Jonas, Jonas, Jonas,

Jonas, Jonas, Jonas, Jonas, Jonas, Jonas, Jon ...'

Bruno saw Jonas reel like a stricken stag, his body spinning. He hit the ground, his arms stretched out as if embracing the mountain on which he had run.

Bruno walked toward him and rolled him onto his back, a terrible breathlessness gathering in his chest. Jonas was dead, his eyes staring sightlessly into the driving rain. Blood trickled from his lips, spreading across his alabaster skin.

Bruno hurled his pistol angrily into the mist, filled with an irrational rage. He felt no sense of accomplishment, only a chilling emptiness as if some essential part of his body had been amputated. It seemed cruel that the man should die with victory almost within his grasp.

He strode back to his motorcycle and was about to kick the engine into life when a sudden thought occurred to him. He hesitated, wiping his face. It wasn't over yet, by God.

He let the motorcycle drop and seized Jonas's arms, pulling the Englishman across his muscular shoulders. For a moment, he stood with his legs braced, testing the fragile body for balance. Then turning toward Buttermere, he set off determinedly into the storm.

The young naval officer felt apprehensive as he hurried along the corridor at the number 10 annexe in Downing Street. He was only twenty-two years old and was spending his first day as an auxiliary member of the Prime Minister's advisory staff. He had just been given a message to deliver to the Prime Minister himself and the lieutenant knew that although Churchill could be charming when the mood took him, his irascibility with junior officers was legendary. The lieutenant was a nervous young man who was easily awed by people in authority and his skin crawled as he tapped lightly on the door of Churchill's map room.

The Prime Minister was seated at his desk, his spectacles perched on his button-like nose, and the officer stood to attention, miserably conscious of the sweat beads gathering on his sallow cheeks.

'Well, what is it?' Churchill said in a remarkably mild voice.

The officer placed the paper he had been given on the Prime Minister's desk. 'Message from General Eisenhower's headquarters, sir. The weather reports are improving. He's given the order for the invasion to begin.'

Churchill took a deep breath and leaned back in his chair. For a long moment he appeared to be deep in thought, then he said, 'So it's now or never, lieutenant.'

'Yes, sir.' The lieutenant paused. 'There's something else, sir. This came in from Section D-14. Jonas Caudale, the Lakeland fellrunner, has just reached Cumbria.'

Churchill's eyes glowed. 'Has he, by God?'

'He arrived at Whitehaven by dinghy, after being dropped from a launch off the north-west coast.'

'How on earth did he manage to cross the Bay of Biscay?'

The lieutenant hesitated. He had a feeling his answer would not be a welcome one. 'He was helped by the IRA, Prime Minister.'

'The IRA?' Churchill frowned.

'They smuggled him out of France on an Irish freighter, then transferred him to the motor launch somewhere near the Irish coast.'

'What on earth are the IRA doing mixed up in this?'

'I really don't know, sir. It seems they just sort of dealt themselves in.'

Churchill rubbed his chin reflectively. 'Jonas Caudale has picked himself some splendid soulmates on his little run, I must say. First, he alienates the French by joining forces with the Communists. Now he's working with Irish revolutionaries.'

'Shall I offer the story to the news agencies, sir?'

'Of course not. We have enough problems without giving free publicity to the damned IRA.' Churchill's plump face was tinged with regret. 'It's a crying shame, it would have made a marvellous tonic for our landing forces, but Jonas Caudale has too many unsavoury connections. I want the story buried. Do you understand, young man? There are to be no further bulletins on the BBC, and no reference in any Fleet Street newspaper.'

'Yes, sir. I'll see to it at once, sir.'

On the morning of June 6th, 1944, after extensive bombing raids on German positions around Cherbourg and Caen, men of 6 Airborne Division landed by glider, capturing two bridges on the River Orne and the neighbouring canal. At dawn, assault forces of the First U.S. Army and the Second British Army attacked the beaches of Normandy in the most crucial offensive of World War Two. Air resistance was slight, apart from Omaha beach, north-west of Bayeux, where the Fifth American Corps encountered considerable opposition. Churchill telegraphed Stalin that despite poor sea conditions in the Channel, the landings had proved successful and the principle obstacles looked like being overcome.

After weeks of preparation and post-
ponement, 'Operation Overlord' was finally
under way.

Greg awoke to find Captain Meadows
gently shaking his shoulder. He blinked,
raising his head. He was sprawled in front
of the inn fire, wrapped in a woollen
blanket. Suzanne lay on the nearby sofa,
sleeping peacefully. Outside, it had stopped
raining and sunlight was streaming through
the open windows.

'It's over, Major,' Meadows said softly.

'Over?'

'Caudale. They've found him.'

Greg threw back the blanket and rose
to his feet. 'Why didn't you wake me?'

'You were exhausted. You needed sleep.
Besides ...' Meadows shrugged. 'Nobody
can help Caudale now.'

'Jonas is dead?'

'I'm afraid so.'

On the sofa, Suzanne opened her eyes
and stared at Meadows expressionlessly.

'When?' Greg's throat felt unnaturally
tight.

'About forty minutes ago. An early
morning fisherman found him by the side
of the lake. He'd been dead several hours.
They're bringing him in now.'

'He made it then?' Greg said idiotically.

It was all he could think of.

Captain Meadows nodded. 'Every step. We've got the ambulance outside. I thought you might like to see him before they cart him off.'

It was a cool day but the downpour had stopped at last and dappled sunlight played across the surrounding hills. In the car-park of the little inn, they watched the sad procession approaching from the lake. Greg saw an attractive young woman in the uniform of a WAAF flight officer, weeping grievously. She was being comforted by a white-haired man in his early seventies. 'Who's that?' he asked.

'Caudale's fiancée, I believe. The gentleman is her father, a local landowner.'

Meadows nodded to the stretcher bearers and they paused as they drew alongside. Greg stepped forward, tugging back the blanket. Jonas's lids were closed and his face looked strangely unreal in death, as if someone had smoothed out the bumps and furrows. There were scratch marks on his skin and heavy contusions around his forehead but Greg had the curious feeling that his eyes might open at any second and flash with their old determined fury.

He let the blanket drop and nodded to the stretcher party to continue. He was silent as he watched them strap Jonas's body into the waiting ambulance. Suzanne

404

reached down, taking his hand.

'What are you thinking?'

'The same thing I've been thinking all along. Why, in God's name, did he do it?'

Thirty feet away, Anne Huntley watched the proceedings through the window of her phone booth, cradling the receiver against her chin. The voice of her editor, Hugh Miller, echoed in her ear. 'So it wasn't Caudale who led those men to their deaths after all?'

'No,' Anne said. 'Naunton Sanders set the whole thing up. He liked Jonas but he didn't want his daughter to marry an ordinary shepherd.'

'He agreed with his wife then?'

'Exactly. Which was why he suggested the fell race in the first place. He wanted to discredit Jonas by getting him disqualified for cheating. He reasoned that it would make him seem less appealing in his daughter's eyes. It was Sergeant Quinlan's job to brief the competitors on the route they had to follow and being a close friend of Sanders, he agreed to give Jonas false directions. Sanders detained Jonas while the briefing took place and Quinlan filled him in independently later.'

'But surely Jonas would have questioned the wisdom of cutting across a frozen lake?'

'Quinlan managed to convince him that the ice was so solid, it would be safe as houses. He was probably right too, if Jonas had made the crossing alone. Unfortunately, it couldn't take the strain of fifteen men running in unison.'

'Why didn't all this come out at the inquest?'

'It did, but Sergeant Quinlan denied it. He was appalled by what had happened and believed his position in the community could be threatened.'

'So nobody believed Caudale?'

'Why should they? He had an emotional interest in the race's outcome.'

'What are you saying? That Jonas Caudale ran back to Buttermere simply in order to clear his name?'

'Not exactly. Who can know what was in Jonas Caudale's mind? But at least it throws a glimmer of light on the turmoil the man was going through. Imagine being exiled from the one place in the world you cared about, separated from the only woman you could ever love, banished from the child you had never seen, and all for something you hadn't done. Was Caudale running to absolve his guilt—real or imagined? Was he doing it to convince the Buttermere people that he deserved a second chance? Was he hoping to confront Quinlan and force him to tell the truth? Or was he trying to give his son something to be proud of, something to remember him by? Maybe it was a combination of all those things.'

'Makes no difference anyhow,' Miller said. 'I've been ordered to kill the story.'

She frowned, turning her back to the phone-booth door. 'Kill it? What do you mean, kill it?'

'Orders from the War Office. Suddenly, Jonas Caudale is taboo.'

'For Pete's sake, Hugh, this is great human interest stuff.'

'I'm sorry, Anne, the matter's out of my hands. The D-notice arrived this morning. "In the interests of national security," it says.'

'Jonas's run had nothing to do with the war.'

'I don't make the rules, I only obey them. However, I did call someone at the War Office press department and get this—apparently the order came from Churchill himself.'

'I can't believe it.'

'You don't have to believe it. All you have to do is get back to London as fast as you can. Now that our troops are finally in Europe, I need all the reporters I can get.' His tone softened. 'Don't be downhearted just because your copy has to be spiked. It's part of the game, you'll learn that in time. See you in the office at nine tomorrow. I'll find something you can really get your teeth into.'

Miller hung up and for a long moment, she stood staring in silence at the stretcher party outside. Then she buttoned her raincoat and stepped into the morning chill.

Greg heard a car approaching from the south and watched it screech to a halt at the little inn. It was an open-topped jeep with two MPs in front. Crouched in the rear, wrists handcuffed and shoulders covered by an army greatcoat, sat Bruno von Hautle. Bruno's face was smeared with mud and his hair stuck up wildly in every direction. He was smoking a cigarette and there was a curious look in his eyes as he watched the ambulance preparing for departure.

One of the MPs climbed from the vehicle and saluted Captain Meadows. 'We found him on the other side of the lake, sir, trying to get back into the hills.'

Greg and Suzanne strolled toward the jeep. Bruno had lost some of his buoyancy during the night but none of his composure. He smiled at them, rolling the cigarette between his fingertips.

'You're too late, von Hautle,' Greg said

with quiet satisfaction. 'Nothing can touch him now.'

'He's dead?' Bruno asked innocently.

'Yes, he's dead. But he made it, just like he said he would. Every step of the way.'

'I had a feeling he might.'

'They found him on the shores of Buttermere early this morning.'

'He kept his promise then.'

'Damn right. He beat you to a standstill. You can never take that away from him, never.'

'I wouldn't dream of such a thing.' Bruno shrugged regretfully. 'He was the best mountain runner I've ever come across. We could have done with Caudale at the Garmische Games.'

'What will happen to you now?' Suzanne asked.

'The usual, I suppose. Interrogation, then imprisonment. There's a POW camp called Grizedale Hall just a couple of valleys from here. The MPs reckon they'll stick me in there. I can think of less pleasant places to spend the rest of the war.'

'And afterwards?'

'After it's over?' His eyes twinkled. 'I have a feeling you'll be seeing me again.'

He chuckled as Greg slipped his arm around Suzanne's shoulder. 'Staking your claim, Major? Well, you'd better be quick.

As a military man, you'll appreciate the folly of delaying an offensive until the enemy has managed to re-group. What was it your General MacArthur said?'

' "I shall return," ' Greg answered tightly.

'That's something you can count on.'

Bruno's teeth flashed as the jeep roared briskly into the Lakeland morning.

Churchill was celebrating the success of D-Day with his wife Clementine when the news of Jonas's death reached him by telephone. He slammed down the receiver and hurled his champagne glass angrily at the fireplace.

His wife stared at him in surprise. She knew the Prime Minister's temper could be fiery at times but it rarely manifested itself in such a violent manner. 'Winston, what on earth is wrong?'

'That shepherd, Caudale, they've just found him on the shores of Buttermere. It looks as though, having reached his objective, his heart gave out under the strain.'

'Oh, Winston, I'm so sorry.'

He opened the French window and strode onto the balcony, leaning against the metal parapet. He could see the ghostly outlines of barrage balloons floating above the streets of London. Somewhere over west, a police siren echoed shrilly. Clementine joined him, gently squeezing his arm.

'I know it's crazy,' he said. 'How many men died on the beaches of Normandy today? How many more will die before we take Berlin? Why should the news of Caudale hit me so hard?'

'Because Jonas Caudale was a symbol of everything we are fighting for,' she told him. 'If our troops show the same kind of spirit as they advance on Germany, then the outcome of this war can never be in doubt.'

Churchill stared at her in silence for a moment, then he reached down and tenderly patted her wrist. His voice trembled with emotion. 'You always know just the right thing to say, Clemmie.'

Epilogue

In the early hours of May 7th, 1945, General Alfred Jodle, Chief of Staff of the German Armed Forces, signed the document of surrender which brought World War Two in Europe to a close. Amid the euphoria which followed the Allied victory, the details of Jonas Caudale's run were quickly forgotten. The D-notice banning media coverage was never revoked and remained in force until its natural expiry date thirty years later.

Greg Anderson left the army in 1946 to head his father's industrial consortium. He married Suzanne Le Gras and they had four sons, three of whom have since taken over the family business. Greg Anderson retired in 1991 and now lives with his wife in Palm Springs, California.

Bruno von Hautle never did leave the English Lake District, nor did he fulfil his promise to pursue Suzanne Le Gras. After internment at Grizedale Hall, he married a local girl and bought a boarding house in the Borrowdale Valley. With Greg Anderson's financial backing, he steadily expanded his business and at the time of writing owns a chain of hotels throughout Cumbria and southern Scotland. The Andersons are frequent visitors and have been for the past fifty years.

Jonas's son, Ambrose, emigrated to British Columbia in 1969 and now works for the Canadian Forestry Service. He has two grown-up children, one a lawyer in Vancouver, the other a headmaster in Red Deer, Alberta.

His mother, Elizabeth Sanders, married a doctor in 1956 and settled in Lytham St. Anne's. After fourteen years, the marriage ended in divorce and she followed her son to Canada where she died of leukaemia in 1977.

Jonas Caudale's achievements were never reinstated in the local record books but in 1979, a small monument was erected on the shores of Buttermere where his body was found. The inscription reads simply:

To Jonas Caudale, who ran home from Switzerland, June 6th 1944.

'Sleep, kindly shepherd, amid whose pleasant pastures lie Sweet peace, and blessed harmony.'

Erected by the people of Buttermere, May 4th, 1979.

This Large Print Book for the Partially sighted, who cannot read normal print, is published under the auspices of

THE ULVERSCROFT FOUNDATION

THE ULVERSCROFT FOUNDATION

. . . we hope that you have enjoyed this Large Print Book. Please think for a moment about those people who have worse eyesight problems than you . . . and are unable to even read or enjoy Large Print, without great difficulty.

You can help them by sending a donation, large or small to:

**The Ulverscroft Foundation,
1, The Green, Bradgate Road,
Anstey, Leicestershire, LE7 7FU,
England.**
or request a copy of our brochure for more details.

The Foundation will use all your help to assist those people who are handicapped by various sight problems and need special attention.

Thank you very much for your help.

Cucksey
Peter